可持续与包容性发展——全球城市的多元实践

2017 年同济大学城市与社会国际学术论坛

论文集

主　编　朱伟珏　周　俭

副主编　钟晓华　邓世碧

同济大学出版社
TONGJI UNIVERSITY PRESS

中国·上海

图书在版编目(CIP)数据

可持续与包容性发展 ：全球城市的多元实践 ：2017年同济大学城市与社会国际学术论坛论文集/朱伟珏，周俭主编. -- 上海：同济大学出版社，2018.10

ISBN 978-7-5608-8100-3

Ⅰ. ①可… Ⅱ. ①朱… ②周… Ⅲ. ①城市社会学-国际学术会议-文集 Ⅳ. ①C912.81-53

中国版本图书馆 CIP 数据核字(2018)第 187893 号

可持续与包容性发展——全球城市的多元实践

2017年同济大学城市与社会国际学术论坛论文集

主编 朱伟珏 周 俭 副主编 钟晓华 邓世碧

责任编辑 荆 华 **助理编辑** 苏 勃 金 言 **责任校对** 徐春莲 **封面设计** 钱如潺

出版发行 同济大学出版社 www.tongjipress.com.cn

(地址：上海市四平路1239号 邮编：200092 电话：021-65985622)

经　　销 全国各地新华书店

印　　刷 上海安兴汇东纸业有限公司

开　　本 787mm×1092mm 1/16

印　　张 12.5

字　　数 312000

版　　次 2018年10月第1版 2018年10月第1次印刷

书　　号 ISBN 978-7-5608-8100-3

定　　价 69.00元

前　言

“城市与社会”国际学术论坛是由同济大学主办，城市与社会研究中心和同济大学社会学系等多家单位共同承办、协办的跨学科国际学术交流盛宴，旨在聚焦前沿城市议题、促进城市研究相关领域不同学科之间的深入交流和广泛讨论，为同济大学学科发展和国际学术研究网络的建立提供强大动力。“城市与社会”国际学术论坛有两种组织形式，一种是集中组织的大型会议，每两年举办一届；另一种是不定期的小型系列研讨会。2015 年 4 月，以“社区・空间・治理”为主题的第一届论坛顺利召开，聚焦中外城市社区在发展演变、转型重构、制度机制等方面的经验与问题，并于会后整理出版了《社区・空间・治理：2015 年同济大学城市与社会国际论坛会议论文集》。2016—2017 年，会议承办方同济大学社会学系和城市与社会中心继续依托学校及本论坛学术委员会的支持，邀请知名的中外学者围绕相关议题举办了 11 期(共 20 余场)“城市对话”系列学术研讨会。在前期积累的基础上，第二届大型论坛于 2017 年 10 月召开，以促成相关领域的跨学科、跨国界对话及交叉学科合作为目标，在理论建构、实证研究、规划实践、政策创新等方面进行多维度学术交流。

近年来，随着城市化、全球化、数字化进程的深入，城市在经济、社会、政治和文化等诸多方面的不平等正在加剧。如何应对这些问题，成为摆在全世界面前的共同命题。联合国新近出台的《2030 年可持续发展议程》及人居 Ⅲ《新城市议程》都将包容性发展作为重要议题，许多全球城市也把建设多元均衡、公平公正、流动活力、安全稳定的包容性社会作为自身战略目标。与此同时，中国的“十三五”规划首次将“包容性发展”加入实现国民经济发展目标所要具备的先决条件。可见，包容性发展已成为全球共识与“中国话语”。基于此，2017 年“城市与社会”国际学术论坛以“可持续与包容性发展——全球城市的多元实践”为主题，聚集来自国内外不同学科的城市研究领域专家与社会研究领域专家，共同研讨国内外全球城市在包容性发展方面的理论建构与多元实践。

本论文集共收录 15 篇文章，根据关注议题的差异划分为五个章节：城市化理论与可持续发展、文化场景与全球城市、移民融入与包容发展、存量更新与多元协同，以及遗产保护与社区治理。

在“城市化理论与可持续发展”章节中，劳伦斯・罗兰-伯格关注西方与中国在城市研究理论方面“延续的断裂性”与“断裂的延续性”问题，致力于推动城市社会学理论向“后西方”转变；莎伦・佐金则探讨了城市主要基于土地控制产生的多个维度与多重矛盾。

在“文化场景与全球城市”章节中，张元皓通过文莱洞和韩流两个案例介绍韩国首尔的城市场景及其意义；吴军对北京的三个城市社区发展的文化动力进行分析；汪弘枫则对上海徐汇滨江和法国里昂汇流区的改造活动进行比较研究，探究文化设施对城市更新的作用。

在"移民融入与包容发展"章节中，水上徹男从历史和现状的角度介绍了日本的"商业城堡镇"中的日裔巴西人社区，以及地方政府针对性的多元文化导向政策；王雪梅以北京海淀区肖社区为例，分析城乡接合部流动人口聚集区的社区生态变迁；洪伟则追溯了穆斯林群体在近代上海地区的发展与融入历史，以及当前城市融入面临的挑战。

在"存量更新与多元协同"章节中，陆勇峰结合上海江浦社区辽源西路睦邻中心周边地区的综合更新，探索了老旧住区更新规划中的多方协同机制；谭露露对成都市小街区的更新思路及其"1＋N"机制进行了反思；刘琦和邹昊阳以上海江湾-五角场副中心为例，研究了协同机制下的大城市副中心演进策略。

在"遗产保护与社区治理"章节中，普拉西多·冈萨雷斯·马丁内斯结合上海虹口港1933老场坊和音乐谷的案例，对遗产原真性重新进行概念化；程情仪和刘佳燕以1999年"9·21"地震后台湾桃米社区的发展为案例，分析社区媒介如何影响了社区的社会资本；张若曦等人通过厦门沙坡尾的案例，探究资本、权力及人文博弈下的历史街区空间再生产问题；郭谌达以上海虹口港为例，对城市历史文化遗产密集区的发展困境及可能的路径进行了研究。

可以看出，本论文集以中国、尤其是上海的案例为主，但也兼顾日本、韩国、法国等国家的城市实践，作者们通过分析具体案例并结合理论，分别从文化场景、移民融入、城市更新、遗产保护等角度，表达各自对可持续和包容性发展的理解。此论文集的出版，不仅是对2017"城市与社会"国际学术论坛的最终总结，也是未来对话与合作的新起点。

编委会

目　录

移民融入与包容发展

存量更新与多元协同

遗产保护与社区治理

本论文集主编:朱伟珏,周 俭; 副主编:钟晓华,邓世碧

城市化理论与可持续发展

Post-Western Theory and Urban Sociology in Europe and in China

Laurence Roulleau-Berger

Abstract Post-Western Sociology is non-hegemonic and critical, constructed from conjunctions and disjunctions, continuities and discontinuities between Chinese and European Sociology which cannot be conceived according to a binary mode. It relies on different knowledge processes: 1) knowledge niches which appear to be specifically European or Chinese intermediary epistemological processes which encourage the partial transfer of knowledge from Europe to China and from China to Europe, 2) Transnational epistemological spaces in which European knowledge and Asian knowledge are placed in equivalence, and 3) the formation of theoretical "common spaces" and "proper spaces".

In this communication we will draw some theoretical and empirical discontinuous continuities and continuous discontinuities between European and Chinese urban sociologies. So we firstly will introduce the question of sociological heritages and circulation of knowledge, for example Marxism' theory and Chicago's School in urban sociology. Then we will describe transnational theoretical spaces through some theoretical and empirical discontinuous continuities between Chinese and European urban sociologies in dealing with the transversal problematic of migration, integration and segregation; we will draw theoretical continuous discontinuities through the problematic of public space, social differentiation and collective action, it also means identify knowledge niches in Chinese and European contexts.

Keywords Post-Western Sociology; transnational epistemological spaces; discontinuous continuities; continuous discontinuities

后西方理论与欧洲和中国的城市社会学

劳伦斯·罗兰-伯格

摘　要　后西方社会学是非霸权和批判的，建立在不能套用二分模型的中国社会学与欧洲社会学的连接与分离、连续与不连续的基础之上。它依赖于不同的知识进程：①知识领域，特别是介于欧洲或中国的认识论进程，它鼓励将部分知识从欧洲传到中国和从中国传到欧洲。②跨国的认识论空间，在其中欧洲知识和亚洲知识并置。③理论的"公共空间"和"适当空间"的形成。

在这一交流中，我们将讨论欧洲和中国城市社会学的一些理论和实证的非连续的"连续性"和连续的"非连续性"。因此，我们将首先引出社会学传统和知识传播的问题，例如马克思主义理论和城市社会学的芝加哥学派。之后，我们将通过中国和欧洲城市社会学方面的一些理论和实证的非连续的"连续性"来描述跨国理论空间，以解决"移民""融合"与"区隔"的横向问题；我们将通过"公共空间""社会分化"和"集体行动"等问题来分析理论上连续的"非连续性"，它同时也表示中国和欧洲背景下的认同知识领域。

关键词　后西方社会学；跨国的认识论空间 ；不连续的"连续性"；连续的"非连续性"

Post-Western Sociology is non-hegemonic and critical, constructed from conjunctions and disjunctions, continuities and discontinuities between Chinese and European Sociology which cannot be conceived according to a binary mode. It relies on different knowledge processes: 1) knowledge niches which appear to be specifically European or Chinese intermediary epistemological processes which encourage the partial transfer of knowledge from Europe to China and from China to Europe, 2) transnational epistemological spaces in which European knowledge and Asian knowledge are placed in equivalence, and 3) the formation of theoritical "common spaces" and "proper spaces". In this article we will draw some theoretical and *empiritical discontinuous continuities* and *continuous discontinuities* between European and Chinese urban sociologies. Then we will introduce the question of sociological heritages and circulation of knowledge, for example Marxism'theory and Chicago's School in urban sociology. Then we will describe transnational theoretical spaces through some theoretical continuities between Chinese and European urban sociologies in dealing with the transversal problematics of *Right to the City and Housing*, *Migration*, *Integration and Segregation*; we also will draw theoretical continuous discontinuities through the problematic of *Public Space*, *Social Differentiation and Collective Action*. It also means identify knowledge niches in Chinese and European contexts, so we will introduce the topic of *Local knowledge and the invention of the City*.

1 What about Post-Western Sociology?

We are at the centre of a global turning-point - distinct from those before and their ephemeral nature - a turning-point in the history of the social sciences[1]. In today's world, the social sciences have become internationalised and have been rejuvenated in other societies such as Asian societies ... Centres of gravity in human science knowledge have been displaced towards Asia - South, East, Central and Pacific Asia - where, in regional forums, intellectuals from China[2]3-23;[3,4], from Japan[5,6], from Korea[7], from India[8] continually discuss the modes of producing epistemic autonomies in a context of non-Western hegemony.

The early construction of dominances and hierarchies between Western, Eastern and Far-Eastern contexts has produced instances of ignorance and occultation of entire bodies of knowledge. Western social scientists have no so much access to the narratives of distant societies such as Japan, China, Korea ... have continually found refuge in ethnocentric positions. However, if Japan, Korea, India ... have been engaged in partial Westernisation processes for several decades and Korea for a little less, the thirty years of Maoïsm closed the gates to China with the result that Chinese intellectuals could not participate in the development of social sciences, a forbidden field from 1949 to 1979.

And we can perceive a diversity of Westernisms - some more Eurocentric, others more Americanocentric - either merging or in tension. As there is a diversity of Westernisms there is also a plurality of Easternisms situated in different epistemic spaces and constructed and ordered into hierarchies according to differentiated political, historical and civilisational processes.

Rajev Bhargava[8] considers of epistemic injustice three forms:

- the imposition of a change affecting the content of the epistemic frameworks
- the alteration of fundamental epistemic frameworks
- the damaging or loss of the capacity of individuals to maintain or develop their own epistemic frameworks

The most pressing task, however, is to investigate the ways in which *continuities and discontinuities*, connections and disjunctions are formed between seats of knowledge located at different places in the world and potentially capable of bringing to light a *transnational intermediate space* that is both local and global.

So new centres of knowledge production are born out of:

a) the refusal to imitate Western epistemic framework

b) a concern to control hybridizations of Western and non-Western knowledge based on the dynamics of the de-territorialization and re-territorialization of non indigenous knowledge

c) the recognition and validation of places of conjunction and disjunction between Western and non-Western knowledge

d) the existence of "epistemic white zones", that is, zones in which the epistemic frameworks constructed in different societal contexts cannot come into contact

In China, the assertion of an epistemic autonomy among sociologists for example means the re-establishment of continuities with epistemic frameworks which had been constructed before 1949 then forgotten. For example Li Peilin and Qu Jingdong[9] distinguish different moments in the scientific history of Chinese sociology in the first half of the 20th century. *The first marxist Chinese sociology* used to rely both on historical materialism and scientific socialism: historical materialism is a kind of "new sociology", a "modern sociology", which distinguishes itself from traditional Western sociology. Then the *social survey movement* corresponds to an important movement hatched at the beginning of the 20th century. It also means, however, the creation of specific paradigms freed from Western presuppositions, and the production of a mosaic of constructivisms [4].

After Post-Colonial Studies, we are purposing to produce *Post-Western Sociology* in this context of globalization and circulation of ideas, concepts and paradigms[10]. *Post-Western Sociology* is first and foremost rhizomatous in that it is constructed from connections between points located in knowledge spaces governed by very different regimes of signs and the non-correspondence of different types of situated knowledge[11]. It does not equate Post-Western Sociologies with "Sociologies of South countries", "Sociologies of East Asia" or "Sociologies of non-Western countries", even should not equate them with "anti-Western sociologies"[12].

Post-Western Sociology is constructed from conjunctions and disjunctions which cannot be conceived according to a binary mode. It relies on different knowledge processes[11]:

a) "Knowledge niches" which appear to be specifically European or Asian and do not signify a transferability of knowledge

b) Intermediary epistemological processes which encourage the partial transfer of knowledge from Europe to Asia and from Asia to Europe

c) Transnational epistemological spaces in which European knowledge and Asian knowledge are placed in equivalence

d) The formation of "common spaces" and "proper spaces"

In this article we will draw some continuities and discontinuities between European and Chinese Urban Sociologies.

2 Heritages and common knowledge in European and Chinese urban sociology

2.1 Marxism and Urban Sociology

Marxism has permeated both French sociology and Chinese sociology.

French School of Marxist Urban Sociology was defined as a critical sociology and appeared ten years after the American explosion of *urban studies* with Raymond Ledrut who published in 1968 *Urban Sociology*, Paul Henri Chombart de Lauwe who created at EHESS the Centre de Sociologie urbaine, Henri Lefebvre, marxist philosopher, who published in 1968 The right to the City et Christian Topalov in 1974 *Real estate developers. Contribution to the analysis of capitalist housing production in France.* Mention should also be made of an article by Manuel Castells published an article in 1968 *Is there an urban sociology*; he makes his entrance alongside other young who critic power centered on the analysis of the capitalist production of the city? urban policies of the State and social movements[13]. In 1981, *French School of Marxist Urban Sociology* is declining after a rapid and short expansion of urban studies. At the end of seventies a new critical urban sociology is emerging by the disciples of Michel Foucault as Isaac Joseph[14] and Murard and Zylberman[15] with the Journal Recherches created by Felix Guattari in 1968 and later with *Annales de la recherche urbaine* in 1978. In the perspective against the hegemony of diverse marxisms Yves Grafmeyer and Isaac Joseph introduced in 1979 in France (Lyon) the Chicago School in urban sociology. They wanted not develop fieldwork sociology about daily life, an urban sociology rid of global theories. This major event in the history of French sociology took place in University Lyon 2. Then in the eighties, in France, the central object of urban sociology became the "problem of the suburbs" which will impose on sociologists a new reflection on the city largely inspired by the School of

Chicago on which we will return; Fran ois Dubet and Didier Lapeyronnie[16] announced that the question of segregation comes to replace that of exploitation. However Edmond Preteceille and Marco Oberti[17] will distinguish several spatial figures of urban segregation, more or less strong and complex according to social categories: ghettos, rich neighborhoods, beautiful neighborhoods, ethnic enclaves, gated communities, gentrified neighborhoods, mixed neighborhoods.

In Chinese sociology we could consider a marxist urban sociology or more precisely a critical urban sociology which still does exist through different topics. The problematic of social division of space and social stratification, new middle classes and gentrification is central in Chinese urban sociology. Through the differentiation of urban lifestyles and the urban modes of consumption the theroetical objective is to improve the stratification of new middle classes[18-20]. Privatization of housing and urbanization in the perspective of critical sociology Guo Yuhua[21], is a way to introduce the awakening of citizens' rights awareness and the formation citizen's in dealing with housing as a private sphere and its identity politics. About urban inequalities, so many studies have been realized about the urban segregation of migrants with the multiplication of urban villages[22]. More recently the concept of new urban underclass is also used to describe the urban poverty. From 1990's the urban economy developed rapidly, living standards in Chinese cities improved greatly but because economic collapse and bankruptcy, unemployment and poverty. Guan Xinping[23] has distinguished four forms of urban poverty : 1) poverty produced by exclusion of subsistence security system. 2)Poverty caused by personal and family reasons. 3)Poverty caused by lay-offs. 4)Poverty caused by business downturn, especially in old industries bases and are old depleted resources and mines. We could add a new form of poverty with the category of homeless.

2.2 Chicago's School Heritage

The Chicago School was very influent in European, especially in French, as in Chinese sociology. It means the birth of the urban sociology.

In France, in 1979, Yves Grafmeyer and Isaac Joseph introduced the work of the Chicago School, then little known in France to introduce a tradition of research in urban sociology very different from the French sociology of the moment. The presentation of this current of research takes place at a time when some French sociologists in the 80s and 90s, including Lyon – and I have been part of it – are starting to work in the neighborhoods – the suburbs – where the questions of crime and deviance, where the first riots take place; these events recall the history of the city of Chicago. The numerous monographs made by Robert Park and his followers focused on the social and spatial trajectories of immigrants, daily mobility, neighborhood relations, associative life, spatial segregation of minorities, juvenile delinquency, gangs, homeless, prostitution ... Issues related to immigration and integration will take on an important status. The introduction of the work of the Chicago

School will lead to the development of a new French urban sociology around similar themes: urban "milieux" and downtown areas[24]; migration and ethnic economies[25,26]; residential trajectories and urban life[27]; youth, marginalization and intermediate spaces[28,29]; ethnicity and social worlds[30,31]; drugs' economy and youth[32]; urban poverty and homeless[33]. These works have privileged methods of ethnographic observation, life stories, case studies, analysis of personal documents .... In the foundation of this urban ecology "*the city is considered as the natural environment of forms of sociability that elaborate daily in a complex game between organization and disorganization, identities and mobilities, frequentation of the similar and experience of the other. In a text that he has always considered as a key moment in his itinerary (Resistances and Sociabilities,* 1978), *Isaac Joseph sketched the outlines of a research program that refocused on the question of urban cultures, by illuminating it. through a close dialogue with the writings of Georg Simmel and Erving Goffman*"[34]Ⅳ.

If in the French urban sociology that developed from the 80s the localized approach could be privileged as in the "community studies" linked to the Anglo-Saxon tradition, we can observe the same movement in Chinese urban sociology since the 80's linked to the influence of Fei Xiaotong. It should also be remembered that the representatives of the Chicago School, Robert Park and his son-in-law Robert Redfield, came to teach sociology in China in 1931 – 1932 and in 1948. Fei Xiaotong in the refoundation's process of Chinese sociology, was strongly inspired by them. The Chicago School is one of the most important scientific community in the history of sociology, has played a major role in the history of Western sociology but also has a continuous influence in non-Western countries, especially in China. Urban sociology and what Zhou Xiaohong[35] identified as social psychology, the two major fields in Chicago school influenced so much the first generation of Chinese sociologists . Chinese sociologists very early know about urban sociology, and so many scientific exchanges Chicago School's reference appears like a theoretical mark, especially in community surveys. The influence of Chicago's School was pregnant in the two contexts, French and Chinese sociologists have mobilized Chicago School to understand urban neighborhoods, peer groups, gangs, communities of migrants, tribe society ... Today Chicago School in Chinese Sociology is taking again a new important status in all studies on *shequ*; Liu Neng[36] showed how Fei Xiaotong, inspired by Chicago School, has developed a space-based sociology where he has used a territorial unit of analysis in rural China especially in three villages in Yunnan in 1940. He purposes to come back to space-based sociology in relying on the methodological concept of«spatial contextuality»connected with the Andrew Abott's sociological theory focused on the analysis of social life and social actions in a specific time-space context.

3 Theoretical continuities in urban sociology and transnational concepts

In this part, we would deal with the continuities of sociological knowledge and transnational concepts of some major theoretical issues in French and Chinese urban sociologies. This approach while not exhaustive is rather eloquent regarding what remains of common knowledge. We have identified the following topics as illustrations of shared theoretical space: the right to the City and housing; migration, integration and segregation.

3.1 The Right to the City and Housing

In France, over the last twenty years, urban renovation and demolition operations have taken place in working-class areas and older districts in several French cities. This signifies the eviction of tenants and the demolition of social housing buildings. For example, in Vènissieux and La Duchère, in the Lyon region, the demolition of towers … represented an important moment in the history of French cities and the construction of urban memories. In 1994, ten towers that had been walled up for ten years in Les Minguettes residential area, Vènissieux, in the agglomeration of Lyon — a city with a working-class background — were destroyed; a symbol of the working-class suburban landscape had disappeared. Between now and 2030, as part of the city's major urban projects, a vast program of urban regeneration is planned: 1 200 housing units will be demolished, 2 000 will be created and 4 000 renovated. During these urban renovation operations, forced removals occur, which then undo protections, suspend residential rights and result in the partial or total loss of community social ties and a protective environment[37]. However, it is important to distinguish here between cases of forced removals and expulsion procedures founded on the illegality of residential situations. The suspension of the right to reside signifies forms of urban eviction; in France, the stated objective of urban renovation and social diversity policies is to fight against urban segregation, but they break up households and re-concentrate the poorest families in new zones of urban relegation. In the case of demolitions, residents express their anxiety for the future and their attachment to a local community, in other words to the uses of urban spaces and practices[37]. Speaking about the right to the city through housing, French sociologists use the concepts of the social effects of eviction, the loss of sociability networks and of belonging to the neighborhood, the feeling of no longer being attached to a local community.

In Chinese cities, *urban villages*, situated in areas of urban transition between cities and rural areas, have emerged in a process of accelerated urbanization where an increasing number of migrant workers, especially youths, are arriving. These urban villages are akin to *slums*, where poor city dwellers live while working in informal sectors. Urban villages can first be defined as informal settlements structured around an illegal housing market (no official leases). How does this informality arise? For Wu Fulong[38], informality results from economic policies based on the development and management of informal regulations, and even more so from overlapping social, political and economic dimensions in the context of urban growth and a dual rural-urban land market. The diversity of urban villages reflects the variations of informality in different cities and differentiated configurations of relationships between state, market, land and city dwellers. Informality translates into sales and lease contracts and practices of an informal nature that define a construction of unregulated or under-regulated housing. These urban villages have also been described as *ant tribes*[22], like Tangjialing in Pekin, as informal housing enclaves in Gaojiabang, or as vertical villages in Liede, Canton. Urban villages, real urban enclaves, reveal new processes of urban relegation and segregation in Chinese cities, and situations of structural exclusion, to which young migrants are also victim. In this process of hyper-urbanization, the demolition of illegal housing and the reconstruction of urban *villages*, where most urban workers live in overcrowded and insalubrious conditions, are then multiplied. The central and local governments still want to put in place forms of political management controlled from above, offset the lack of infrastructure and address sanitation in these urban enclaves, all without considering the practices, uses and needs of urban village residents, and while committing to mobilize residents during urban renovations. Within the framework of urban policies, demolitions are envisaged as spatial reconfigurations radically changing the ecological structure of cities, denying residents' relationships with their communities, their social ties, to violently impose removals upon them. After the time needed to rebuild these urban villages, the least affluent migrants cannot access the new housing, whose rent is very high, nor access social rental housing[39]. They are then subject to expulsion from Chinese cities. Above all, the demolition of urban villages signifies the destruction of neighborly relations and social networks. Furthermore, outside urban villages, in other older districts being transformed in Chinese cities due to the strong growth of real estate development and land pressure housing judged to be dilapidated is destroyed, and owners are also expulsed. Yang Chen[40] showed how, in the process of urban renovation in Caoyang, the first working-class neighborhood constructed in 1950 in Shanghai, workers lost the right to job, the right to occupy the community space, the right to residential mobility to be confronted to social injustice and inequality in spatial occupancy. In 2011, *Nangfang Dushibao* reported the suicide of a villager in Changsha, Hunan Province, following the refusal of her claim for housing compensation. Property rights only last 70 years in China, expropriation is common, and suicides are multiplying.

French and Chinese sociologists analyze the "right to the city" and housing in similar terms, by questioning social and spatial eviction. They illustrate how, in both contexts, urban renovation policies based on demolition appear to disregard the poorest, most destitute and "voiceless". The loss of housing is considered as a loss of ties, attachment, roots in places and communities of destiny, and a loss of self that may provoke suicides in the Chinese example.

3.2 Migration, integration and segregation

The process of urban integration in sociology is often related to the question of migration that we will introduce here. First, the assimilation approach characterizing the Chicago School's studies of immigration[41] described how migrants could use adaptation strategies to be settled in urban enclaves, then they would usually leave these places, be involved in competition for space with other social groups, and develop their own social trajectory. Park and Burgess dealt with the concept of urban integration and segregation. The question of upward social mobility among second-generation migrant communities was broached: the assimilation theory initially showed how the children and grandchildren of migrants gradually acceded to the social statuses of the host society and that this process had an element of irreversibility about it.

Today in European cities Chicago's School's theory still could be mobilized to analyse some ascendant social trajectories of migrants, for example new entrepreneurs and traders. But about children of immigrants Chicago's School's theory is not adapted. In the neighborhoods of European cities, particularly in the working-class suburbs of French cities, spatial, social and economic segregation have increased over the last twenty years. In 2011, young people of North African origin took more than eleven months to get their first job, compared with six months or seven months for those of French descent, and twenty-four months on average to access a stable employment contract, compared with fifteen months for those of French descent. After three years of active life, youths of North African origin occupied more precarious jobs than those of French descent. So, the Chicago School's theory is not adapted to children of immigrants in Europe today. For children of immigrants, intergenerational mobility seems to be increasingly less linear and may give rise to "segmented assimilation" [42] that reflects the irregular, reversible, unexpected, multidimensional and differentiated aspects of urban and economic integration[29,43].

In Chinese Cities the internal migration of young Chinese – more and more stratified – is fundamental to understand the transformations of the regime or urbanities. The Chicago School's theory still makes sense in certain situations to understand the process of social mobility of Chinese migrant workers[44,45] and also of new international migrants in big cities, for example, successive waves of Arab and sub-Saharan traders in Guangzhou[46] and Yiwu. But this theory cannot be used to analyze the process of social disqualification for the new, less-qualified, young, internal migrants, who form a new urban underclass and experience a new poverty in "urban villages", the "ant colonies"[22,47], or new urban villages which appear on the outskirts of megalopolises; some of them are constrained to leave big cities and go back to their *laojia*. Secondly, young internal migrants graduates gain access to skilled jobs in Chinese mega-cities as technicians, executives in private or public Chinese enterprises and in international enterprises, but most of them remain migrants and are in situations of job and housing insecurity; they designate themselves as *beipiao* 北漂(nomads in Beijing). These young people, the majority of whom do not have an urban *hukou*, are victims of employment discrimination by local authorities: for example, a young graduate with a rural *hukou* cannot easily get to an urban job; young graduates are forced into informal jobs or situations of unemployment[48].

We can understand the assimilation's theory in China still is influent in urban sociology to analyze the urban process of integration and segregation. In France some sociologists have been more focused on the tension between mobility, captivity and sedentarity[26,49]. But in the two academic contexts, through the figure of *young internal migrant in China* and the figure of *the descendant of immigrant* in Europe theoretical continuities are located around the challenge to understand the complex urban life constructed on the oscillation between isolation, segregation and partial integration in the City[50]. In European cities, social, ethnic and economic boundaries as well as new urban hierarchies are appearing and producing diffracted inequalities and situations of injustice. So we have to consider the intersectionality between spatial integration/segregation, socio-economic integration/ segregation and ethnic integration/segregation.

Now in French urban sociology we are talking more and more about the «cosmopolitan condition»[51];it means for new migrants - asylum seekers and refugees - the circulations produced by globalization impose experiences rather ordeals of national, ethnic, religious, linguistic, social and cultural borders, resulting in a cosmopolitan condition in European cities. Confronted with recurring risk situations, menaces and uncertainty, the most threatened and exposed new migrants are compelled to cross a succession of borders where, each time, lives are exposed, put in danger, after having fled wars, the Taliban... The most at risk migrants are then obliged to stay, for a relatively long time, in liminal situations in European cities that do not necessarily evolve towards stable situations.

In this part about migration, segregation and integration we have observed some discontinuities continuities between Chinese and European Urban Sociologies.

Chinese and European sociologists converge in the way of thinking together, migration, social differentiation and discrimination in big Cities. In the tow contexts, the less endowed migrants in terms of social capital and economic and symbolic resources are defined as subjected to the forces of political and economic measures in a context of hyper-competition, uncertainty and globalization. But Chinese sociologists are using the concepts of *social structures*, *interactions and guanxis*, *and individual strategies*[52] to understand the migratory experience in Chinese cities; for example, they analyze how the less endowed migrants, in terms of social capital and economic and symbolic resources, are subjected to the forces of political and economic measures; they consider available networks of trust and community solidarities, the strategies to find social and spatial anchorage in economic spaces[53]. And French sociologists are using the concepts of *structural processes*, *individuation and subjectivation*, *agency and capabilities*; for example, we have noticed a proliferation of biographical bifurcations in trajectories structured in the conjunction of professional mobility and spatial mobility, where migrants are using individual and collective capabilities to exist in the city.

4 Theoretical continuous discontinuities: public space, social differentiation, collective action

Public space therefore highlights new forms of inequality when confronted with social risks and the way in which they are increased in it. It shows how individuals owning economic, social and legal goods and their own selves co-exist alongside others who have fewer resources and less support and do not own their own selves to the same extent. Public space has been conceived as being a primitive stage for politics upon which identities and group memberships come into contact and tension with each other[54]. In this part we will draw theoretical continuous discontinuities in European and Chinese urban sociologies through the following topics: public space and urban differentiation, public space and collective action.

4.1 Public space and urban differentiation

Public space and social inequalities in Western Europe

In European sociology, even if public space is represented as being traversed by inequalities with those individuals and groups ignored by democracies confronting those whose social identity has been recognised by them, it is defined as being increasingly punctuated by situations of alarm, violence and suffering which reveal situations of structural emergency and zones of anomie within the society. These are linked to economic, cultural and social disruptions which produce social contempt, self-abandonment, solitude, silence and demands for meaning and recognition. Violence in the public space is partially engendered by the processes of social stigmatisation — for example refugees, migrants, homeless - and it expresses social conflicts which are related to the non-respect of implicit rules of mutual recognition, that is, depriving individuals of rights and inter-subjective recognition of their capabilities and performance[55].

Public space is therefore dealt with as the place of political stakes and the object of investigations undertaken by those who directly manage social risks — giving orders, disciplining and moralising. This phenomenon characterises societies represented and experienced as risk societies in which the Other must be protected in order to protect the self. European sociologists thus analyse measures of public action advancing the idea of a multiplication, sharpening and miniaturisation of the forms of intervention and social and political instrumentalisation regarding those who appear "excluded from the interior" in the eyes of those who think of themselves as "included". These measures are analysed as constituting increasingly numerous controls, supervisions and mediations which contribute to the crumbling of the boundaries between public and private. They reveal a process of the State continually taking control through the management of social risks.

In the European urban society, sociologists conceive public space as the first goods accessed by every citizen. In democracies damaged by unemployment, poverties and racisms, public space is conceived as being the privileged place for the expression of social conflicts, inequalities, uncertainties and the non-recognition of the Other. Although the public space of European sociologists is defined as being fragmented by poverties and discriminations, although it is the object of multiple interventions, it is also conceived as showing how, today, plural forms of socialisation and de-socialisation overlap, co-exist and diverge revealing the vulnerability of a crumbling salaried society, an evolving urban society in which social, cultural, religious and other differences are continually aggravated. Public space demonstrates how the "excluded of the interior" and the "included" rub shoulders or avoid each other and how they do not inhabit completely separate universes. Thus, public space enables one to understand, at the micro-level, how recognition and contempt of the Other are reflected in a democracy which has been deformed by various forms of unemployment, poverty and discriminations.

New socio-spatial and economic divisions mean a reduction in the experiences and ordeals of urbanity. Increasingly large inequalities and distances separate social groups facing differentiated access to the social, economic, material and virtual resources of the contemporary city. In the European Cities social affiliations define specific forms of appropriation and control of public space, even forms of its privatisation by the upper classes organised around the principle of social homogeneity, strong closure strategies based on class togetherness with forms that vary according to the feeling of belonging[56]. Marco Oberti and Edmond Prèteceille[17] also have identified the relationships of the upper and upper middle classes to the social mixing of populations. French sociologists have done a lot of research in poor districts, especially the "banlieues ouvrières" and in the desindustrialized cities where are taking place the entangled and cumulative processes of relegation[57] in which a new urban underclass has formed and where the public space is one hand occupied by solidarities and on another hand fragmented by social conflicts. In France the great social housing crystallize spatial figure of the concentration of poverty, but we must consider a plurality of neighborhoods. Economic flexibility and job insecurity, ethnic and class discriminations are distancing young descendants of immigrants from labour markets and public space. Working class suburbs in French cities more and more look like «urban ghettos»[58].

The emergence of public space in China

The public space issue is approached in rather different terms in China given the authoritarian political regime. Although Chinese sociologists often employ the risk society notion, the notion of public space is less used since there is very little research into the public space which is emerging in Chinese society. Whereas, in the past, public space and political space tended to flow together[59], the two spaces are now very slowly moving apart, leading to the gradual emergence of individuals with rights and entitlements and the ability to operate autonomously and take responsibility in a developing public space ... This public space appears to be very different to a democratic public space even if this controlled public space can be invested by rural and commercial associations and people's organisations. In an analysis of the conditions for the forming of a public space, Zhang Jing[60] invites us to revisit the fundamental sociological theoretical issues, such as domination, by introducing the notion of civic domination in opposition to authoritarian domination. She pursues her line of reasoning with citizenship referring to the public consciousness of the members of a society and their capacity for autonomy, solidarity and civility before posing the question of the policy of recognition of individual identities.

So we could consider a public space in new gentrified districts[19] where new Chinese middle classes are occupying public space from strong closure strategies based on class togetherness with forms that vary according to the feeling of belonging. The public space in poor neighbourhoods is produced by internal migrants who are developing survival strategies but is still controlled by State and local governments. Anyway political control and mutual control are still active in the interactions in urban public space in Chinese cities[61].

In the public space in big cities – especially in Shanghai – old people are very present and organizing new forms of intra and intergenerational solidarities in creating ONG for caring in health of inhabitants, social and cultural activities ... Chinese sociologists[62] are taking account in this new phenomena to rethink the regime of urbanities in the Chinese City. In the public space in big cities especially in Shanghai old people are very present and organizing new forms of intra – and intergenerational solidarities by creating NGOs to take care of inhabitants' health, social and cultural activities ... Chinese sociologists are taking into account this new phenomenon to rethink the regime of urbanities in the Chinese city. Zhu Weijue[62] uses theories of social networks and social capital in the sense of Robert Putnam and Bian Jie, based on relationships of trust and reciprocity, to examine forms of social solidarity in *shequs*, starting with the mobilization of district residents and health-care professionals for the elderly. Although district medical facilities were planned within new urban policies, new social health inequalities appear between populations who have access to health care and those without the right, especially migrants without hukou.

Chen Jin[63] demonstrates how displaced populations internal migrants and foreigners and old people are quite excluded from urban life in public spaces because they do not have a collective memory of these places. He connects the concepts of space, place and memory to understand the urban and temporal transformation in Chinese urban society. Chen Jin[64] also illustrates how relationships between memories and places are structured from processes of embeddedness, disembeddedness and re-embeddedness of memories and places in urban modernization, particularly in two water towns, Tongli and Zhenze. The memories of residents in older neighborhoods are reconfigured in spatial and temporal continuities between places of "yesterday" and of "today", with cultural heritage activities.

4.2 Public space and collective action

Public space appears to be a place of distance and proximity, civility and incivility, negotiation and exchange, revolts and mobilizations.

New Social Protests in China

More and more export-focused companies have closed and their workers, most of them migrants, have been laid off. Young migrants have protested and faced the police, in particular in the Pearl and Yangtse delta cities, such as Shenzhen, Dongguan, Huizhou. Now, riots and urban social movements occur in all Chinese provinces. Second-generation of migrants bear the sufferings and humiliations of their parents and, while outraged, have developed a set of skills to resist and fight oppression and injustice. They are also increasingly conscious of their social rights and their level of aspirations is higher and higher[65-67]. Workers, often from the same communities, are lodged in factory dormitories, giving them the possibility to set up collective actions[68] to fight for their rights and express strong resentment against the involvement of foreign capital. These workers fight their local government and global capitalism, while young migrants develop new working-class *cultures of resistance* in urban public space.

The social conflicts and the collective struggles in the Chinese cities are centered on the property rights, object of social conflicts in the cases of demolition and expulsion of the populations. Since the 1990s, in addition to the mobilization of landlords following the housing reform, other forms of protest related to housing have emerged: protest against the destruction of entire neighborhoods and the violent eviction of their inhabitants; the creation of homeowners' committees as intermediary actors in the *shequ*[69]. Shen Yuan[70] showed how a citizen movement related to the right of property was born from the claims of the urban middle class in China for civil and political rights. The emergence of homeowners' movements has revealed tensions and social conflicts in the public space that have led the city-dwellers linked to the emerging middle classes to mobilize in an increasingly organized way. The development of skills among urban residents to mobilize for the resistance around the right of ownership reflects the way in which new forms of accessibility to the public space are being built and new demands for public recognition.

In the Chinese public space about the protests of the owners (and demonstrations anti-demolition[71] the analysis of the theories of social movements to study the organization, mobilization and strategy of various manifestations is based on the theory of resource mobilization, political opportunities and frameworks of action. Several researchers questioned the "success of the protests", particularly against demolitions to acquire land that has become a massive phenomenon in the context of economic transformation.

Collective action and riots in European Cities

Democracies are slowly crumbling under the assaults of unemployment, labor insecurity and discriminations. Public space in cities has become the main place to express individual and collective fears and uncertainties as well as social contempt. Social conflicts happen when citizens — especially descendants of immigrants and migrants - are confronted to racism and discrimination, can no longer deal with social and economic situations of *double-bind* challenges they have to face. Institutional, urban and socio-economic violence create eviction and stigmatisation, especially against young unemployed people from working-class housing projects and migrants who feel vulnerable to racism, unemployment and a society which does not give them any space.

In Western European cities, such as those of France, Italy or Spain, the decline of working-class movement, the disparition of French communist parti have produced a gaping hole, it means the non-participation of working-class to the political life, especially by young people. The disparition of organization and representation of working-class et the development of urban precariousness have produced social conflicts originate in different political, social and economic spaces. Since 1981 numerous riots are a moment of "political actualization" to resist to multiple forms of domination for "weak and vulnerable groups" when new forms of collective action are built on the margins of the conventional political field, when feelings of injustice combine with requests for respect [32,55]. Rioting is then a way to enter the public space. Urban riots express a demand for justice and citizenship and they can be seen as the exacerbation of local micro-mobilisations, or as revolts against being ascribed to irrelevant, inaccurate or unwanted roles. These riots cannot be reduced to being infra-political, they illustrate the fragility and vulnerability of political representation and the failure of former social regulations. They are not only the consequences of a crisis, they could be the turmoil accompanying the birth of a new society. In recent years, acts of urban violence have been on the rise again while the economic situation has deteriorated in working class neighbourhoods. This sater of urban riots in France shows that vulnerable, stigmatised, scorned and forgotten populations demand a new social and public recognition.

Now in segregated neighbourhoods Islam could appear as a resource for poor people, for activist involvement for the descendants of immigrants struggling for public recognition and defending their honor. For Julien Talpin and Franck Fregosi[72] ordinary Islam can appear as a vector, a support or a brake on activist engagement; associations defended Islam's values have been created to produce non-religious social work and humanitarian support, to articulate French citizenship and Islamic involvement. Muslim women are producing specific capabilities in producing new public spaces in segregated neighborhoods via the creation one new Internet medias where they are promoting an equal and just City for them and their children. In Paris, Marseille and Lyon, Muslim women are connected each other via social networks in doing an invisible political work from the bottom, they do appear as *moral entrepreneurs*[73] in mobilizing a repertoire of social, cultural and religious resources.

In the Post-Western Sociology we have observed *some continuities discontinuities* between Chinese and European Urban Sociologies. European and Chinese Sociologists have increasingly been led to think of collective action urban movements and riots as representing a whole in the present day societal context. If they have in common the consideration of different demands for recognition in public space of Chinese and European citizens, Chinese sociologists are more focused on the consciousness of «weak groups»and the authority of Chinese State about social movements.

5 Local knowledge and the invention of the City

In European urban sociology, in this case French, like in Chinese sociology, situated sociological reasoning is constructed to address the key questions of the discipline, for example: How is the city manufactured? How does urban citizenship invent itself in urban "fringes"? These questions belong to a specific French sociological tradition that has no equivalent in China. In this perspective, the city is thought of as being structured around a plurality of urban orders that are constantly being redefined and renegotiated by escaping too-normative and universalist a conception of the city to address the moral boundaries within the city and the movements from one urban space to another, from one place to another. A hierarchy of spaces and places described as "central" or "peripheral", "marginal", then appears, in which city dwellers invent the city from skills and knowledge born in spaces of weak legitimacy, where the cities work on themselves. In the context of the development of "economies of arrogance"[74], city dwellers are constantly confronted with double-bind situations between injunctions to take their place in the city and difficulties accessing spaces of strong urban legitimacy, where social and moral systems capturing "selves" and linked to emotional capitalism result in new forms of urban subordination, where the manufacturing of urban citizenship occurs through appropriation, invention, the "remote" reinterpretation of spaces, more or less spaces of strong political and economic legitimacy. The multiplication of situations of social and economic exclusion in European cities, especially in pauperized districts, generates spatial captivity and can also give rise to the production of invisible activities in urban interstices, to spatial combinations, circulations, appropriations of places that react to one another, from one city to another. Although European cities are today making evictions and expulsions, "communities of destiny"[75] and communities of experiences are also being formed from liminal socializations "at the city's edges", where unemployed youths, migrants, refugees, the voiceless ... place themselves, rally together, act to assert their humanity. This is in line with the conception of a negotiated urban order made from the instable and precarious structure of a plurality of local orders in spaces of unequal legitimacy and societal interstices in a city constantly being redefined. We introduced the concept of intermediate space to consider adhesion or non-adhesion between urban worlds[28,29]; the intermediate space contains both what seems "to make residue" and what seems "to make invention" in the city, depending on whether social worlds are coming apart or touching.

For example, in youth groups from working-class districts in European cities, social roles are defined by managing situations of instability and crisis, by peer, neighborhood, religious, cultural and family solidarities in intermediate spaces. Liminal socializations illustrate unique, plural, microbial, minor practices, revealing individuals who are both dominated but capable of inventions, the "art of making do" or tactics of the "weakest" against the "strongest"[76]. Of course, liminal socializations suppose a previous process of primary socialization and secondary socializations and theoretically demonstrate that there is no "in" or "out" but instead a continuum of hierarchical positions between them, coexisting as part of a bigger whole. These intermediate spaces see the emergence of cultures of uncertainty, even cultures of roaming made from the diversity of individual experiences constructed in situations of precariousness and from collective skills developed through managing situations of crisis, eviction, expulsion[49], from a fear of tomorrow, when the days ahead are uncertain. These cultures are structured around the ability to carry out makeshift repairs, to salvage, to exchange a service for another, or a good for another. At the basis of these cultures, there is the ability to reverse the situation, to anticipate while remaining close to one's own identity. Cultures of uncertainty demonstrate survival strategies and the management of weakened identities, what counts is to "face up" to situations of eviction, expulsion. Cultures of uncertainly are also made from these solidarities and loyalties to peers and can rely on ethnic and inter-ethnic solidarities.

Today, new intermediate spaces are being born, constructed from forms of solidarity and hospitality of European citizens regarding asylum seekers and refugees who are engaged in forms of collective action within the associations receiving them. Cosmopolitan cultures of hospitality are constructed in forms of intercultural exchanges and sharing of identities from here and elsewhere in transnational intermediate spaces.

This approach to the city has continuously been addressed in other French works. Alain Tarrius[26] proposed a paradigm of mobility to understand a city escaping urban policies; he suggested the notion of circulatory territory to show how territory contains identities and alterity, how margins, interspaces, peripheries overturning the topics of centrality, are established. Indeed, the concepts of circulatory territories, intermediate spaces, shattered the normative center/periphery pair to consider new urban cosmopolitanisms, to understand how to inhabit the transnational[77], to see mobile populations, diasporas, roaming, nomadism that reveal how the orders of mobility and sedentariness are constantly superimposed in increasingly complex assemblages and transnational networks. Considering the variety of forms of precariousness, Michel Agier[51,78-79] addressed these forms, questioning how societies, groups or social backgrounds "make the city", based on research into townships, favelas in Brazil, refugee camps and villages[51]. He also showed that the city invents itself in empty spaces of the naked city that appear during "invasions" (massive land-occupying movements by poor populations), on urban margins, in transit cities, humanitarian camps and facilities where populations who are forced to move live.

This way of manufacturing and inventing the city from margins, urban interstices and intermediate spaces reflects a current of French urban sociology inspired by a pragmatist sociology of action that has no equivalent in Chinese sociology. This can be described as a discontinuous discontinuity between French and Chinese sociology, even between knowledge niches, when we speak of urban margins, of intermediate spaces.

Conclusion

In European and Chinese societies we can observe some similarities about Right to the City and Lodging, segregation and integration processes, we also can understand how the socialist trajectory and the democratic one do influence in different ways the construction of public space. Sociologists are using common theory to explain urban worlds but they always are confronted to the necessity to be focused on global and local, general and singular realities. What makes urban specificity in Chinese and European societies for sociologists? For example the process of hyper-urbanization in China or the integration of asylum seekers and refugees in European cities. Even sociologists are involved in a process if internationalization, even we are travelling transnational academic spaces, local knowledge and traditions do influence "sociological eyes", for example our way of thinking space and time, mobility and immobility, centers and margins, State and citizenship ... So we have seen how some theoretical and empirical *discontinuous continuities* and *continuous discontinuities* between European and Chinese urban sociologies are producing Post-Western sociology.

About the author

Professor Laurence Roulleau-Berger is a Research Director at CNRS, Triangle. She is also the French Director of the International Associated Laboratory CNRS-ENS Lyon/CASS "Post-Western Sociology in Europe and in China" Ecole Normale Supérieure de Lyon-Triangle.

Bibliographie

[1] Dufoix, S. Les naissances académiques du global (Global's academic births) [M]// Caillé, A.,

Dufoix, S. Le tournant global des sciences sociales. Paris: La Découverte, 2013:27-44.

[2] Li Peilin. Sociology and the Chinese Experience[M]// Li Peilin, Li Qiang, Ma Rong. Sociology and Chinese Society. Beijing: Social Sciences Academic Press of China, 2008.

[3] Zhou Xiaohong. China Studies: Possible Stand and Paradigm reconstruction[J]. Sociological studies, 2010(2).

[4] Xie Lizhong. Houshehuixue (Post-sociologie) [M]. Beijing: Presses Académiques des Sciences Sociales, 2012.

[5] Nishihara, K. Phenomenological sociology in Japan and its significance for contemporary social research[M]// Elliott, A., Katagiri, M., Sawai, A. Japanese social theory. From individualization to globalization in Japan today. London and New York: Routedge Publishers, 2013.

[6] Yasawa, S. Civilizational Encounter, Cultural Translation and Social Reflexivity: A Note on History of Sociology in Japan[M]// Seung Kuk Kim, Li Peilin, Shujiro Yasawa. A quest of East Asian Sociologies. Seoul: Seoul National University Press, 2014: 131-167.

[7] Han, S.-J., Shim, Y.-H. Redefining second modernity for East Asia: a critical assessment [J]. The British Journal of Sociology, 2010, 61(3): 465-488. Kang Jung. Academic Dependency: Western-centrism in Korean political science[J]. Korean Journal, Winter,2006: 115-135.

[8] Bhargava, R. Pour en finir avec l'injusticeépistémique du colonialism[J]. Socio, 2013: 41-77.

[9] Li Peilin, Qu Jingdong. History of Sociology in China in the First Half of the Twentieth Century[M]. Beijing: Social Sciences Academic Press, 2011.

[10] Roulleau-Berger, L., Li Peilin. European and Chinese Sociologies. A New Dialogue[M]. Leiden: Brill Publishers, 2012.

[11] Roulleau-Berger, L. Post-Western Revolution in Sociology. From China to Europe [M]. Leiden&Boston: Brill publishers, 2016.

[12] Xie Lizhong. What is Post-Western Sociology? [M]// Xie lizhong, L. Roulleau-Berger. The fabric of sociological knowledge. Explorations of sociological knowledge. Beijing: Peking University Press, 2017.

[13] Topalov, C. Trente ans de sociologie urbaine, Un point de vue fran çais. Métropolitiques [EB/OL]. (2013-10-16). http://www.metropolitiques.eu/Trente-ans-de-sociologie-urbaine.html.

[14] Joseph, Isaac. Disciplines àdomicile. L'édification de la famille [M]. Fontenay-sous-Bois: Recherches, 1977 (28).

[15] Murard, Lion et Zylberman, Patrick. Le Petit Travailleur infatigable. Villes-usines, habitat et intimités au XIXe siècle[M]. Fontenay-sous-Bois: Recherches, 1976.

[16] Dubet, François et Lapeyronnie, Didier. Les Quartiers d'exil [M]. Paris: Seuil, 1992.

[17] Oberti, M., Préteceille, E. La ségrégation urbaine [M]. Paris: La découverte, 2016.

[18] Zhou Xiaohong. La classe moyenne chinoise: réalitéou illusion? (Chinese middle- class: reality or illusion?) [M]// Rocca, J. L. La sociétéchinoise vue par ses sociologues (Chinese society through its sociologists'eyes) Paris: Les Presses de sciences Po, 2008: 141-161.

[19] Chen Yingfang. City Chinese logic[M]. Peking: Joint Publishing Company, 2012.

[20] Zhang Dunfu. The marketization of housing and its social consequences: Housing consumption of the urban Chinese middle-class and lower class[J]. Journal of Lanzhou University, 2010, 38: 106-113.

[21] Guo Yuhua. Individualization in China under Compressed and Contradictory Modernity [J]. Temporalités, 2018(26).

[22] Lian Si. Mazu (Ants) [M]. Cuilin: Guanxi Normal University Press, 2009.

[23] Guan Xinping. Contemporary poverty issues and the characteristics of poverty in China[M]// Li Peilin. Chinese Society-Change and transformation. London and New York: Routledge Publishers, 2012.
[24] Grafmeyer, Y. Habiter Lyon. Milieux et quartiers du centre-ville[M]. Lyon: PUL, 1991.
[25] Peraldi, M., dir. Cabas et containers. Activités marchandes informelles et réseaux migrants frontaliers (Shopping bags and containers. Informal merchant activities and borders' migrant networks) [M]. Paris: Maisonneuve et Larose, 2001.
[26] Tarrius, A., in collaboration with Missaoui, L. Les nouveaux cosmopolitismes. Mobilités, identités, territoires (New cosmopolitanisms: Mobilities, identities, territories) [M]. La Tour d'Aigues: l'Aube, 2000.
[27] Authier, J. Y. La vie des lieux; Un quartier du Vieux-Lyon au fil du temps[M]. Lyon: PUL, 1993.
[28] Roulleau-Berger, L. La ville-intervalle: jeunes entre centre et banlieue (The interval-city: youths between center and suburbs) [M]. Paris: M ridiens Klincksieck, 1991. Reedited in 1993.
[29] Roulleau-Berger, L. Le travail en friche. Les mondes de la petite production urbaine (Redefining the notion of work. The worlds of small-scale urban production) [M]. La Tour d'Aigues: Editions de l'Aube, 1999.
[30] Payet, JP. Coll ges de banlieue. Ethnographie d'un monde scolaire [M]. Paris: Méridiens Klincksieck, 1995.
[31] Boubeker, A. Les mondes de l'ethnicité. La communautéd'expérience des héritiers de l'immigration maghrébine (Ethnicity's worlds. The common experience of maghreb immigration's heirs) [M]. Paris: Balland, 2003.
[32] Kokoreff, M. La force des quartiers (The disadvantaged areas' strength) [M]. Paris: Payot, 2003.
[33] Pichon, P. Survivre la nuit et le jour. La préservation de soi face au circuit d'assistance[J]. Politix, 1996, 34(2).
[34] Grafmeyer, Yves et Joseph, Isaac. 4 èmeédition. L'École de Chicago. Naissance de l'écologie urbaine [M]. Paris: Flammarion. 2004.
[35] Zhou Xiaohong. Contribution and Limitation of Chicago School [M]. Chengdu: Social Science Research, 2004.
[36] Liu Neng. Field research methodology reconsidered: reading Earthbound China's Introduction[M]// Ma, Rong, et al. Fei Hisao-Tung and China's sociology and anthropology. Beijing: Social Sciences References Press. 2008: 789-798.
[37] Deboulet, A., Lafaye, C. La rénovation urbaine, entre délogement et relogement. Les effets sociaux de l'éviction[J]. L'Année Sociologique, 2018(1): 155-183.
[38] Wu Fulong. Housing in Chinese Urban Villages: The dwellers, Conditions and Tenancy Informality [J]. Housing Studies, 2016, 31(7): 852-870.
[39] Zhao Yeqin. The Logic of the Illegal Housing Market and Living Uncertainty: The Case of the Demolition of Illegal Constructions in an urban village in Shanghai[C]. Communication in 2017 City and Society International Forum, Tongji University, [2017-10-28].
[40] Yang Chen. History, Identity, Space: Three dimensions of the Research on workers' Villages[J]. Time + Architecture, 2017(2): 10-15.
[41] Park, R. E., Burgess, E. W., McKenzie, R. D. The City. Suggestions for investigations of Human Behavior in the Urban Environment[M]. Chicago: The University of Chicago Press, 1925.
[42] Zhou, M. Segmented assimilation: issues, controversies and recent research on the new second

generation[J]. International migration review, 1997, 31(4): 825-858.

[43] Roulleau-Berger, L. Migrations, plural economies and new stratifications in Europe and in China [M]// Li Peilin, Roulleau-Berger, L. China's internal and International Migration. London and New York: Routledge Publishers, 2013: 269-275.

[44] Li Peilin. Chinese Society-Change and transformation [M]. London and New York: Routledge Publishers, 2012.

[45] Li Chunling. Institutional and Non-institutional Path: Different Processes of Socio- economic Status Attainment of Migrants and Non-migrants in China[M]// Li Peilin, Roulleau-Berger, L. China's internal and International Migration. London and New York: Routledge Publishers, 2013: 26-40.

[46] Liu Haifang. Mapping the New Migrants between China and Africa: Theoretical and Methodological Challenges[M]// Li Peilin, Roulleau-Berger, L. China's internal and International Migration. Oxon and New York: Routledge Publishers, 2013: 234-245.

[47] Liu Ziqin. Les jeunesdiplômés chinois à l'épreuve de la précarité. Mobilités, accès àl'emploi et rapport au travail[D]. Thèse de sociologie soutenue le 28N novembre 2014 sous la direction de L. Roulleau-Berger, ENS Lyon.

[48] Roulleau-Berger, L., Yan Jun. Travail et migration. Jeunesses chinoises àShanghai et Paris[M]. La Tour d'Aigues: L'Aube, 2017.

[49] Roulleau-Berger, L. Migrer au féminin[M]. La Tour d'Aigues: L'aube, 2010.

[50] Hannerz, U. Exploring the City: Inquiries Toward an Urban Anthropology. New York: Columbia University Press, 1982.

[51] Agier, M. La condition cosmopolite [M]. Pairs: La découverte, 2013.

[52] Li Peilin, Li Wei. The Work Situation and Social Attitudes of Migrant Workers in China under the Crisis[M]// Li Peilin, Roulleau-Berger, L. China's internal and International Migration. Oxon and New York: Routledge Publishers, 2013: 3-26.

[53] Liu Yuzhao, Tian Qing. Entreprises familiales rurales et gestionéconomique enChine: le cas de Baiyangdian (Rural family businesses and economic management in China: the Baiyangdian case) [M]// Roulleau-Berger, L., Liu Shiding. Sociologies économiques française et chinoise: regards croisés (French and Chinese economic sociologies: crossed perspectives). Lyon: ENS Editions, 2014: 51-62.

[54] Joseph, I. La ville sans qualités[M]. La Tour d'Aigues: Editions de l'Aube, 1998.

[55] Roulleau-Berger, L. La rue, miroir des peurs et des solidarités (The street: miror of fears and solidarities) [M]. Paris: PUF, 2004.

[56] Grafmeyer, Yves, Authier, Jean-Yves. Sociologie urbaine[M]. Paris: Nathan, 2008.

[57] Grafmeyer, Yves. Sociologie urbaine[M]. Paris: Nathan, 1994.

[58] Lapeyronnie, Didier. Ghetto urbain. Ségrégation, violence, pauvretéen France aujourd'hui [M]. Paris: Robert Laffont, 2008.

[59] Zhang Jing. Evolution politique et justification des normes de légitimitédans le discours social (Political evolution and justification of legitimacy norms in social discourse) [M]// Roulleau-Berger, L., Guo Yuhua, Li Peilin, Liu Shiding. La nouvelle sociologie chinoise (New Chinese sociology). Paris: Editions du CNRS, 2008: 381-411.

[60] Zhang Jing. Dual integration of social order: analysis of a case of property right dispute[M]// Roulleau-Berger, L., Li Peilin. European and Chinese Sociologies: A new dialogue. Leiden: Brill Publishers, 2012: 223-235.

[61] Fan Jingyu, Heritage Community Interaction, Conflict and Social Integration[C]. Communication in 2017 City and Society International Forum, Tongji University, [2017-10-28].

[62] Zhu Weijue. Social Influencing Factors of the Health of the Elderly: An Empirical Study Based on Comprehensive Survey Data of Shanghai Community. In Zhu Weijue ed, Communauty studies and planning in Shanghai[M]. Beijing: Social Science Academic Press (China), 2016.

[63] Chen Jin. Community Changes and Community Comparative Study: Memory, Location, Identity) [M]// Zhu Weijue. Communauty studies and planning in Shanghai. Beijing: Social Science Academic Press (China), 2016.

[64] Chen Jin. Modernitécompressée, mémoires et lieux dans deux villes d'eau, Tongli et Zhenzi[J]. Temporalités, 2018, 26.

[65] Liu Neng. Theoretical Thoughts on Contemporary Chinese Massive Collective Actions: Observations from Empirical Cases[J]. Open Times, 2008(3): 110-123.

[66] Liu Neng. Collective Actions in Changing Contemporary Chinese Society: An Overview of Three Waves of Collective Actions in the Last Three Decades[J]. Academia Bimestris, 2009(4): 146-152.

[67] Cai He, Liu Linping, Wan Xiangdong. Chengshi hua jingcheng zhong de nongmin-gong: laizi zhujiang sanjiaozhou de yanjiu (Migrant workers in urbanization process. A research from the Pearl River delta[J]. Zhongshan daxue shehui xue wenku, 2009.

[68] Pun Ngai, Hu H. L. Unfinished Proletarianization: self, Anger, and Class Action Among the Second Generation of Peasant Workers in Present-Day China[J]. Modern China, 2009: 436-493.

[69] Merle, A. Homeowners of Beijing. Unite! the construction of a collective mobilisation[J]. China Perspectives, 2014(2): 7-15.

[70] Shen Yuan. Vers les droits du citoyen: la défense des droits des propriétaires comme mouvement citoyen dans la Chine contemporaine[M]// L. Roulleau-Berger, Guo Yuhua, Li Peilin, Liu Shiding (dir). La nouvelle sociologie chinoise. Paris: Editions du CNRS, 2008.

[71] Lü Dewen. Meijie yunyuan, dingzi hu yu kangzhen zhengzhi: Yihuang shijian zai fenxi (Media Mobilization, Demolition-Resistant Families, and Contentious, Politics: Reanalysis of the Event of Yihuang) [J]. Shehui, 2012(3).

[72] Talpin, Julien O'Miel, Franck Frégosi, L'islam et la cité. Engagements musulmans dans les quartiers populaires[M]. Villeneuve d'Ascq: Presses Universitaires du Septentrion, 2017.

[73] Becker H. S. Outsiders: studies in the sociology of deviance[M]. New York: The Free Press of Glencoe, 1963.

[74] Favereau, O. Arrogance de l'économie et économie de l'arrogance in Enriquez, E. (dir), L'arrogance. Un mode de domination néolibéral[M]. Paris: Editions in Press, 2015.

[75] Pollak, M. L'expérience concentrationnaire. Essai sur le maintien de l'identitésociale (The experience of concentration camps. An essay on the upholding of the self) [M]. Paris: Métailié, 1990.

[76] Certeau, M. De. L'Invention du quotidien, I: Arts de faire (The invention of daily routine, I: Arts of doing) [M]. Paris: Gallimard Folio, 1980.

[77] Bastide, L. Habiter le transnational. Espace, travail et migration entre Java, Kuala Lumpur et Singapour[M]. Lyon: ENS Éditions, 2015.

[78] Agier, M. L'Invention de la ville. Banlieues, townships, invasions et favelas. Amsterdam[J]. Éditions des Archives Contemporaines, 1999.

[79] Agier, M. Les migrants et nous[M]. Paris: CNRS Editions, 2016.

[80] Agier, M. Le couloir des exilés. Etreétranger dans un monde commun. Editions du Croquant[M].

Bellecombe-en-Bauges: Editions du Croquant, 2011.

[81] Burgess, Ernest W. et Bogue, Donald J. (dir.). Contributions to Urban Sociology[M]. Chicago: University of Chicago Press, 1984.

[82] Chang Kyung-Sup. China as a Complex Risk Society. Risk Components of Post-Socialist Compressed Modernity[J]. Temporalités, 2017(26).

[83] Chombart de Lauwe, Paul-Henry. Paris. Essais de sociologie, 1952-1964[M]. Paris: Éditions Ouvri res, 1965.

[84] Grafmeyer, Yves et Joseph, Isaac. L'École de Chicago. Naissance de l'écologie urbaine[M]. Seyssel: Champ Vallon, 1979.

[85] Kokoreff, Michel. Sociologie des émeutes[M]. Paris: Payot, 2008.

[86] Ledrut, Raymond. Sociologie urbaine. Paris: Presses universitaires de France, collection Le Sociologue, 1968.

[87] Lefebvre, Henri. Le Droit àla ville[M]. Paris: Anthropos, 1968.

[88] Li Peilin. La modernisation orientale et l'expérience chinoise[J]. Socio, 2015(5): 25-45.

[89] Park, R. The urban community as a spatial pattern and a moral order[M]// Park, R., Burgess, E. W. The urban community[M]. Chicago: University of Chicago Press, 1926.

[90] Peraldi, M., dir. Cabas et containers. Activités marchandes informelles et réseaux migrants frontaliers (Shopping bags and containers. Informal merchant activities and borders' migrant networks) [M]. Paris: Maisonneuve et Larose, 2001.

[91] Wu Fulong. Informality and the Development and Demolition of Urban Villages in the Chinese Peri-urban Area[J]. Urban Studies, 2013, 50(10): 1919-1934.

[92] Wu Fulong. Housing in Chinese Urban Villages: The dwellers, Conditions and Tenancy Informality [J]. Housing Studies. 2016, 31(7): 852-870.

社会可持续城市：自主性、融合与生存[①]

莎伦·佐金

摘　要　本演讲以有关过去几年城市经历的著名影像开头——自然灾害中的城市、战争中的城市、作为公民空间的城市，勾勒出城市中包含的或者正在场所中发生的社会矛盾。城市是极端富裕和贫穷、环境破坏和可持续性、一元管理和多元参与、包容和排斥同时存在的地方。这些矛盾很多基于对土地的控制：作为巨大的特定经济集中地，城市控制着农村的产品；在城市中控制着土地的人和机构成为一种永续的权力结构，它所带来的增长既可能有着社会的可持续性，但也可能破坏社区共同体。我们能定义城市居民真的需要什么吗？“诉求”到底是什么样的？这个演讲将“诉求”解释成自由、向上的社会流动、不感到无聊以及原真性，它们也和联系、根基、自主性矛盾地结合在一起。对“自主性”的深入探索引出了有关当前一些重要因素和进程的影响的讨论，例如来自城市外部的投资（外商直接投资或者海外投资，尤其在房地产开发方面），从“创新城市”到私人短期房屋租赁以振兴经济的“全球工具包”，国家-地方政府权力的组织以及城市绅士化。最后一个问题是，考虑到文化、经济以及永续的权力结构，当前以“智慧城市”为目标的政策是否更好？

关键词　诉求；可感的悖论；自主性；社会可持续性

Socially Sustainable Cities: Autonomy, Integration, Survival

Sharon Zukin

Abstract　Beginning with well-known visual images of urban experiences in the past few years — cities in natural disasters, cities at war, and cities as civic spaces — the presentation outlines the social contradictions that cities always embody or "put into place." Cities are places of extreme wealth and poverty, environmental destruction and sustainability, oligarchy and democracy, and tolerance and intolerance. Many of these contradictions are based on the control of land: cities as enormous specialized economic concentrations control production in the countryside, and the people and institutions who control land in the city become a permanent power structure that manages growth in ways that may be both socially sustainable and destructive of communities. Can we define what city dwellers really desire? What does "desire" look like? The presentation interprets "desire" for freedom, upward social mobility, lack of boredom, and authenticity in terms of a paradoxical combination of connections, roots, and autonomy. Looking more deeply into "autonomy" raises questions about the influence of several important contemporary factors and processes, such as investment from outside the city (foreign direct investment, or overseas

① 本文根据莎伦·佐金教授在2017“城市与社会”国际学术论坛上的发言整理、翻译，英文稿经演讲者审阅。文稿编辑者：邓世碧，上海同济城市规划设计研究院助理研究员；校对：钟晓华，同济大学社会学系副教授。

investment, especially in property development); a "global toolkit" of revitalization strategies, from "city of innovation" policies to private short-term rentals of housing; the organization of national-local state powers; and gentrification. The final question is whether current policies that aim at a "smart" city will be better, in terms of culture, economy, and the permanent power structure.

Keywords desire; tangible paradoxes; autonomy; socially sustainable

你们或许知道,对于城市的未来,城市社会学家并不像城市规划师或政府官员那么确定。我们通常是提出启发性问题的人。我们会提出,如果要实现幸福、安全、包容和可持续,有哪些问题必须被解决。我今天的演讲尝试解构"城市是什么",提问"当前的城市环境是什么""对于世界上的城市,我们知道什么""我们可以在合作的讨论中引入哪些比较"?城市是经济、文化、社会全球化进程的发生之地,面临着如何整合地方利益和全球利益的问题,因为有些时候全球化的进程会对地方社会整合模式产生破坏性的影响。

1 比较是可能的吗?

我问自己的第一个问题就是,是否有可能比较不同的城市?对于世界上的城市,我们了解些什么,即使我们没有机会去那里?今天,我们在包括数字媒体、社交媒体、电影、电视、各类出版物等在内的各种各样的媒体上看到很多的城市形象,并且发现这些形象对我们而言是如此熟悉。我们不仅对这些地方感到熟悉(至少在视觉上熟悉),同时也看到了全世界城市景观出现千篇一律的形象:出现在世界某个区域的高楼大厦,逐渐地扩散到其他地方;兴起于香港、曼谷的城市购物商场逐渐出现在上海;在过去二至五年里面蓬勃发展的联合办公空间、创业孵化空间和加速器,也逐渐在全世界范围内扩展,从纽约、伦敦蔓延到了北京和成都。因此,存在一种全球性的城市话语(urban language),它至少对于那些受过最良好教育、社会流动性最高的城市人群来说是很熟悉的。

但是,我们也看到一些令人伤感的城市形象在全球变得人尽皆知:比如,给环境可持续发展带来巨大问题的自然灾害(图 1)。很多城市都建在水滨——河边或者海边。无论是在纽约、上海、伦敦,还是在世界上很多的城市,人们都被迫面对这样一个紧迫的问题——不断在水边建造新建筑的同时,我们怎么可能建设一种可持续性?对纽约与上海而言,这个问题更为严峻,因为这两座城市的很多重要的新建筑物都仍然出现在水滨。

我们对于让人非常悲伤的战争图像也同样记忆犹新。我们都不希望看到自己社会的战争景象,也为世界其他地方被摧毁的城市感到悲哀。但在当前,被战争摧毁的城市形象对于我们而言真的再熟悉不过了(图 2)。

来源：https://www.cnbc.com/2017/08/28/underwater-metropolis-photos-of-houston-before-and-after-historic-flooding.html.

图 1　自然灾害：飓风哈维，休斯敦

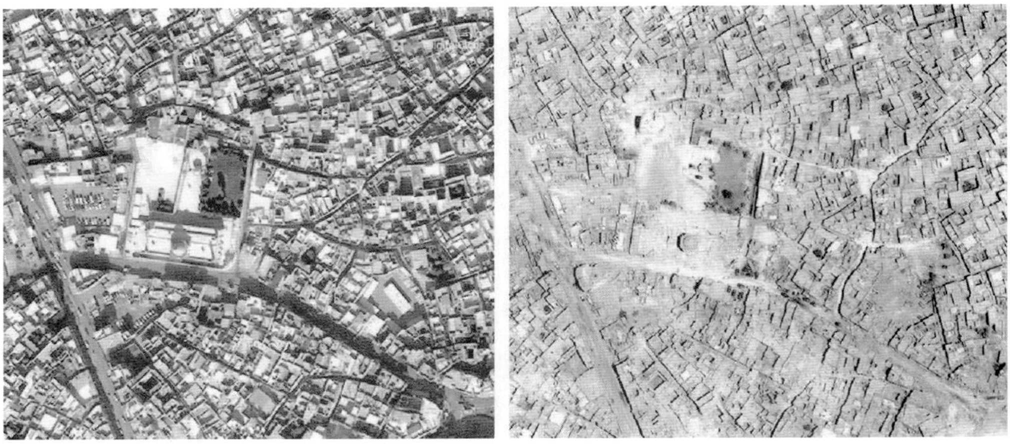

来源：https://www.washingtonpost.com/news/worldviews/wp/2017/07/20/a-birds-eye-view-of-the-ruins-of-mosul/? utm_term=.274c5543bc4f.

图 2　战争：卫星上看到的伊拉克摩苏尔大清真寺

注：左图拍摄于 2015 年 11 月 13 日，右图拍摄于 2017 年 7 月 8 日(数字地球)

我们同样非常熟悉那些被用来展示市民要求的中央公共空间的场景，无论是 2011 年开罗的“阿拉伯之春”(图 3)，还是发生在纽约的“占领华尔街”的情景(图 4)。全世界都对这些场景很熟悉，我们不能也不该忘记它们，因为它们也是各个城市社会对社区包容与社会可持续性的鲜活诉求的一部分。

来源:http://www.nytimes.com/2011/01/31.

图 3　开罗解放广场,2011

来源:Richard Rosen 摄

图 4　占领华尔街,2011

2　城市化进程中的“城市”?

在 21 世纪的某个节点上,预计 80%的世界人口都会生活在城市里面。那么,在这样一个城市化的世界里面,“城市”究竟意味着什么?如果你去看美国最优秀的地理学家们的作品,你会发现“城市”的定义有非常强的功能主义色彩,它基于关于土地的权力。但是,以一种更加复杂的方式来看的话,它也是一个基于“对立”的定义。城市集中了各种各样的资源,将各种行动进行了极端而良好的专门化,还包含了远远高于其他人类聚居类型的非凡的多样性——可能是经济、人口、文化类型或者生活方式的多样性。我们也看到,在城市中有两种不同的城市文化都被称为“世界主义”(cosmopolitanism):比较传统的一种是“世界性地极致化”(worldly sophistication)。21 世纪的上海就是一个很好的例子。相对农村居民而言,城市居民对于自己直接接触的环境之外的世界了解更多。过去二十年里，随着越来越多的农村居民移居到城市、越来越多的跨国移民发生在欧洲、美国、非洲、拉丁美洲的城市中，人们从一个地区移居到另一地区的城市中，“世界主义”的另一层意义变得越来越重要，那就是世界性地融合(worldly integration)。这层含义表明，城市的文化也是全球的文化，是由不同的移民文化所组成的。

我的学生总是要求我明确地定义城市，那我就试试吧。“城市”是一种物质的景观，同时也是参与不同的经济活动的人的功能性地聚集；它还是一系列与居住于城市边缘和农村的人们不同的文化形式。

但是，“城市”也是矛盾的，城市本质上就是充满矛盾的。例如，城市环境是脆弱的，因为我们是如此依赖电力、数字化沟通、对自然环境的重塑。但城市同时也是有弹性的，因为它们是人口的高密度聚集。因此，我们可以提问：对于人类的未来而言，城市是好还是坏？

2.1 具体的悖论

罗伯特·博勒加德(Robert A. Beauregard)是城市规划专家，他最近出版了一本书，叫《城市时代的城市：异议》(*Cities in the Urban Age: A Dissent*)，书中谈到，城市包含四个悖论：

城市聚集了社会中最多的财富，与此同时又展现出非常明显的贫穷。城市是破坏自然环境的，因为我们使用、并且浪费了太多的能源和资源；但城市又具备规划更好的环境可持续性的能力。城市通常由精英团队或者寡头来管理，但同时城市又是人们聚集起来表达民主诉求的地方。在城市中，人们包容陌生人并在平等的基础上互动；但也是在城市中，人们表达不包容性，因为他们与那些生活方式、语言、宗教不同于他们的陌生人生活得太近了。

为什么城市会有这么多悖论呢？是因为我们无论是资本主义国家还是社会主义国家，或者介于二者之间，都具有某些形式的资本主义经济吗？还是仅仅因为城市是一个不断扩张的大型人类聚居区？或者因为它是一种被称为“城市”的东西？只要有“城市”的条件存在，往往就会催生这些悖论，而不论我们的政策是什么样的？

2.2 土地与权力

如果大家认同这样的观点，即在任何形式的人类聚落，尤其在城市中，土地是权力的基础，那么我们就必须问：城市里面究竟衍生了那些类型的权力？我们有通过在一个地方整合生产与消费带来的权力。对生产和消费的掌控成为控制土地的人的权力来源。

城市也是交易所根植的地方——无论这种交易是商品的还是资本的。因此，许多城市中的权力(power in the cities)以及城市的权力(power of cities)是建立在偏远地区和城市政府的整合的基础上的。换言之，城市实际上是整合各种类型的全球流动的一个端点或节点。

但是，第三点，城市中往往有一个永恒的权力架构在控制着土地。人民在更替、个体在更迭，但是控制土地的基础机构几乎没有变化。

社会学家约翰·罗根(John Logan)和哈维·莫洛奇(Harvey Molotch)在他们多年前出版的《都市财富——空间的政治经济学》(*Urban Fortunes*)一书中就写过了相关的内容。他们把城市看作一个推动增长的机器，这种增长是基于一个对土地进行开发、再开发、重新开发的连续过程，涉及新的用途、人群、经济，但一直保持不变的是：由控制土地的权力架构来决定什么活动会成为新增长的一部分。每个社会中的机构略有差异，但通常来讲，这种永恒的权力架构包括城市政府、房地产开发商和土地的所有者。在欧洲、美国、中国的城市中都可以看到这样的组合。对于不同的机构，权力份额分配可能有所不同，但一定是这三个群体才能真正做出决定城市增长方式的基本决策。所以，城市里存在这样一对非常有趣的权力架构的组合：政府的权力架构统治着某块领土(rule of territory)，有时候有一个金融的权力架构控制着上面的土地(control of land)；而在有些情况下，会存在一个同时控制政府和土地所有权的永恒权力架构。如果整合了这两种形式的权力，就有可能会产生非常强有力的社会整合——这就引出下一个问题，当其权力非常强大的时候，这种永恒的权力架构如何能够创造包容性？如何能够创造社会的可持续性？权力架构能够通过强制达到整合吗？或者它能够通过“诉求”(desire)来强迫服从吗？

2.3 美学诉求？超越还是固守？

在各个城市行走的时候我拍过很多照片。这两张是我最近在布鲁克林绅士化的街区中拍摄的(图 5，图 6)。我们能通过这两张照片来理解城市景观是如何利用美学的诉求来实施整合的吗？

左边是一家餐厅门口的画像，看上去像是一位墨西哥艺术家的一幅画，但是看起来非常奇怪，甚至激进(图 5)。这幅画代表了什么呢？是代表了某种文化革命吗？还是代表了一种新的美学？但是在同样一个社区，仅仅几个街区之外，就是另外一种美学——我们所熟悉的、在上海或者世界上许多其他城市都能看到的情景：人们穿着黑色 T 恤、坐在大的木质桌子边、在笔记本电脑上工作，喝着啤酒或咖啡等等(图 6)。这些都发生在布鲁克林的一小片区域中，同一个城市中的同一个社区。我们应该如何解释这些现象？这个社区里的人们到底想要什么？

图 5　Crown Heights，Brooklyn

图 6　Crown Heights，Brooklyn

下面两幅图，一幅是南京的一个非常时尚的书店(图 7)，一幅是一个因为没有取得经营许可证而在去年关闭的上海小商店(图 8)。你可能会说：“这不就是一些店铺吗？它们能超越什么？”这两个空间中蕴含的抗争(rebellions)是什么？在这两种空间中，人们想要表达某种东西吗？他们是想要表达一种对更加包容的城市文化的诉求吗？

图 7　南京先锋书店

图 8　上海街边被关闭的无证商店

2.4　城市能否支持人们的愿望？

城市中的“诉求”是什么意思？人们想要什么？我们如何发现人们想要什么？以及怎么样才可能通过他们的诉求去塑造包容和可持续性？我认为，人们所希望建成的“美好城市”包含四个主要的目标：第一个目标就是拥有自由的空间。什么叫“自由”空间？就是人们能够在这些空间里面展现他们认为代表了“自由”的行为，能够拥有社会生活的自由。第二个目标是移居到城市的人们持续追求的东西，那就是实现向上的社会流动：养家糊口、生活得越来越好，拥有更好的居住条件、交通条件，以及所有好的城市规划能带给他们的益处。第三个目标就是加入城市生活这个大舞台上，观看街道上的行人、观察和体验所有迁徙到城市中的人们所带来的文化多样性。人们有时候通过品尝来自不同地方的食物、有时候通过逛不同的商店、有时候通过在公共空间中与来自许多不同地方，但是同样在这个城市有归属感的人们待在一起来体验这种多样性。第四个目标就是人们对于城市中的原真性的追求，这点我在《裸城》(*Naked City*)一书里面曾提及。这个其实是一个矛盾的诉求，因为尽管我们知道城市总是在不断发展变化，还是希望与他人建立联系、扎根于社会。这四个主要目标乍一看非常简单，但其实非常复杂。

有一种形式的原真性依赖于人们建立本地的社会网络、本地的相互依赖性，从而创造地方认同感。在当前的欧洲和美国的城市里，这种在本地生活的归属感非常强，但在中国却不是那么强——你可能会说，你住在市中心、住在郊区、住在这个或那个区(district)，但是你或许没有那种住在某个有别于其他地方的、特定的社区(neighborhood)的感觉。另外一种形式的原真性要求有稳定的住房(secure housing)，无论你是房屋所有者还是租赁者。在地方层面上使人们感觉相互联系在一起的社区连接是很有必要的。但也必须使人们在某种程度上感觉本地社区具有决定自身命运的自主性。

但是，我们的城市是否真的是自主的？以纽约为例：外商在纽约房地产领域的投资比例非常之高(图 9)——在外国投资者拥有纽约如此多的房产的情况下，普通的纽约市民能否决定他们自己的社区事务呢？又或者，如果没有足够多的社会住房给人们去住，他们当然不能产生“自主”的感觉。比如说在纽约，如果价格高昂的、私人所有的公寓更多的话，对于租户来说意味着什么?他们就没有“自主”的感觉。如果在纽约或者其他城市存在一个非常大的系统、在其中人们以投资为目的购买公寓并且短租出去,对于这些人的邻居的自主权又意味着什么?这些问题在美国和欧洲的城市很严重,可能在中国也同样如此。

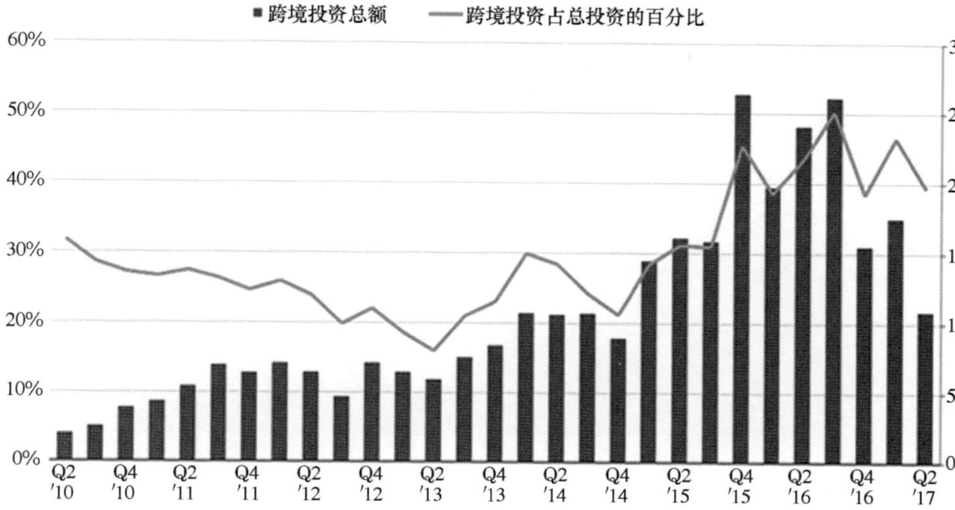

来源:https://therealdeal.com/2017/08/29/the-long-view-nyc-real-estate-is-addicted-to-foreign-cash-the-withdrawal-symptoms-aint-going-to-be-pretty/

图 9　2010—2017 年外商在纽约投资房地产的情况

影响城市自主性的第二个因素是政府的国土结构。美国不仅有一个非常强有力的联邦政府,还有非常强有力的州政府。美国有五十个州(相当于中国的省),州政府控制着城市的政府想要控制的很多功能,包括房屋租赁、公共交通、教育等领域,住在城市里面的人依靠州政府制定的政策来生活。

影响社区自主性的第三个因素是绅士化,即通过对房屋和商店的再开发使得高收入群体置换低收入群体。以纽约为例,我们看到市场力量、建筑物业主所驱动的绅士化——而本地政府并不想逆转这样的趋势(图 10)。在阿姆斯特丹,我们看到政府推动的绅士化:城市政府以打破贫困集中为由驱赶外国移民,以此来提高住房和商店的层次(图 11)。在上海,或许存在一种由市场、政府和建筑物业主三个因素驱动的复合型绅士化,通过使新资本、新用途和新移民流入某些特定的区域带来实现(图 12)。这些城市中,有没有哪个帮助社区变得自主、变得具有社会可持续性了?

图 10　纽约市场驱动的绅士化

来源：Alice Arnold 摄

图 11　阿姆斯特丹政府驱动的绅士化

图 12　上海市场、政府和建筑业主共同驱动的绅士化

3　“智慧”(Smart)的城市会具有社会可持续性吗?

近来有很多关于“智慧城市”的讨论,我们应该问问,它们是否能帮助社区变得具有社会可持续性?如果你能跟上我的思路,你就会明白,我认为一个智慧的城市实在需要由控制人们的诉求而非“什么对人们有益”之类的抽象概念所掌控。当我们激励城市中的“创新”的时候,我们应该问一下,谁会从这个创新中获益?如果城市要建设“创新街区”,谁将住在那里,谁又将在那里工作?

演讲者简介

莎伦·佐金(Sharon Zukin),美国纽约市立大学布鲁克林学院和研究生院社会学教授。

文化场景与全球城市

首尔的场景与新文化社区[①]

张元皓

摘　要　城市场景是一个用来解释城市场所中特定生活方式的新概念。一个场景可以被描述为五个组成部分。它们是:①社区;②物质结构(比如歌剧院或钓鱼小屋);③带有种族、阶级、性别、教育标签的人的集合;④这些标签的特定组合以及使这些人产生交集的活动(例如参加同一场音乐会);⑤他们所展现的价值观和意义。城市景观的生产者是居民、商业人士和到特定城市场所的游客。他们同时也是这一场景的消费者。从这个意义上说,他们共享相同的文化身份和品位,而相同的文化身份和品位使他们发展出文化社区。

根据社区理论,城市场景可以提供一个整合了基于场所的方法和基于网络的方法的新视角。这是因为城市场景既嵌入在特定的场所,又以居民、商务人士和游客的关系网络为基础。

本文用城市场景的概念分析首尔新兴文化社区的出现。在此基础上,探讨首尔文化社区的两个实证案例,即文莱洞和韩流场景。文莱洞的案例展示了居民、艺术家和游客如何能在共同的艺术品位的基础上发展出文化社区。韩流场景是一个跨国文化社区的例子,它共享韩国流行文化的内容,比如韩国流行音乐和韩国电视剧。本文结合实例,表明城市社会学中城市场景方法的重要性。

关键词　城市场景;文化社区;文莱洞;韩流场景

Scenes and New Cultural Communities in Seoul

Wonho Jang

Abstract　Urban Scene is a new concept to explain specific lifestyles in the urban places. A scene can be characterized as five components. They are: 1) neighborhood, 2) physical structures (like operas or fishing lodges), 3) collections of persons labeled by race, class, gender, education, 4) specific combinations of these and activities (like attending a concert) that join them together, 5) the values and meanings they express. The producers of urban scenes are residents, business persons, and visitors to the specific urban places. They are at the same time the consumers of the scene. In this sense, they share common cultural identities and tastes, which lead them to develop cultural communities.

Regarding community theory, urban scene can provide a new perspective integrating the place-based approach and network-oriented approach. It is because urban scenes are imbedded in specific places as well as based on networks among residents, business persons and the visitors.

This paper analyzes the emergence of new cultural communities in Seoul with the concept of

① 本文根据张元皓教授在2017“城市与社会”国际学术论坛上的发言整理、翻译。文稿编辑:邓世碧,上海同济城市规划设计研究院助理研究员;校对:钟晓华,同济大学社会学系副教授。

urban scene. In so doing, the paper deals with two empirical cases of the cultural communities in Seoul, the case of Mullae-dong and the Korean Wave scene. The case of Mullae-dong shows how residents, artists, and visitors can develop cultural community based on common artistic tastes. Korean Wave scene is an example of transnational cultural communities sharing the cultural content of the Korean Wave, such as K-Pop and Korean drama. With the cases, the paper will suggest the importance of the urban scene approach in urban sociology.

Keywords urban scene; cultural communities; Mullae-dong; Korean Wave scene

1 城市景观(Urban Scenes)的概念

城市景观是城市设施的集合,却不是自然地集合。它是通过社交型的消费的乐趣而致力于意义实践的场所,是有共同认知的居民、商人和游客的消费产生的社会组织,事件、活动、态度都是场景的一部分。在这里,我们看到不同的群体协作形成一种文化,而且这些群体共享一种文化品位。我们可以想象纽约的 SoHo 区,很多本地居民和艺术家共同居住在那里;现在韩国、日本也开始通过同样的方式来发展文化艺术场景,画廊不断演变场域身份,从而成为都市文化的组成部分之一。所以,游客、居民和艺术家有相同的文化身份认同,在这里做生意的商人也有这种身份认同。这就是城市文化场景的概念,图 1、表 1—表 4 是对这一概念的系统解释。

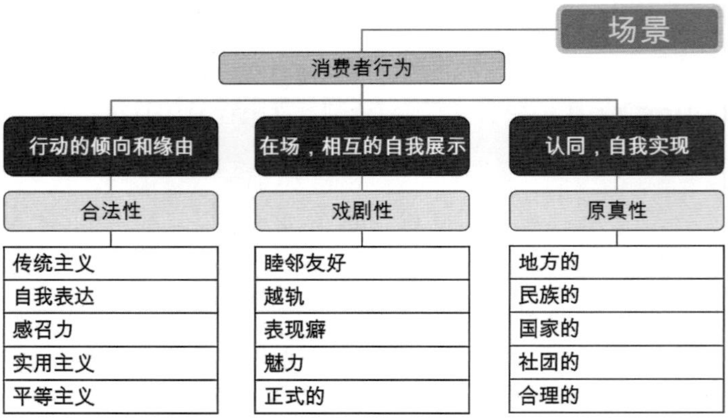

图 1 场景的法则

表 1 场景的次级维度:戏剧性

次级维度	例子	设施样例
魅力	站在戛纳红毯上,看着路过的明星	时装表演/设计师、美容院、电影节、赌场、珠宝店、夜总会
正式性	穿着礼服或打着白色领带、身着燕尾服去看歌剧	正式服装和礼服租赁、精致餐厅、戏剧公司
睦邻友好	参加社区管弦乐队的演出	家庭小旅馆、市民和社会组织、中小学、水果和蔬菜市场
表现癖	在肌肉海滩看举重运动员	成人娱乐、夜总会、时装表演和设计师、健康俱乐部

表 2　　场景的次级维度:原真性

次级维度	例子	设施样例
地方的	在芝加哥蓝调的里程碑处——棋盘休息室——聆听蓝调音乐	历史遗址、垂钓的湖和池塘、古董商、景区观光服务、运动团体和俱乐部
民族的	感觉到斯坦利兄弟的阿巴拉契亚口音	民族餐馆、民族音乐、民间艺术、语言学校
法人的	抨击布兰妮·斯皮尔斯的表演,因为她是一个公司创造出来的	市场调研、管理咨询服务、快餐店、百货公司
国家的	参观葛底斯堡战场	政治组织、大使馆和代表团、历史遗迹
合理的	在天文馆中陶醉于人类理性的宇宙视野	科学研发服务:大学、水族馆、人权组织、图书馆和档案馆

表 3　　场景的次级维度:合法性

次级维度	例子	样例设施
传统主义	正如你所相信的那样,在维也纳国家歌剧院中肯定能听到演奏莫扎特	宗族社会、历史遗址、古董商、博物馆、图书馆和档案馆
实用主义	参加一场能够带来积极结果的慈善音乐会,或者在工业博物馆里尽情享受高效生产的价值	快餐店、仓储俱乐部、超市、商务及秘书学校、便利店
平等主义	享受工艺品市场对民主的影响	人权组织、社会倡导组织
自我表达	聆听一位爵士音乐家只有在某个特定时刻才能即兴发挥的演奏	舞蹈公司、瑜伽工作室、身体穿刺、时装表演/设计师
感召力	观看一场芝加哥公牛队的比赛,因为迈克尔·乔丹的个人魅力而非因为自己是芝加哥人	服装及配饰设计师、音乐团体和艺术家、观众运动、舞蹈公司

表 4　　场景与传统城市空间的对比

空间	场景	社区	工业园区
目标	体验、社交	生活必需品、基础服务、住房	工作、产品
代理	消费者	居民	生产者
物理单元	设施	房屋/公寓	公司
社会联系的基础	生活方式/情感	在附近出生或者成长、长期居住、遗产	工作/生产关系

2　场景与城市社区

这种城市场景能够带来或促进城市社区的发展。我们常说,因为城市化的发展,有些社区消失了。这也是其他社会学家常常在讨论的。但是,赫伯特·甘斯关于社区的研究、巴里·威尔曼的网络研究,都认为社区没有消逝。社区研究是指对一定的社区区域、一定的时间里面发生的事情的研究。这里面有很多不同的概念，比如说基于空间的研究，还有一个是关于网络的研究。沟通交流技术的发展让研究者提出“基于网络的研究”这个比较新的概念。我认为，借助城市场景概念，可以通过基于空间和网络的研究促发城市社区的再发展、复苏或者重获新生。

大家知道，城市的场景肯定是在某个确定的地点，比如说特定的居民区、商业区等等，但是城市场景还应该包括游客——他们来这里旅游，实际上和当地居民、商人之间产生了网络关系，也成为网络的一部分，共同建立了网络的规则。所以我认为，城市场景是一个很好的概念，可以让我们以更新的视角来研究城市，重建场景中的城市网络。给大家举两个例子。

3 案例1：首尔文莱洞

这个地方曾经是工厂集聚地（图4、表5）。因为中产阶级化和消费主义，很多在弘大做视觉艺术的韩国艺术家们搬去了租金相对便宜的文莱洞，使那里变成了一个新的艺术社区。但艺术家们需要和工厂工人以及受到房价上升影响的当地住户们作斗争。艺术家们试图通过一些新的艺术特征来展示文莱洞的艺术特性（图5）。他们邀请工人、居民来举办各种各样的庆典、艺术节（图6），还邀请居民、工人参与到他们的艺术领域中，比如开设艺术教育机构（图7）。文莱洞艺术节现在已经成为最流行的艺术节之一。当地的居民和政府官员认为这个创意不错，觉得确实可以在工厂的旧址上建立起艺术空间。

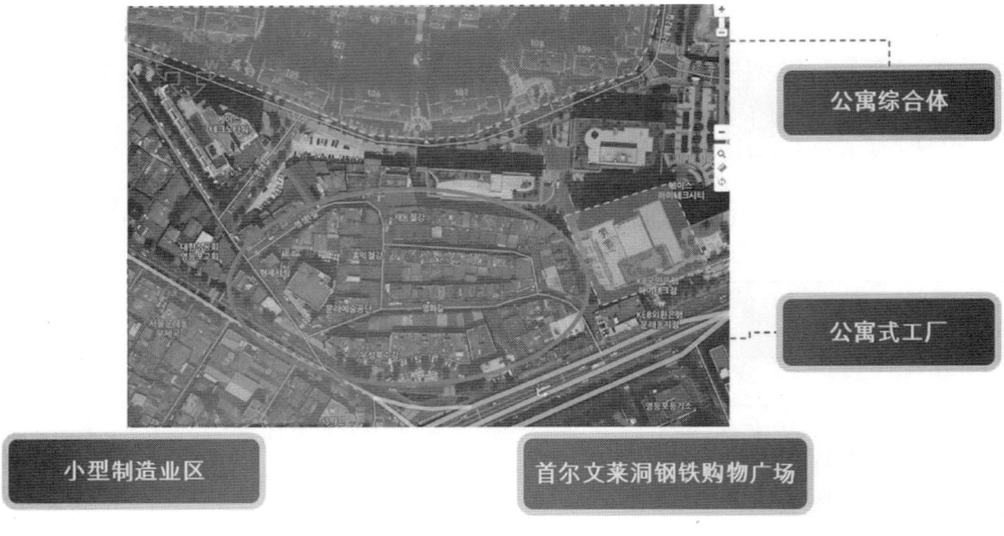

图4 文莱洞所在地

表5 文莱洞艺术社区的形成过程

时期	实质
1979年之前	韩国军队的电影制作中心
工厂大楼建造于1979年	钢铁购物商场的发展
20世纪80年代	1988年首尔奥运会之前，对建筑用钢的需求上涨，制造工业促进了经济发展

续表

时期	实质
20 世纪 90 年代	政府提议他们搬到始兴市的综合体，很多就搬了
21 世纪早期	首尔艺术空间文莱（由首尔艺术与文化基金会运营）在这里开幕，导致艺术家们逐渐但是平稳地向这一地区流动
2010 年至今	文莱艺术成为一个著名的艺术节，大约有 250 名艺术家，以及 22 家饭店和咖啡馆注册在文莱艺术村中（2015 年 4 月数据）

城市景观塑造了三方参与者：当地居民、商业从事者和游客。很多游客慕名而来参观文莱洞，感受艺术节的艺术氛围和艺术家们的艺术特性。居民本身也越来越倾向于和艺术家们交流。所以艺术家、商人、居民和游客在文莱洞形成了一种的新的城市艺术场景。虽然我们不是确定地说这里已经变成了一种新的文化社区，但我认为这是一种方法，可以基于同样的文化特点或者文化品位开创一种文化社区。这是第一个例子。

图 5　文莱洞的创意艺术

图 6　文莱洞艺术节

图 7　文莱洞的艺术教育

4　案例 2:首尔的韩流场景

第二个案例是韩流。它是一个共享韩国流行文化背景——如韩国流行音乐和韩国电视剧的跨国文化社区的案例。全球本土化文化,即在全球化的背景下受到国际影响并创造出新的本土文化,但是新的本土化文化可以被全球性地消费。这是一个全球化和本土化的复杂组合。韩流就是一种全球本土化文化。因为韩国实际上也受到来自日本的、欧洲的和美国的文化影响,其他地区的文化也受到韩流的影响。所以现在出现了一种新的文化,包容了这些国际文化的新融合,在这个地方,韩流变成了新的流行消费文化的标杆。我下面介绍一些典型的韩流场景(图 8)。

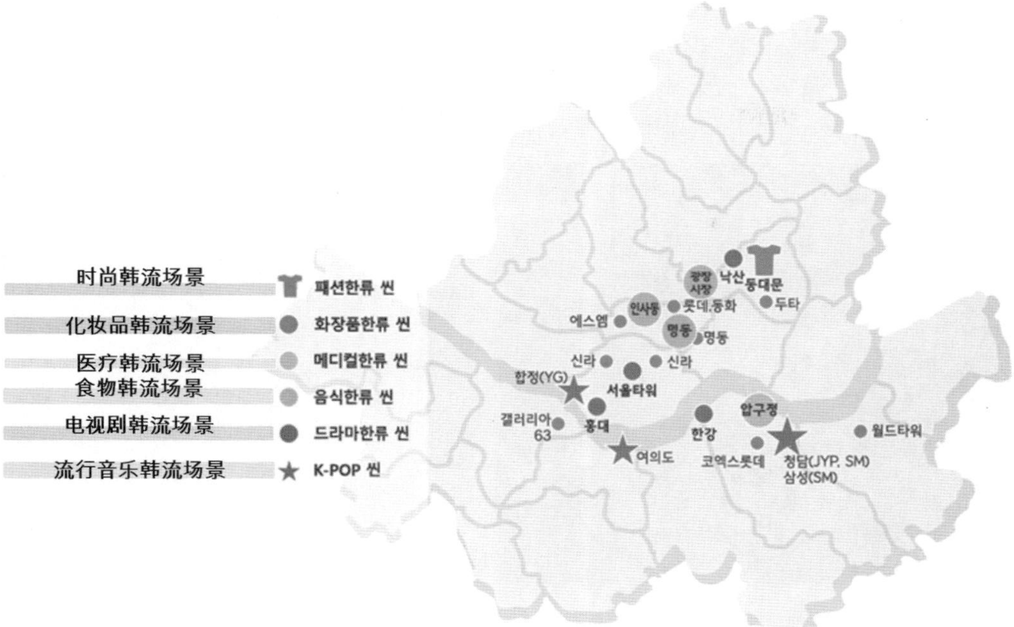

图 8　韩流场景分布图

4.1　韩国流行音乐场景

SM Town 是一家韩国流行音乐经纪公司，JYP 是一家非常有名的经纪公司。有很多粉丝来参观它们的大楼，拍很多明星的照片。很多中国、韩国粉丝都会聚集在这些地方，而且跨越国别成为朋友(图 9)。在明洞有一个 YG 公司(BigBang 的经济公司)开的餐厅——

图 9　韩国流行音乐粉丝常常聚集在经纪公司楼外，并跨越国别而成为朋友

K-PUB餐厅(图 10),很多粉丝都拥到这里。这种组合会产生一种全球本土化的文化,因为一个特殊的爱好而产生了一个新的群体。我去了那里许多次,发现那里会聚集很多韩国人、日本人和中国人,虽然他们不能很流畅地交流,但是我认为他们聚在一起的这种方式可能会引起一种跨国的全球本土化,就是建立在他们共享的文化认同之上的国际化文化社区。

图 10　韩国流行音乐经纪公司开的饭店,来自亚洲的人们聚在这里一边吃喝一边交谈,讨论偶像团体的新闻

4.2　电视剧相关的韩流场景

N 首尔塔对于希望宣誓永恒之爱的情侣而言,是一个浪漫的朝圣之地。人们挂了很多“爱之锁”在那里的栏杆上(图 11)。弘大的街头艺术在外国人中非常有名。在这块区域会有很多外国人,尤其是年轻人聚集起来欣赏街头艺术表演。我也去过那里很多次,好几次看到这样的场景(图 12),来自不同国家的人们聚集在街头观看表演。

这种韩流的表现形式或许在未来可以创造出新的跨国文化共同体,这也是未来很可能出现的一种既有国际融合又有本地化特点的新情况,也可能是将来民主的一种新形式,因为世界各地的人,尤其是年轻人比较喜欢通过这样的音乐或戏剧来解决一些新问题。所以我认为这是非常重要的。

毋庸置疑,不同的摩擦与冲突使得这种交流传播减弱了。但是我们仍需要文化交流,因为我们需要中立地、客观地了解彼此地不同文化,因为中立的理解是解决冲突问题的唯一方法。如果不了解彼此,我们就无权发表任何言论——这是哈贝马斯关于协商民主的开端。所以我认为这种跨国文化共同体真的非常重要,韩流和韩国首尔将在未来共同体的文化交流中发挥很好的作用,促进国际合作、和平发展。

图 11　N 首尔塔和上面的“爱之锁”

图 12　弘大的街头表演和围观人群

延伸阅读

[1] CLARK T N. Can Tocqueville Karaoke? Global Contrasts of Citizen Participation, the Arts and Development[M]. England: Emerald Group, 2014.

[2] SILBER D A, CLARK T N. Scenescapes: How Qualities of Place Shape Social Life[M]. Chicago: The University of Chicago Press University of Chicago Press, 2016.

演讲者简介

张元皓(Wonho Jang)，韩国首尔市立大学社会学教授。

场景制造:北京三个城市社区发展的文化动力分析

吴　军

摘　要　以往的区域发展研究很少涉及具体的设施、人群、活动、价值观与生活方式等地方文化特征的研究,而主要是从传统的经济发展要素,如土地、资金和劳动力等入手,研究它们与经济增长和社会发展的驱动作用。可以说,早期的区域发展研究带有很强的物质要素传统和弱文化色彩。但是,随着后工业社会的来临,这种研究传统逐渐发生改变。本文以中国最具有后工业城市色彩的北京作为分析对象,选取其中三个不同文化特征类型的社区,来探索后工业城市社区复兴的驱动力。它们分别为:以创新创业文化为特征的中关村创业大街、以创意文化为主的798艺术区、以传统文化为主的南锣鼓巷。本文从这些地方的文化场景特征角度入手考察,包括设施、人群、活动等形成的场景,以及场景中蕴含的价值观和生活方式等。这些要件构成了地区文化特质,正是这些特质吸引了诸如创新创意等高级人力资本聚集,形成新企业和新业态,带来经济增长和社会发展。

关键词　场景制造;北京;城市;社区发展;文化动力

The Development of Three Different Cultural Communities in Beijing from Scene Dynamics

Wu Jun

Abstract　The traditional research of regional development rarely involves specific local cultural characteristics, for example, amenities, activities, organizations, norms, values, etc. The researchers mainly focus on land, capital and labor when they explain the dynamics of economic growth and social development, while they often overlook the roles of culture and arts. With the advent of the post-industrial society, this research tradition has gradually been changed. This article chooses three different communities in Beijing to explain the drivers of local development from cultural scenes or local cultural characteristics, including Zhongguancun community characterized by the culture of science and technology innovation, the 798 art community and Nanluoguxiang community characterized by traditional culture. Local cultural characteristics include the following dimensions: facilities consumer oriented, diversity of population, characteristic activities, these factors combined to form the scenes, and the values and way of life in the scene. It's these local cultural features play very important during the process of the gathering of senior human capital, especially for the IT talents and arts crowd. These will bring regional prosperity, including jobs increasing, new industries and social development.

Keywords　scenes making; Beijing; cities; development of community; cultural dynamics

1 增长发展动力:"生产要素"VS"消费要素"

一片空旷的土地上如何形成城市?为什么有的地方可以发展起来而有的地方则会"销声匿迹"?同时,为什么居住在不同城市的人们,或者同一城市里不同社区的人们,他们的态度和行为往往会有显著差异?这些都是城市增长与社区发展研究中探讨的经典问题。在现有的研究文献中,社会科学家们大致给出了两种答案。一种观点认为,在空旷的土地上,土地本身、资金注入、劳动力流入等生产性因素决定了这一地区是否能够发展成一个城市,是否会演变成一个繁荣的社区。恰恰相反,另一种观点则认为,决定这一地区增长与社会发展的是消费性因素,比如公园、超市、博物馆、图书馆、艺术馆、画廊、创意集市、咖啡厅与酒吧、特色餐厅等设施与活动,以及不同文化价值取向与生活方式的人群聚集等消费性因素;正是这些消费性因素决定了本地区是否发展、是否能够变成具有活力的城市社区[1]。

简言之,到底是生产带来增长发展,还是消费带来增长发展?这是关于不同地方发展模式的争辩。事实上,在不同的国家、城市和社区的不同时期,生产和消费带来增长发展都可以找到很多案例来支持。从时间层面来看,工业化时期,城市与社区增长发展普遍依赖生产性要素,如土地、资金和劳动力等。到后工业时代,文化消费因素慢慢崛起并快速地上升到更重要位置。从跨国层面来看,现今的发达国家更加倾向于文化消费因素导向的发展模式;相反,在发展中国家里,生产性要素仍然起着决定性作用。但是,并不是所有的发展中国家的城市都是如此。具体到中国,在幅员辽阔的国土范围内,增长发展的水平是极其不平衡的。我们既有能与欧美发达国家城市媲美的城市,如北京、上海和深圳;同时,我们也有很多比较落后的中西部城市。因此,无论是生产型的增长发展模式,还是消费型的增长发展模式,在当代中国都可以找到鲜明的例子[1]。

不过,随着后工业社会的来临和全球化的推动,文化消费因素在地方发展中的作用越来越明显。这个结论已经被美国的社会科学研究所证明。代表学者有哈佛大学城市经济学家格莱泽、多伦多大学创意管理专家佛罗里达和芝加哥大学城市社会学家克拉克。但是,文化消费因素也不是自然而然就组合成为一种发展动力的。更多的时候,文化消费因素是与生产性因素"互动"才能转化为增长发展动力。在这个互动过程中,不同元素的多样组合可以形成不同场景,简约的说是文化场景(cultural scenes),即价值观与生活方式+设施(活动)。正是这些独特的场景定义了一个城市、一个社区的特征。不同的场景同时又反过来对场景里面的人们的态度与行为产生不同的引导作用。

2 一种新的理论分析框架

事实上,文化在定义城市和社区增长发展中的角色在理论和实践上已得到广泛的认可。最新的研究文献探索文化艺术如何链接人与地之间的"互动"构成一个场景从而来聚集相应人群和企业,带动城市与社区的增长发展[2]。典型代表来自芝加哥大学社会学系特里·克拉克(Terry N. Clark)领衔的跨国团队。他们认为,对于地方发展的解释应该从哈维·莫洛奇(Harvey Molotch)所描绘的地方政治经济学(a political economy of place)分析框架转移到文化消费的政治学理论(a political theory of consumption)框架上来。前者强调的增长发展思维突出诸如土地、资本和劳动力等经济性因素，但这种“地方，地方，地方”的想法并不完整[3]。他们进一步追问道，这个地方“在哪里”“有些什么”“有什么人群会来这里”等更为具体的问题。要解决这些问题，必须要回到地方的文化范畴。经典增长发展元素与地方文化要素如何结合才能生产生出有利于发展的场景。

同样，来自美国和世界范围内其他学者也找到了强有力的证据，并认为，地方增长发展越来越由文化、价值观、设施、活动以及人群等消费因素决定[4]。比如，很多数据显示城市的创新力、包容度、多样化和创新创意群体对于城市增长发展具有强大的驱动作用[5]。从另外一个角度来说，高级人力资本的流动逻辑也从注重工作机会等转移到自我表达、社会参与、文化消费、休闲娱乐以及生活方式等文化因素上来[6]。在克拉克教授的带领下，新芝加哥学派城市与社区研究学者们在过去近二十年的讨论和总结过程中归纳出了场景理论(a theory of scenes)。场景理论在强调地方和强调文化的相对对立模型中找到了一个平衡，认为地方、设施、人群、价值观与生活方式等都非常重要。这些分散的元素可以进行组合，如通过文化表演等串联起来，构成一个活生生、有意义的场景。因此，由不同的设施、人群、活动等构成和结合可以产生不同场景，由此带来地方增长发展[7]。从增长发展的角度去理解，场景理论可以算是在承认生产因素比如土地、资金与劳动力等作为基础之上，去思考与探索文化艺术怎么盘活这些力量来推动地方发展。

场景理论中的“场景”一来源于“Scenes”的翻译。根据“场景”在电影中的应用来看，它包括对白、场地、道具、音乐、服装和演员等影片希望传递给观众的信息和感觉。在场景中，各个元素的关系是相互有机关联，同质元素布局之间有必然的出现关系，异质元素布局之间将表达颠覆性的思想。克拉克将这种现象引入城市社会的研究中，进而形成了场景理论。[8]场景的构成有多重维度，但至少可以从以下 6 个维度来把握：① 居住区(neighborhoods)，而不是城市、大都市区、州、省或民族等；②物质结构(physical structures)，更多是指向生活文化娱乐设施(amenities)，如舞蹈俱乐部、俱乐部沙龙和购物商场等；③ 人群(persons)，不同种族、阶级、性别、教育、职业和年龄等；④1－3 的特殊组合和嵌入组合中的活动，如青年创业沙龙或朋克音乐会等；⑤这四个因素所表达的符号意义和价值，这种价值可以定义地方发生的经验中什么是重要的；⑥公共性(publicness)——而不是独特个性，强调由公共空间所展现的场景，它们对过路人和活动热衷者来说是可获得的[9]22-23。事实上，“场景”这个概念已经超越了设施与活动集合的物化概念，它是一种涂尔干所描绘的社会事实，是作为文化价值观的外化符号而影响个体行为的社会事实。

场景理论的研究体系建立在主观认识和客观结构两大体系上[4]。客观结构由被研究区域中的生活文化设施(amenities)构成。通常，我们将拥有大量商铺的城市区域称为商业区，拥有大量工厂的城市区域称为工业化。场景理论中客观结构的概念类似于此，不过更为细化。比如，咖啡馆、酒吧、书店、博物馆、艺术画廊，以及朋克音乐会、文化沙龙、娱乐俱乐部活动以及音乐艺术节等等。主观认识体系是指场景中蕴含的价值观范畴。比如，自我表达(express-self)、传统主义(traditionalism)、时尚魅力(glamor)等[9]24-25。

以鼓励自我表达和时尚魅力的场景为例。一种好的场景可以作为强有力的纽带，把艺术家群体与经济表现连接起来。以两个艺术家为例，即艺术家 A 和艺术家 B。每位艺术家每周工作时间相同，所使用的工具相似(电脑、绘画颜料、软件等)。艺术家 A 生活在生机勃勃的场景，如倡导自发行为(个体自我表达与创意)、上演令人惊喜的秀(魅力与形式)以及鼓励不拘泥于传统等。艺术家 B 生活的场景刚好相反,传统、死板和守旧的环境。艺术家 A 工作在一个比较肥沃的艺术土壤(场景)里:在这里,我们可以想象,开放的即兴创作与冒险、对创意多次失败的理解与包容、许多创意与技术分享的机会与交流、乐意克服传统偏见与刻板印象(stereotypes),回归原初与质朴的经历与体验……这种场景,有利于激发艺术创造,有利于产出高质量的艺术作品,从而形成创意经济。这种现象用“艺术红利”来形容,恰当不过。

对于企业组织更是如此。在两个案例中,肥沃的土壤“孕育”的公司 1 和艺术家 A,比公司 2 和艺术家 B 更富有成效,更具有生产力。从这个意义上讲,它们的输出结果会更有价值,而土壤就是本文所说的场景。艺术家群体和这些公司所产生价值的多少与场景的不同有关;不同设施的组合会形成不同的场景,不同的场景孕育着不同的价值观与生活方式。在这些案例说明,场景发生变化,其他变量的经济输出结果也会随之变化[10]71-121。

3 三个不同文化特征社区场景的比较

为了具体阐述场景作为一种新动能,本文选择了北京三个不同文化特征的社区,从场景视角来探讨地方发展动力。它们分别为:以创新创业文化为特征的中关村创业大街、以创意文化为特征的 798 艺术区以及以传统文化为典型的南锣鼓巷。事实上,北京作为一个后工业城市,拥有很多的典型文化场景,比如红色文化(爱国主义)场景、教育科研文化(高校聚集区)场景等。由于篇幅限制,本文将讨论三个案例来说明场景动能。

3.1 中关村创业大街:传统图书城商业街到创新创业文化圣地

中关村创业大街的前身是北京海淀图书城。2013 年,海淀区政府决定对图书城经营业态进行调整,按照“政府引导、市场化运作”的方式,将图书城打造成创新创业孵化社区。入驻的创新创业孵化机构有 40 多家,包括车库咖啡、联想之星、飞马旅、创业家、天使汇等。创业大街不仅定位于建设创业服务集聚区、科技企业发源地、创业者文化圣地,还要打造具有极强科技感、展示度、时尚感的创新创业特色景观大道,吸引培养一批具有国际影响力的世界一流创业孵化服务机构,致力于缔造全球知名的“Inno Way”。

本文认为,中关村创业大街作为一种独特的创新创业场景,既是一种科技创新人才的空间聚集,也是科技企业与产业的业态融合。在这样的场景里,创新创业产生更多绩效。比如,印娃(inwow)移动打印公司创业过程①很好地诠释了场景动力作用。

印娃是创业大街孵化出的众多公司中的一个,创始人李兵是做传统的复印机,起初对互联网行业并不在行,当时来创业大街只是抱着一个简单的想法:“如果复印机能够做成移动复印会怎样呢?”于是,他来到创业大街,在极短时间内完成了公司注册、融资、产品开发、品牌设计以及市场推广等。据介绍,从“创意”变成现实产品再到市场也就三个月时间。传统

① 随着移动互联网的发展,智能手机的功能越来越强大,收集逐渐取代了 PC 成为新的办公工具,越来越多人不局限在办公室办公。移动互联网在改变世界的实践,打印服务却依然自顾自地走自己的老路。而传统的打印服务,在这个时代已经难以满足移动办公的人群的打印需求。用户通过印娃 APP,将存放在云端或手机端的文档与线下打印终端建立连接,可以随时随地享用文件打印服务,享受更便捷、更潮流、更专业的打印服务。

的创业过程至少需要一年时间。这种高效且便利的场景，正吸引聚集着科技人才和公司。据不完全统计，像李兵这样的创业团队在创业大街孵化出1600多个。

这种场景里，除了高效与便利外，还有这人才密集的特点。比如，中午十二点提交一份用人需求，七个小时后，就可能有一名来自BAT（百度、阿里巴巴和腾讯）的顶尖工程师到岗，开始为你自己的创业公司工作。这个听起来几乎天方夜谭的场景已经成为现实。这就是中关村创业大街社区场景孕育的可能性。正如创业者们所说，这里给每个人有创业梦想的人提供了“一切皆有可能”的实践意义。

图1　中关村创业大街街区景观

从发展态势来看，中关村创业大街已经初步形成了独特创新创业场景，吸引与聚集着各种创新创业资源，成为北京城市创新创业的一个地标、一种品牌，也成为全国创新创业者心目中的圣地与文化家园。但问题的关键是：到底中关村创业大街社区场景包括哪些要素呢？本文从以下几个方面来概括。

（1）定位于社区层面，而非城市

从社会学角度，社区是放置在一定地理空间上的社会，强调互动、认同与网络组结合功能等。在特定的时间里，创新创业群体、设施与活动等放置到一定空间位置里并形成一种有机且紧密网络联结，而非松散或物理堆砌。比如梦想者、创意者、高校与科研机构、行业领军企业、IT人才聚集、天使投资、创业金融、各种孵化器以及政府补贴优惠政策等组合形成的一种独特场景。这些共同构成了一种创新创业文化，一种专属于创新创业者的亚文化群体与生活格调（生活方式）。

（2）设施：创业咖啡馆＋便利设施＋互联网大企业

物理结构是创新创业场景形成的载体。中关村创业大街的物理结构有三类设施：

其一是以创业咖啡馆为典型代表的众创空间，仅创业大街上有45家，包括周围的有上百家。这些咖啡馆不但为创业者提供办公、公司注册、法律咨询、技术支持等服务，还经常举办各种沙龙，邀请各领域顶级的企业家、创业者、投资人做深度分享；甚至，有些咖啡馆还成立创业基金，资助创业团队；还有的咖啡馆提供员工招聘等。

其二是以生活休闲消费为导向的便利设施，如咖啡馆、书店、特色小食店、果汁店、超市、健身房、主题酒店、银行、移动打印以及清洁高效的餐厅等。据不完全统计，这样的便利设施有成百上千个，这些设施也都比较受创新创业者青睐，除了对生活便利的满足之外，还构成了一种格调、一种创新创业者特有的生活方式。

其三是靠近互联网大企业或分支机构。创业大街社区里有百度、阿里、腾讯、小米以及联想等这样的互联网企业的分支机构，以及清华、北大、人大等高校，为创业大街提供了各方面高端人才与资源。

图 2　中关村创业大街创业咖啡馆内景

(3) 数量庞大的创新创业活动

创业大街自 2013 年开办以后，整个社区呈现出“天天有路演、日日沙龙”的局面，这些活动包括创业沙龙、讲座培训、政策宣传、展示陈列、路演推广、创业比赛以及其他等。据不完全统计，在两年多的时间里，创新创业活动超过 1600 场，平均每天有两个以上的主题创新创业活动，参与人数达到 16 万之多(表 1)。

表 1　中关村创业大街创新创业活动类型划分

年份	创业沙龙	讲座培训	政策宣传	展示陈列	路演推广	创业比赛	其他
2014 年上半年	22	11	0	6	13	2	0
2014 年下半年	122	100	30	14	40	18	0
2015 年上半年	113	134	6	23	45	6	3
2015 年下半年	102	151	21	22	34	12	10
2016 年上半年	47	157	14	3	20	4	3

来源：http://www.z-innoway.com.

(4) 多样性创业人群

从来源地来看，有北京土生土长的青年、取得北京户籍的新北京人、部分高学历海归以及“北漂”等。从学科背景来看，创业者学科背景多元，知识面跨度广，有做 IT 计算机与软件开发的，有搞音乐与艺术的，还有做平面设计的，还有的做核动力研发的。从行业分布来看，

图 3　中关村创业大街的入驻创新创业机构

有互联网、IT、教育、医疗、智能家居、汽车以及生活服务等几十个行业。总之，这些多样性的人群是创业大街社区活力的重要来源。

（5）中关村创业大街的“价值观”：一切皆有可能的精神

中关村创业大街的社区文化、以创业孵化为核心的物理设施、各类创业活动、多样性人群等，都透出激情和憧憬。如果要用一句话来概括创业大街的价值观和生活态度，不妨归纳为“一切皆有可能”。这里有在国内堪称最优秀创业人才、最新的信息、最知名的风险投资机构和最好的服务，这里是将梦想变成现实的最佳场所。印娃（inwow）移动打印创业过程就很好地诠释了这一点[11]。这里诞生了很多创业神话，这种神话激励着更多的人选择这里创业。这不是一条只有咖啡馆的“街”，也不仅仅是创业大潮中的昙花一现，在这背后，是一个关于“一切皆有可能”文化圣地。

3.2 798 艺术区:从工业厂房到文化创意中心

在仅仅半个世纪里(1957—),位于北京朝阳区酒仙桥街道的大山子 798 社区经历了翻天覆地的变化,从原先的北京华北无线电联合器材生产工业社区,到废弃破旧的城市社区,再变成如今生机勃勃的世界级艺术区[1]。现如今的北京 798 社区聚集了超过 400 多家的艺术馆和画廊工作室,甚至一些世界闻名的艺术馆在 798 社区设立了分支机构,比如 Guy&Myriam,Ullens Foundation 和 Pace Gallery[12]。

毫无疑问,这是一个世界范围内城市社区发展从工业生产主导型向以文化艺术消费进行社区复兴的经典案例[12]。这样经典的案例触及了一个核心的研究议题,到底是什么因素驱动着一个地方能够从一个封闭生产工业厂房转化为开放型的文化社区,从一个自发形成的艺术区转化为城市文化旅游的重要吸引物?恐怕,这个问题是很多关注后工业社会城市与社区发展的学者们普遍关心的问题。本文尝试从场景动力分析的角度对这一案例进行分析。

(1) 社区特点

798 艺术区位于北京城乡接合部地区(大都市郊区)的酒仙桥街道大山子社区,故称"大山子艺术区"(DAD-Dashanzi Art District),是原来国有企业无线电工业生产厂区所在地,占地面积约 30 多万平方米,其中 20 世纪 50 年代风格建筑面积为 97 230 平方米,包括约 2 万平方米的锯齿形包豪斯风格建筑。798 艺术区从 2002 年开始至今,经历了一个快速变化的过程,包括规模变大和功能变化。2003 年只有 30 多家艺术机构和个人,到如今的 400 多家。空间从最初的厂区部分空间扩展到整个园区;功能则从一个艺术家聚集区转变成了现当代艺术画廊聚集区,从艺术作品的创造转变成了现在的艺术作品的展示区和流通区[13]29-30。

图 4 798 艺术区的包豪斯风格厂房外景与内景

(2) 艺术家工作室与画廊

798 艺术区成功地实现了由生产工业区向艺术消费社区的转变。798 艺术区最初的入驻设施是艺术家工作室,而画廊是随着艺术区的逐步形成而进驻的。画廊的入驻,彻底改变了这里最初的艺术家群体聚集单一形态。

除了画廊外,在仅仅为 30 多万平方米的空间里建设了众多设施,还有艺术家工作室,涉及雕塑、环境设计、摄影、手工艺术、表演、服装设计、精品家居设计、影视传媒、特色书店、餐饮、酒吧等。根据学者刘明亮 2003—2009 年做的田野调查,在此期间,艺术家工作室高峰期达到 51 家,画廊的数量一直上升到 160 多家,其他艺术机构和精品店商铺都在处于上升趋势。我们最近的调查显示,798 艺术区各类文化艺术机构总数已经达到了 450 多家,其中工作室、画廊和展演设施就达 200 个,这些设施主要用来创造、展示和交流。

除了画廊、艺术工作室之外,798 艺术区还有大量的商铺和餐饮,经营范围包括特色书店、创意首饰、原创服饰、刺绣、旅游纪念品等;餐饮主要包括咖啡厅和饭店。

(3) 艺术家群落

艺术家的聚集形成了不同的艺术群落,众多的艺术群落形成了今天的各种艺术社区。这也成了当今都市文化的一个重要组成部分。总的来说,艺术家群落维持在 40 人左右。艺术家是 798 艺术区的开创者,但不一定是这里的最终留守者。他们与艺术区的关系总像一个怪圈:他们的入驻,给区域注入活力,使该区域的土地在短时间内得到升值,同时房租提高;反过来,艺术家又会因生活成本提高和喧嚣环境而被迫迁移,去寻找下一个适合他们生存的区域,然后进入另一轮循环。艺术家的聚集与离散,可以直观反映艺术区的整体变化。

(4) 798 艺术区的"价值观":自由表达精神

街头涂鸦是 798 艺术区倡导鼓励自由表达价值观念的典型体现。在 798 艺术区的很多墙面和角落,都有各种涂鸦的存在,它们已经成为艺术区的一道风景,很多参观者都在此拍照、留影。这些涂鸦,既有艺术家的作品,也有游客的作品;既有组织的创造,也有随时而随意的涂抹。欧美社会流行的涂鸦(graffitist)往往代表了一种对现实生活的发泄或嘲讽,通过这种形式表达自己。在 798 艺术区,涂鸦更多的是一种对外宣传的途径,因为进入艺术区,各种涂鸦已经暗示游客进入了一个不同于普通生活地点的区域,涂鸦既是一种点缀,也是艺术区作为当代艺术所持有的反叛、突兀和自由表达的一种象征。

图 5　798 艺术区的墙头涂鸦"西游记"与"红军毛笔"

从 798 艺术家群落聚集来看,他们一般会选择大都市的城乡接合地区。这里除了租金价格便宜、建筑风格独特、地理环境优越外,与城中心之间也保持着一定距离,某种程度上反映了艺术家对于对现代城市紧张生活的一种厌恶与反叛及追求独立个性、脱离俗世的一种"乌托邦"式的生活理想。

3.3 南锣鼓巷社区:从胡同四合院到文化旅游区

南锣鼓巷是一条胡同,位于北京中轴线东侧的交道口地区,北起鼓楼东大街,南至平安大街,宽 8 米,全长 787 米,于元大都同期建成,至今已有七百四十多年的历史,是北京最古老的街区之一。它是我国唯一完整保存着元代胡同院落肌理,规模最大、品级最高、资源最丰富的棋盘式传统民居区,也是最富有老北京风情的街巷。现在已经变成了北京旅游文化名片,每天吸引着大量的游客。

(1) 社区特点

在元大都"左祖右社,面朝后市"的城市格局中,南锣鼓巷是"后市"的组成部分。整个南锣鼓巷建筑以胡同、四合院形态为主,呈现出棋盘式的城市建筑格局。除了胡同和四合院外,这里还有大量的个性酒吧、咖啡馆、餐厅、各种手工艺商店。如今的南锣鼓巷,商业兴盛,市场繁荣。

图 6 南锣鼓巷社区的胡同与四合院

(2) 胡同和四合院

从南向北,西面 8 条胡同是福祥胡同、雨儿胡同、帽儿胡同等;东边 8 条胡同是炒豆胡同、前圆恩寺胡同、菊儿胡同等。这些胡同名称是明朝以后逐渐演变来的。里坊是中国古代居住区组织的基本单位,也是城市规划建设的基本单位。在先秦称为"里",后改为"坊"。元大都规划设计沿用里坊制,全城分为 50 坊,坊与坊之间是宽阔平直的街巷,犹如棋盘。时至今日,元大都里坊构造在八百多年的历史变迁已面目全非,但南锣鼓巷社区完整地保存着元大都里坊格局[14]。

以四合院为主的名人故居。这些名人故居经过保护和修缮变为城市重点文物。比如,僧王府是清代僧格林沁的王府。齐白石故居、茅盾故居、蒋介石行辕等。其中,菊儿胡同是南锣鼓巷最北头东边的一条胡同。1990 年,建筑大师吴良镛主持设计菊儿胡同危房改造工程,有机更新了这条古巷中的小胡同,使其既保留了老北京四合院的神韵,又适合现代人居住。1993 年被联合国授予"世界人居奖"。

沿着南锣鼓巷和各条胡同的各类商铺。有些商铺临街,有些设在民居深处。这些商铺多以传统手工艺为主,如吹糖人、捏泥人、烙画葫芦、制作陶瓷、绘制脸谱、画鼻烟壶等;还有一些生活类的创意休闲酒吧、餐馆、书店等[15]。除了这些设施外,这里还有艺术机构,比如中央戏剧学院、中国国家话剧院、北京美术家协会、蓬蒿剧场、七色光儿童剧场、老物件博物馆等。这些设施不仅吸引了大量游客,而且还是创意人群的重要来源[16]。

(3) 四类不同的"人群"

人群是城市社区发展的驱动力,不同人群对于社区发展的推动作用不同。活跃在南锣鼓巷的"人群"分为四类[16]。一类是商家和手艺人。这里的商家比较有创意能力,有的是传统手工艺者,有的是时尚设计师、服装师等。二类是旅游参观者,平时日均人次有 2 万左右,节假日高峰期能达到日10万人次以上。三类是常住居民，由汉族、满族、回族、蒙古族等多民族组成。四类是各级政府机关派出机构、社区组织和事业单位的工作人员。1个街道办事处、8个居委会和社区服务站。还有大量的社会组织，比如"月圆古巷"志愿放映队、社区志愿服务队。

（4）南锣鼓巷场景"价值观"：传统与闲适淡雅的生活方式

传统主义是南锣鼓巷社区最为典型的写照。传统的历史意识是本地居民、商家和多数游客普通感受到的南锣鼓巷价值取向。历史意识指人们对过去事物有意识的记录、欣赏、追寻、思念[16]。南锣鼓巷保留下来的元明胡同肌理、青砖老树、古色古香的四合院等构成的北京传统文化场景，体现着地道的"北京味道"，特别受游客青睐，尤其是来北京的外国人比较喜欢到这里闲逛。

同时，胡同与四合院为基础形成的闲适淡雅生活方式，也是吸引游客的重要原因。在北京这样大都市里，人们每天都会面临着各种竞争带来的巨大的心理紧张，通过闲淡平和的生活予以疏解是必要的。南锣鼓巷的设施、活动、价值观等正体现了这样一种暂时抛离大都市紧张的闲适淡雅生活方式（至少在部分人的想象中是这样）[17]。

3.4 三个城市社区场景的比较分析

以上三个案例讨论了北京三个城市社区发展的场景动力，即由设施、人群、活动、这些元素组合形成特定场景以及场景蕴藏的价值观与生活方式，将作为一种新动力，吸引着创新创意人才等优秀人力资本聚集，催生新兴产业集群，从而带来经济增长和社会发展。

从设施活动来看，三个案例中社区场景内容也有着较大差异，比如中关村创业大街的设施活动以创业咖啡为主的众创空间，活动以创业沙龙、讲座培训、政策宣传、展示陈列、路演推广和创业比赛等。798艺术区的设施以艺术家工作室和画廊为主，配套一些混合经营咖啡馆和餐厅，活动以产品展示和艺术沙龙为主。南锣鼓巷社区相对比较传统，以民居胡同和四合院为主，活动多以传统节日庆典为主。

从人群来看，三个城市社区都具有人口多样性特点，不同地域来源与不同专业背景的土著、海归、北漂、新北京人、游客、艺术家、画家等分别聚集到不同社区，比较包容和多样。

从价值观层面来看，中关村创业大街场景凸显了科技创新创业文化，其呈现的"一切皆有可能"和"创新创业作为人生情感体验"等价值观，影响着青年毕业大学生群体的城市流动；而798艺术区以画廊和艺术家工作室的场景给予创意阶层自我表达的自由和都市乌托邦理想的实践；南锣鼓巷靠着其独有的胡同与四合院等元素集合呈现出地道的"北京味"，传统主义、闲适淡雅民居生活方式，吸引着社会大众，尤其是来北京的外国游客。

表 2　　北京三种不同类型社区文化场景特征比较

案例	设施	人群	活动	价值观与符号意义	公共性
中关村创业大街（科技创新文化）	创业咖啡馆与众创空间	土著、海归、北漂、新北京青年、游客	路演、发布会、创业沙龙、投资会	一切皆有可能、创新创业情感体验	免费开放
798 艺术区（创意文化）	艺术工作室、画廊、混合咖啡馆或餐馆	艺术家、画家、游客	产品展示与艺术沙龙	自我表达精神、乌托邦式的理想	免费开放
南锣鼓巷（传统文化）	胡同、四合院	游客、商户、居民	传统文化节、旅游节	传统主义、闲适淡雅	免费开放

4　三个社区场景制造的机制分析

很显然，无论是中关村创业大街创新创业社区，还是 798 文化创意区，抑或南锣鼓巷传统文化旅游区，这些地方如今均重新焕发生机，其中，文化场景培育与塑造发挥着重要的作用。然而，在具体的某个文化场景的形成过程中，政府、市场和社会三种力量都涉及，但侧重点不同。有的是政府“自上而下”的强力推动，比如中关村创业大街；有的是艺术家群体“自下而上”的自发形成，比如 798 艺术区。不同的主导力量所形成的文化场景不同，对于地方发展的结果也有所不同。

在三个案例中，政府的推动力最为关键，那种“地方、地方、地方”的概念尽管重要，但是，“政策、政策、政策”在三个社区场景形成中扮演着极其重要角色。现实中，往往那些扶持力度大、政策密集的地方，其发展会更快。比如，中关村创业大街仅仅在 2 年时间里就完成了传统图书商业街区向创新创业孵化基地的转变，当地政府从租金减免、宽带水电补贴、间接投融资、外包服务政策支持等全方位支持。即使在自发形成的 798 艺术区也如此。其成立之初，是由于中央美院等艺术家自发聚集，后来城市改造中，引发政府的关注，并介入保护下来，变成了今天的北京文创中心。

进入后工业时代后，城市经济结构的重组使得城市作为制造业中心的作用基本被终结，取而代之的是城市成为第三产业的基地和消费场所。政府急需要一种新的“抓手”来维持增长和更好的社会发展。同时，对于城市废弃空间改造升级，有利于城市面貌改善的迫切需求。这两方面做好了，权力的合法性和官员政绩才能被“认可”。这对于官员的提拔来说至关重要。这就是场景形成的第一大动力，来自政府和官员的政绩考量，从传统的房地产、基础设施建设领域向社区公共文化服务转变。本文把这种特点称为场景形成机制的政治性。这种政治性有时候被地方官员理解成为“政治正确”。

对于市场经济组织来说，创意文化是新的经济增长点，创意经济的年增加值已经取代了很多传统行业变成北京城市发展的支柱性产业。因为后工业的城市已经俨然成了一部娱乐机器。这是城市社区场景制造过程中的重要动力。

不同于前两者，对于社会大众来说，文化艺术就是一个消费利益的表达。他们在物质生活大幅度提高的今天，对文化艺术消费提出了更多的需求；同时，他们也需要文化消费的便利性、低价性和参与性。这样的要求和过程往往是由社区精英（艺术家）和代表大众利益的社会组织所推动；这方面往往在当下北京城市发展中表现得比较弱。

表 3　　三个城市社区场景制造形成机制的比较

场景制造的推动力	中关村创业大街	798 艺术区	南锣鼓巷
政府 （政治性）	中央和地方政府大力支持，把这里打造成中国创新创业的标杆； 政府干预恰到好处	地方政府政策鼓励文化创意产业发展； 管理控制文化艺术发展方向； 中后期政府开始介入	市政府的文物建筑保护与街道社区改造升级； 初期政府介入较少
市场经济组织 （经济性）	传统图书行业与电子卖场转型到现在的众创空间，探索一种新的营利模式； 市场运作恰到好处	盈利为目的的文化艺术机构，配套的餐饮服务经济，以及旅游创意经济； 中后期出现过于“商业化”	特色休闲餐馆、酒吧和旅游创意产品商店； 中后期出现过于“商业化”
社会大众（社会性）	青年大学毕业生和部分科技企业高管的创业体验； 社会大众参与积极	社会大众旅游文化消费； 艺术家思想表达，以及高房价的社会底层反应； 中后期出现过于“商业化”	社会大众的旅游文化消费； 大众一致参与比较多

表 3 简单地比较了三个案例社区在场景制造过程中具有的政治性、经济型和社会性。为了阐述每一个参与主体展示的力量，让我们分别从每一个个案中挑选一个特性来做简单讨论。在中关村创业大街的发展过程中，从一开始就是政府的强力介入与推动。它的前身是海淀图书城和电子产品卖场，房屋产权归属在不同私人业主手里，比较分散；当地政府为了建设创新创业中心，通过成立国有公司来强力回购房屋产权，然后再把收回的房屋进行整体规划与设计，低价出租给创新创业机构。在中国，在市中心黄金地段，也只有政府的力量才能在极短的时间里促成土地和房屋等不动产统一。因为土地从一开始就属于国有，这一点不同于欧美的土地私有制。高效率的土地征收和房屋征用，为随后的创新创业社区规划发展奠定了基础。另外，中关村创业大街 2014 年开街以来，国务院总理及科技部、教育部和北京市政府多位领导不断来此考察，并给予很多优惠政策支持。

798 艺术区场景形成作用力有所不同。在其发展过程中，一开始主要是由艺术家群体自发聚集形成。由于它本身是废弃工厂，并且处在城市边缘地方，因低廉租金和宽大空间吸引了一批艺术家入住。发展到一定程度后，产生了一些经济影响，特别是旅游效应，更多的文化艺术机构及相关产业也就介入。市场主体开始发挥重要力量，商人通过投资主导社区的基本发展方向。再后来，798 艺术区达到一定影响后，北京市政府开始更多介入。政府角色开始对 798 社区进行管制，甚至，对社区发展的艺术也有控制手段，艺术也展现了更多的国家政治性[1]。南锣鼓巷社区的发展是一个复杂的动力体系。从近 20 年来的情况来看，主要是受到三类政策影响：其一是关于历史文化街区保护，其二是关于居民社区改造与腾退，其三是关于旅游商业发展[16]。前两者的主导力量是政府,后者主要是商户和社会大众。

总之,无论社会怎么变化,政府、经济和社会都是场景生成的三种主要参与力量。当场景生成的政治性、经济性和社会性达到一个平衡点的时候,一个良好的文化场景的动能才能发挥最大作用,地方发展的动力才有可能出现。如果政治组织支持一种场景与价值观,但是企业组织或是社会大众不迎合这种场景与价值观的走向,那么,该社区活力就很难出现。甚至,社区反抗也有可能就在这个时候出现。同样,如果场景是一个从下到上的(bottom up)过程,政府管理者在一定时间内往往也会介入。当从下到上的这种发展不顺应他们的利益时候,政治控制和管理就会变得更强。因此,一个稳定能够发展起来的场景往往是符合多方利益的[16]。三个案例中所制造出来的场景,都是在政府、市场与社会之间正在趋向一种平衡点,虽然很难说是已经找到,但是至少是向这种方向在发展。这为本地区发展提供了生命力。

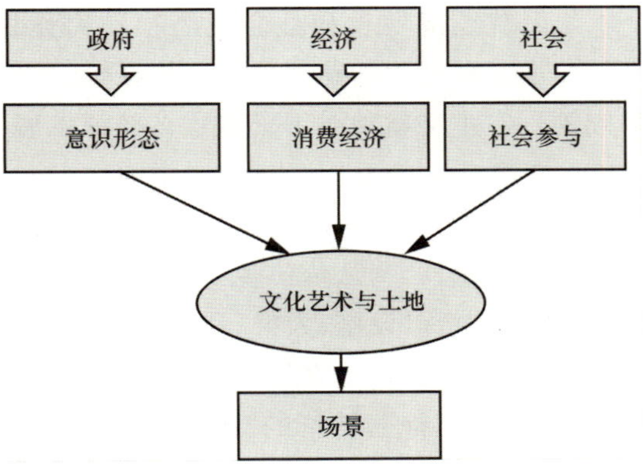

图 7　一个良好的城市社区场景制造机制分析模型[1]

5　对于城市政策的一些建议

一片空旷的土地(或废弃厂房)如何变为繁荣的城市社区?工业社会的城市政策与后工业社会的城市政策有着完全不同的发展逻辑。前者可以通过工业园区建设、房地产和 CBD 商务区开发等,吸引企业入驻,提供就业机会,促进人口流入,推动经济增长;人口跟随企业"走"。后者是利用文化艺术与土地、人力资本等要素"互动",形成场景,吸引创新创意等高级人力聚集,带来新企业,推动经济增长和社会发展;后者是企业跟随人力资本"走",而且除了经济增长,还会出现更好的社会发展。如果说,前者注重城市建设的数量与速度,那么,后者更注重城市建设的品质与可持续性。

事实上,随着后工业社会来临,城市发展路径已经开始从传统增长机器模型向娱乐机器模型转变。前者的推动主体是政府与开发商,后者是本地社会大众;前者强调的土地与建筑开发利用,后者推动的是文化艺术消费[1]。那么,在这样的发展框架下,一个城市社区怎么样才能获得增长发展呢?文化艺术的确已经成为城市发展的一种新思维[18]。同时,只有当参与主体政府、市场开发商和当地民众持有相同文化发展理念时,一个城市社区才能获得真正的健康增长发展。如果政府试图开发一个市场不愿意投资的文化社区主题,这样的城市建设就不可能获得市场的支持。如果政府和开发商试图建设社会大众不认同的城市社区文化理念，那么本地居民就不会参与进来[19]。在中国北京、上海和深圳等发达城市里，类似失败的案例不在少数。当然，本文具体分析的三种城市社区发展案例相对来说是比较成功的。三个社区场景制造的共同点都是朝着政府、市场和社会一致的文化发展理念，尽管个别阶段可能有略微的差异。

三方力量如何快速达到在文化上的利益平衡是场景形成的关键。一个好的、稳定的社区场景制造要依赖信任的建设，无论是政府对于市场经济组织和社会大众的信任，还是民众对政府的信任，这些都是社区场景制造最为关键的力量[1]。从这个角度来讲，培育地方的社会信任和网络资本至关重要。总之，只有文化发展符合政府文化方针，各种参与主体在利益上达成平衡时，一个有生命力的社区文化场景才能出现，才能真正聚集到人群和企业，才能驱动本地区的经济增长和社会发展[1]。

最后谈一谈场景理论对于中国城市发展的意义。克拉克教授提出的场景理论建立了微观文化动力学，深化了对文化在经济增长和社会发展中动力作用的认识。社会学家马克斯·韦伯从宗教社会学的角度分析文化的动力价值。他在《新教伦理和资本主义精神》一书中讨论了新教伦理为基础的资本主义精神对于资本主义经济发展的重要性。经济学家迈克尔·波特是从产业的角度分析文化在提升国际竞争力中的作用。他在《国家竞争优势》一书中认为，基于文化的优势是一个国家的最核心的竞争力。克拉克教授则从文化消费角度，将此前学者从精神层面对文化的理解，转为从价值观与生活方式层面去理解文化的内涵，从而将文化理解为生活化的结合体，是指以设施、人群、活动等形成的场景，以及场景中的价值观与生活方式，对于创新创意等高级人力资本聚集的意义。

韦伯的“新教伦理与资本主义精神”、波特的“国家竞争力理论”更多地从国家的视角分析文化对促进经济社会发展的作用；而克拉克更多是从社区这样的微观层面，从设施、人群和活动等，分析文化在促进经济社会发展中的作用力。如果说，韦伯的社会学理论，波特的竞争力理论更多是宏观文化动力学，那么克拉克的场景理论则更多是微观文化动力学，其深化了对文化在经济社会发展中动力作用的认识[11]。

场景理论还强调不同文化要素的协同性和真实性。场景理论不是孤立地讨论单个设施，而是强调设施、活动、人群等元素的协同有机组合。场景理论还强调不同设施所体现的真实性，被本地居民所认同的真实性，这也是城市创新动力的重要源泉。场景理论的这些观点对当前我国的城市建设有很强的针对性。一是有助于匡正城市建设普遍存在的热衷于建设高档文化设施，忽视日常生活文化设施建设的现象；二是有助于避免单纯注重文化设施建设，忽视设施配套组合，以及组合后的价值观与生活方式意义；三是热衷于引进文化设施，忽视从本地区发掘特色文化资源，即地区真实性的复原而非模仿或抄袭[11]。

最后，值得注意的是，尽管场景理论对于中国城市政策有着很强的指导意义，但在具体的运用上，也存在一些局限性。因为该理论本身主要是对美国、加拿大、韩国、法国等发达国家城市发展的研究基础上提炼出来的概念和术语，缺乏对于发展中国家城市发展转型的材料分析。因此，在运用的时候，应该注意：一是立足中国现实，分析中国问题；二是创造性地转换成中国概念体系和表达方式；三是吸收现代科技成果，特别是互联网技术在城市、社区生活的深刻影响，将现实空间与虚拟空间的研究结合起来；四是要注意，诸如北京与上海这样的大城市存在着工业与后工业的混合业态，城市内部也存在着二元社会结构，场景的形成更多了复杂性。

作者简介

吴军,(1984—),北京市委党校(北京行政学院)社会学教研部副教授,博士,北京人口与社会发展研究中心人员;浙江大学人文学院-浙江省城市治理研究中心博士后、杭州国际城市学研究中心研究人员,研究方向:城市与社区研究。本研究得到北京社科基金研究基地北京人口与社会发展研究中心项目“北京创新创业社区发展的文化动力机制研究”。

参考文献

[1] 吴志明,马秀莲,吴军. 文化增长机器:后工业城市与社区发展的路径探索[J]. 东岳论丛,2017(7).

[2] SILVERD A,CLARK T N, YANEZ C J N. Scenes: Social Context in an Age of Contingency, Social Forces[J]. 2010, 88(5): 2293-2324.

[3] CLARK T N. The City as an Entertainment Machine[M]. Amsterdam: Elsevier Press, 2004.

[4] GLAESER E L, GOTTLIEB J D. Urban Resurgence and the Consumer City[J]. Urban Studies, 2006, 43(8): 1275-1299.

[5] FLORIDA R. The Rise of the Creative Class-Revisited: Revised and Expanded[M]. New York: Basic Books, 2014.

[6] 吴志明,马秀莲. 流动的三种文化逻辑:解读高校毕业生大城市聚集[J]. 中国青年研究,2015(10): 72-77.

[7] SILIVER D A, CLARK T N. The Power of Scenes: Quantities of Aamenities and Qualities of Places [J]. Cultural Studies, 2015,09(13):425-449.

[8] 吴迪. 基于场景理论的我国城市择居行为及房价空间差异问题研究[M]. 北京:经济管理出版社,2013.

[9] CLARK T N. Can Tocqueville Karaoke? Global Contrasts of Citizen Participation, the Arts and Development[M]. England: Emerald Group, 2014.

[10] SILVER D A, CLARK T N. Scenescapes: How Qualities of Place Shape Social Life[M]. Chicago: The University of Chicago Press, 2016.

[11] 祁述裕. 建设文化场景、培育城市发展内生动力[J]. 东岳论丛,2017(1).

[12] ZHANG Yue. Governing Art Districts: State Control and Cultural Production in Contemporary China[J]. The China Quarterly, 2014,21(9):827-845.

[13] 刘明亮. 北京798艺术区:市场语境下的田野考察与追踪[D/OL]. 中国艺术研究院,2010.

[14] 新华网. 南锣鼓巷社区[EB/OL]. (2006-08-15). http://www.bj.xinhuanet.com/bjpd_sdwm/2006-08/15/content_7781820.html.

[15] 张纯,张敬甯,陈平,王缉慈,吕斌. 地方创意环境和实体空间对城市文化创意活动的影响[J]. 地理研究,2008(2).

[16] 刘东超. 场景理论视角上的南锣鼓巷[J]. 东岳论丛,2017(1).

[17] 朱家溍. 故宫退食录(上)[M]. 北京:故宫出版社,2009.

[18] 吴军. 文化动力:大城市发展新思维[M]. 北京:人民出版社,2016.

用文化机构带动城市更新

——以上海徐汇滨江和法国里昂汇流区改造为例

汪弘枫

摘　要　随着城市经济、产业、生态、环境的调整，城市的面貌和功能在不断变化和更新。本文特选了中法两个不同的地块的转型实践，以比较的方式，通过分析两个地块的历史沿革、相关的政策和文化设施在新地块中文化设施的使命来阐述在城市区域功能调整中，在旧工业区的改造升级中文化设施的所能起到的带动作用。

关键词　城市转型；上海西岸；里昂汇流区；新博物馆学

Urban Renewal Promoted by Cultural Institutions —Take the Renovation of the West Bund Area in Shanghai and the Confluence Area in Lyon for Example

Wang Hongfeng

Abstract　Urban appearance and function are in the stage of constant adjustment and improvement due to the development of economy, industries, ecological environment, etc. In order to illustrate that cultural institutions can play a leading role in urban transformation and renovation, this article analyzes and makes comparison of the history, policy application, culture and facilities of two selected areas respectively from France and China.

Keywords　urban transformation; Shanghai West Bund; Lyon confluence area; new museology

历史沿革、生活习惯、文化习俗、经济发展等各种因素时时刻刻影响着城市风貌，而建筑作为构成城市风貌的要素，对城市的形象又起着举足轻重的作用。每个时代都会有各自标志性的建筑，它们代表着当时的文化、科技和艺术。正如法国艺术社会学家蕾蒙德·穆兰女士说的："最近三十年来，博物馆取代了中世纪的大教堂、'黄金时代'（17 世纪）的宫殿和 19 世纪的火车站，成为时代的标志[1]63。"

穆兰女士的这句话也从侧面向我们阐述了不同时代占据统治地位的权力象征，因此博物馆就是现今文化和创意产业大爆发时代的最完美的代言人。

在当今社会，博物馆已不仅仅是城市的地标，它的社会作用和文化效应日益凸显。在文化战略已经上升到国家策略的当代中国，在政策的扶植下，在各级政府职能机构的鼓励下，大大小小、种类繁多的博物馆层出不穷，中国的博物馆在 21 世纪第一个十年的尾声迎来了建设高潮。以上海为例，依据上海文广局官网的信息，截至 2015 年上海全市拥有除美术馆之外的各类博物馆 122 家，另有美术馆 56 家，其中近 40%（21 家）的美术馆成立于 2010 年之后(全法兰西岛拥有博物馆及各类文化场所131处[①])。上海美术馆的数量还在持续增长，2016年又有5家美术馆注册成立[②]。上海各类博物馆数量激增源于以下两点：其一是城市面貌更新的需求，这主要与后世博时代如何利用好为数众多的世博场馆有着密切的关系。其二则是与城市经济结构转型，以及由此产生的工业遗迹的再利用有关。与之相比，远在法国里昂的汇流区的改造项目自1999年立项以来，区域的更新也是大刀阔斧，在文化设施的建设上除了2014年年底开幕的“汇流博物馆”之外，还有原糖厂改造的当代艺术中心，该中心自2003年起就是“里昂双年展”的主展馆。如果说“徐汇滨江”的定位是文化展览、艺术产业、都市休闲区，那“汇流区”的“野心”则要大了不少，里昂市政府希望将这段两河夹击的半岛打造成城市的副中心，“罗纳大区”的大区政府办公楼也落户在这片重新规划的土地上，使该地区成为集行政、文化、办公、教育、商业、休闲、居住各功能为一体的里昂新地标。

不难看出，上海和里昂在城区改造，区域功能翻新中殊途同归，都通过引入重量级文化设施向地块注入新活力，为其赋予新的使命，进而带动区域功能转型。笔者会利用以下有限的篇幅以历史、政策等方面为切入点来剖析中法两座城市在各自实践中的异同点。首先中法两国的文化政策会帮助我们更好地理解这个以“博物馆”为时代标志的当今社会的政策背景；当然法国学者弗朗索瓦·梅雷思的“新美术馆学”理论会帮助我们更好地理解，城市的设计者和决策者决定将博物馆、美术馆这类重要文化设施安置在城市边缘地带，甚至是以前的无人区的缘由；然而，这些区域的发展也非尽善尽美，所以我们将在文章的最后一部分分析一下这两个区域的问题。

1 地块的历史沿革

历史上这两个地块都属于城外“工业区”，居住区域外的“无人区”，得益于其得天独厚的地理位置，无论是里昂的汇流区还是上海的徐汇滨江都是城市陆、航运中转站，货运中心和产业中心，当然也有各自的特色，下面描述这两个地块的历史沿革。

1.1 里昂汇流区的历史变迁

如果上海徐汇滨江的工业历史可以上溯到晚清，里昂汇流区的历史则更为悠久。该地块的发展也可以分为几个阶段：

第一阶段：早在18世纪(1771年)的时候，工程师米歇尔·安托万·佩拉什先生就着手开发位于罗纳河与索恩河夹击形成的狭长半岛上的汇流地区，在他去世以后(1779年)，由他创办的佩拉什公司继续开发工作，直至1841年才全部完工(图1)。

第二阶段：随着工业化的深入，铁路也获得了长足的发展，得益于两河夹击、得天独厚的地理位置，里昂市选择在汇流区的佩拉什区建设火车站，以便将航运和铁路运输衔接起来，成为当地重要的货运和客运枢纽。虽然佩拉什火车站的选址考虑了运输的便捷，但是它横跨在半岛北部将主城区与汇流区拦腰斩断，使之成为地道的工业区，随后里昂市政府将糖厂、屠宰场、批发市场等重要市政、工业设施都建设在这个区域中。

① 汪弘枫统计于法兰西岛旅游局官网。

② 该数据由汪弘枫依据上海市社会团体管理局官方网站发布的信息统计。

第三阶段：从上个世纪末开始，里昂市政府决定再利用这片土地来扩大里昂中心城区的面积。改造项目自 1999 年立项以来，成为里昂市乃至全法国城市风貌更新、功能调整、产业结构再造最重要的项目之一，当地政府也致力于将汇流区打造成生态、环保、节能的示范区，并使之成为里昂市的文化、休闲和商业中心（图 2）。

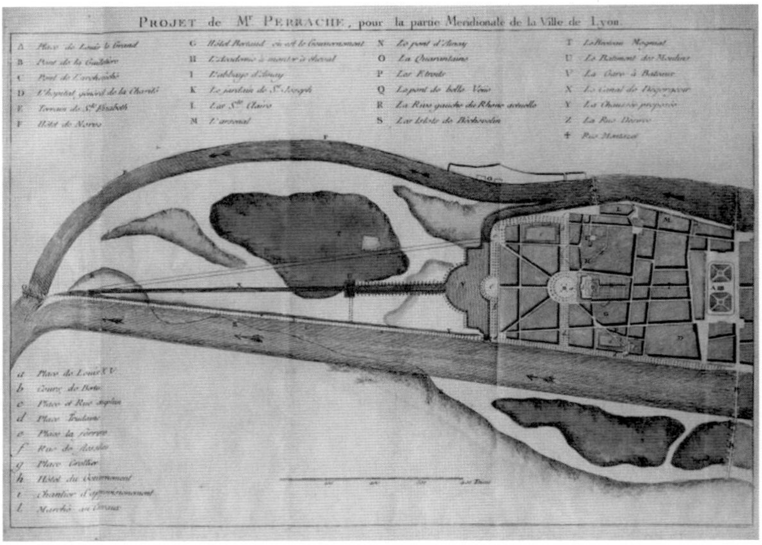

来源：法国文化部，里昂市档案馆

图 1　佩拉什先生的开发计划图

来源：La confluence Lyon, dossier de Presse [EB/OL]，里昂，里昂智慧城市战略办公室 SPLA Lyon Confluence，2012 年 10 月.

图 2　里昂天主教大学校区效果图

1.2　上海徐汇滨江的历史变迁

上海徐汇滨江的发展主要可以分为以下几个阶段：

第一阶段：太平天国时期徐汇滨江地区被英、法租界共同占有。1908 年，法国商人开通了上海法租界经过宝昌路（霞飞路）和姚主路（天平路）直抵徐家汇的有轨电车。1914 年，上海法租界向西扩张，新扩展的法租界带动了徐家汇地区的商贸发展与环境品质提升，徐汇滨江地区形成当时的商贸中心(图 3)。

第二阶段:中华人民共和国成立后至改革开放前(1947—1978 年)以工业建设为主导的发展模式。20 世纪六七十年代以来,随着城市化进程的推进,徐家汇成了工业聚集区,由市区通往吴泾的龙吴路两侧,一字排开了水泥、造纸、洗涤剂等企业及 10 多个码头。工业的建设带来了经济的提升,同时也带来了不少环境问题(图 4)。

第三阶段:改革开放后至现在(1978 年—现在)由社会经济活动中心发展为国际经济、金融、贸易中心。改革开放之后,徐汇滨江地块继续保留原有工业,并引入商业、居住与公共服务设施,形成区域的社会经济活动中心。2003 年徐汇滨江开发提上日程,依托西岸文化走廊、西岸传媒港等主导产业的导入,打造上海文化、传媒产业中心,造就新世纪国际大都市发展的新中心。2010 年世博会的召开,为徐汇滨江地块的发展带来新一轮契机。

来源:徐汇区档案馆

图 3　八十年前,从即将降落的飞机上俯瞰龙华和浦江西岸

来源:徐汇区档案馆

图 4　20 世纪 50 年代,实现水陆联运的北票码头

从上述两个地区发展的历史沿革我们不难看出其中有不少共同之处,比如都是处于城市的边缘地带,都是城市的航、陆运中转的交通枢纽,得益于便捷的交通体系,地块上的工业

也随之高速发展。然而，随着时间的推移，两座城市的经济、产业结构都发生了转变，随着城市化的加剧，原来的城市边缘慢慢被融入中心城区。近期，健康理念，生态、环保概念广受推崇，越来越多的居民开始关心自己和家人的健康和城市的生态环境，人与城市的关系也随之发生了改变。之前地块上高污染、高能耗的工业企业也陆续搬离，如何将这些地块重新纳入城市肌理，如何为它们定位，调节使用功能，如何为这些“无人区”新增附加值，都是城市的决策者需要考虑的问题。我们将在接下去的章节中初略分析两地政府对地块的定位和出台的相关的扶植政策。

2　政策导向和目标

当代社会的发展伴随着城市化进程的不断加剧，城市可利用空间也变得越来越宝贵。在本章节里，我们会分别阐述两国政府为改造地块制定的相关政策和目标。

2.1　法国文化政策和里昂汇流区改造的相关目标

法国作为文化大国，长久以来一直注重本国的文化发展和文化扶植，历届政府也在文化发展上投入了大量的资本，也出台不少法令和政策来扶植本国文化的发展。最有代表性的就是著名的“1% 法令”：凡是由政府出资的公共建筑项目预算的 1%都必须被用来采购艺术品[1]146。法国政府也非常重视博物馆的发展，因为博物馆作为一座城市重要的文化活动空间，建筑只是它的外壳，而真正决定一座博物馆成功与否的是它藏品的价值，以及它展览的质量和数量，当然博物馆的公教能力也越来越被重视。作为文化大国的法国在博物馆的建设、馆藏的丰富上是不遗余力的。为了保证和鼓励文化事业的发展，即便在经济衰退的今天，法国文化与传媒部 2016 财政年度的预算还是达到了 73 亿欧元，比上年度增加了 6%[2]4。

我们不难看出法国政府鼓励文化发展的信心和决心，里昂市政府也希望使城市迈入欧洲一流城市行列。20 世纪 70 年代，因为经济结构的调整，里昂的汇流区日趋萧条。在 20 世纪末，在时任里昂市市长雷蒙・巴尔(于 1995—2001 年在任)先生的领导下，里昂市政府将眼光投向了汇流区，启动了该区域的改造，并将其作为向“新世纪献礼，开启第三个千禧年的钥匙[3]”。他也认为，“如果里昂错过了汇流区的开发项目，则将永远是一座不入流的外省小城[3]”。汇流区的改造项目于 1995 年由里昂市政府启动，由中央和里昂当地政府会同私营资本共同出资。从 2003 年起，索恩河岸的改造成为区域第一期改造的重点，并按照以下目标推进改造：

(1) 构建丰富的公共空间；

(2) 便于社会各阶层居民混居；

(3) 平衡区域功能(住宅、办公楼、商业、文化、教育、休闲等)；

(4) 建设可持续发展城市。

汇流区第一期改造项目占总项目工程量的 40%，总投资额达 12 亿欧元，未来将在 41 公顷的土地上建成 40 万平方米的建筑，该阶段 80%的工程量已在 2016 年完成[4]。

2.2　上海徐汇滨江改造的相关政策

目前在文化发展已上升为国家战略的中国，其实早在十多年前就已经定下未来国家文化发展的战略基调。2006 年 3 月 28 日，李长春同志就提出了“新文化发展观”的理论；随后，为了在新的形势下更好地明确艺术发展的方向，李长春同志又在 2010 年 6 月 17 日发表了名为《正确认识和处理文化建设发展中的若干重大关系，努力探索社会主义文化发展道路》的文章[5]104。

就地方而言，二十多年来上海市政府已经不满足于仅仅将上海打造成中国的金融中心，同时也提出了成为 21 世纪世界设计之都的目标。而在最新上海市 2040 年城市总体规划中也明确指出：到 2040 年，上海要建设成为卓越的全球城市，国际经济、金融、贸易、航运、科技创新中心和文化大都市。为了实现该目标，一方面，上海市政府致力和鼓励文化场馆建设，目前上海市拥有的博物馆总量已超过了大巴黎；另一方面，着手打造有影响力的文化、艺术活动和项目。

2016 年 11 月 30 日，上海市市政府颁布了《黄浦江两岸地区发展“十三五”规划》(以下简称《规划》)的通知，对未来提出了新的要求：

> 聚焦黄浦南外滩地区、徐汇滨江-浦东前滩地区、世博园区、浦东新(华)民(生)洋(泾)-杨浦滨江南段等重点发展区域，大力完善基础性开发，稳步推进功能性建设，力争在“十三五”期末，将这些区域打造成为黄浦江两岸特色鲜明的城市亮点。

该《规划》对“徐汇滨江”的未来发展提出了具体的要求：

> 徐汇滨江。坚持规划引领、文化先导、产业主导的基本思路，加快形成独具魅力的文化传媒区、国际一流的商务商贸区、充满活力的滨水新城区。

“十三五”期间“徐汇滨江”的主要任务是(图 5)：

> 进一步拓展西岸文化走廊品牌内涵，扎实做好“美术馆大道”设施建设、更高水平举办各类活动。

我们从上述的政策和目标中不难看出两个地区的政府改造现有地块的意愿和决心，很巧合的是两个国家的政府都制定近乎类似的改造战略，也就是通过对地块上工业遗迹的改造和再利用，用文化设施来带动地块的转型。为什么相距千里的两国政府都殊途同归的选在原工业遗迹上建设重要的文化设施？下一章节中将会就该问题作出解答。

3　用文化设施带动城市转型

先来看看这两座城市是如何利用区域重要的文化设施来带动城市区域转型的。首先，将像博物馆这样的重要文化设施建在城市边缘是非常契合“新美术馆学”理论的。弗朗索瓦·梅雷思在《新美术馆学起源史》一文中是这样讲述“新”美术馆选址的：

> 这些“新”美术馆位于大城市中的贫困街区，或是处于贫民窟之中，也可以在传统工业衰退转型的老工业区，或者是乡村，都是经典博物馆尚未涉足的城市边缘地带[6]43。

“新美术馆学”之所以认为应该将博物馆这类文化设施安排在城市的边缘，是因为：

> 针对社会精英的圣殿般的博物馆，已经所剩无几了，“新博物馆”要和精英逻辑，以及参观者(与博物馆间的)被动关系划清界限。‘新博物馆’要成为服务于全体民众的工具，这里的民众既是参与者又是使用者[6]35。

所以，所谓的“新美术馆”是要服务于大多数人的，而不是仅仅服务于精英阶层的，“新博

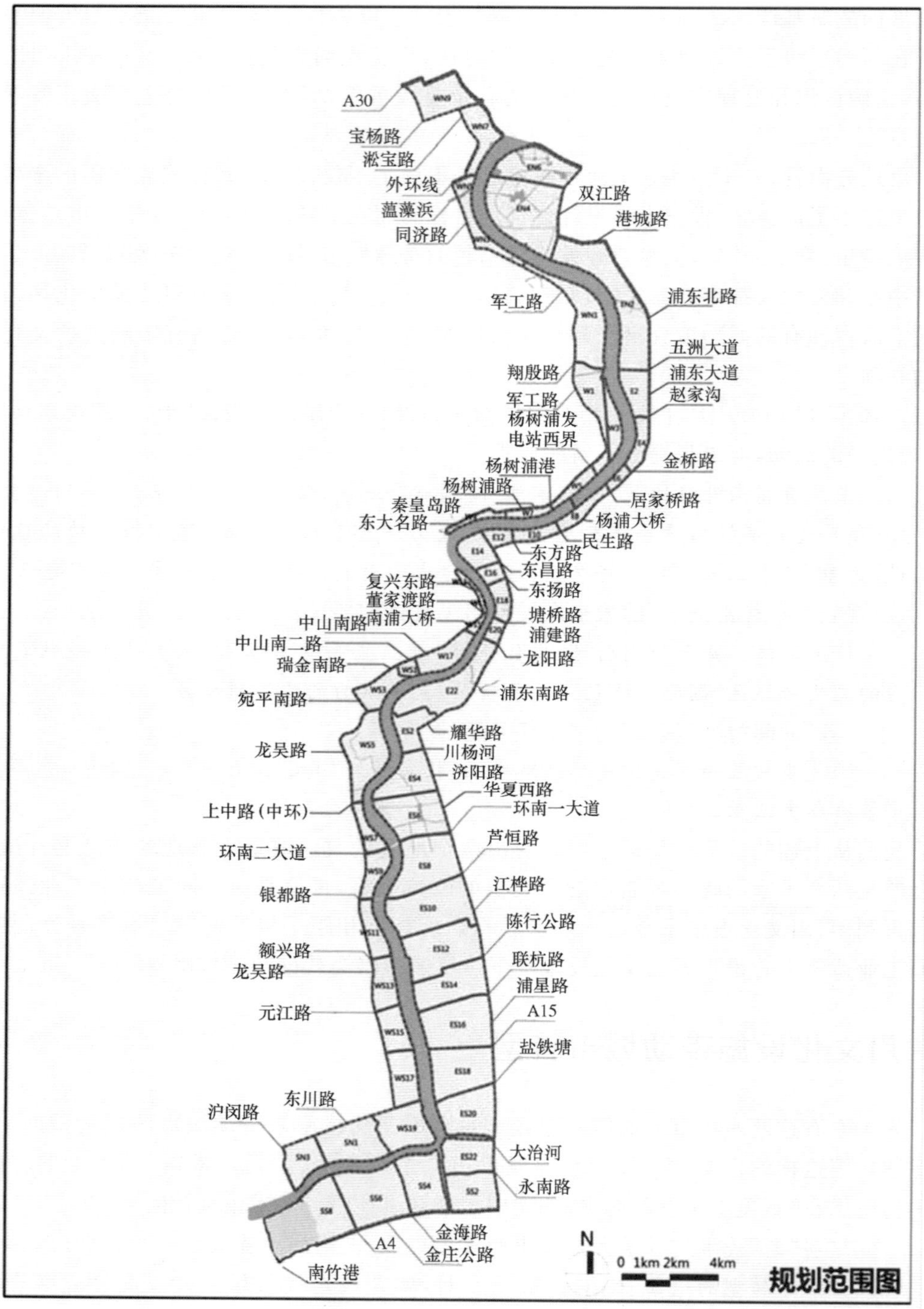

来源:市政府关于印发《黄浦江两岸地区发展“十三五”规划》的通知

图 5　黄浦江两岸地区“十三五”发展规划范围

物馆”的任务也是要吸引和服务于大多数的人群,让普通“老百姓”也有兴趣进到博物馆来,看他们可理解的展览。而无论是里昂的汇流区和上海的徐汇滨江的改造规划上都尽量避免使之成为功能单一的城市飞地,而是有活力、有生命力和生活气息的全新城市地标。因此,两国的规划中都涉及住宅项目的植入,汇流区改造的一大目的就是"增进社会各阶层的融合",因此在商用的住宅项目中会提供一部分的社会住宅,以便各个社会阶层的居民可以在汇流区混居,并且做到宜居,使他们都能享受到区域内的文化、公共设施。这也为区域内的文化设施保有了相当数量的观众,同时也为这些文化机构提出了新的要求——如何满足来自不同阶层人群的文化需求?

3.1 汇流区文化设施的实践——以汇流博物馆为例

首先来看看里昂市政府在汇流区的改造项目中赋予了文化设施怎样的使命。汇流区的改造项目就是通过商业和文化设施的植入,将原工业园区单一的产业结构和使用功能进行再创新和丰富,住宅项目的安置又激活了街区的活力和生命力,使之不会在周末沦为死气沉沉、渺无人烟的"无人区",而"汇流博物馆"(图 6)就是第一期改造规划中的点睛之笔。

将重要的文化设施植入到该地区,用来带动区域业态转型,使里昂不单单在市中心拥有市立"美术馆"等重要的专门展馆,在城市的边缘地带也同时拥有了如"汇流博物馆"等重要的现代化文化场所,使城市的文化设施得以平均分布,不但错落有致,而且内外有序。这样也可以造成城市人口的双向流动,以博物馆为代表的文化设施在这里不单单起到文化功能,同时也肩负着社会效应。

图 6 "汇流博物馆"主体建筑

作为里昂的自然、历史和科技博物馆,为了满足各类人群的文化需求,汇流博物馆的 4 个常年展厅的设想和布置都独辟蹊径(图 7)。每个展厅都按照一个独立的展览来策划,都是独立的一个完整故事,而展厅与展厅之间又有着一定的关联,这样既保持了博物馆叙事的独立性,又兼顾整体性,一方面很好地解决了"汇流博物馆"跨学科展品同时展出的难题,也方便了观众观展,不强制观众按部就班地按照预设的既定参观路线,循规蹈矩地步步深入,而是将问题抛给了观众,让他们在参观中找寻问题的答案。在这里观众不是被动接受而是主动获得,也完全不会因为跳过一件重要展品,而造成叙事的割裂和不连贯。而不同类型、跨学科的展品被陈列在同一空间内,就仿佛是为同一"论点"服务的不同"论据",不会因为学科的不同而显得突兀或者格格不入,况且"博物馆可以通过跨学科,让所拥有的遗迹承担起社会化角色,也可以通过对它所在的乡村或城市的社会环境、环境、城市发展问题的认知,同时通过博物馆持续的教育工作和传播知识的方法来实现对社会结构改变的探讨[6]44"。博物馆不仅仅是人类共同精神或物质财富的陈列室，它更应该是一个论坛，一个开放的、民主的对话和讨论的平台。

“汇流博物馆”在“为人民服务”上可谓是不遗余力，在展览的布置上除了使用传统的，殿堂式的陈列方式之外，还通过不同的手段和方法来调动参观者除了视觉之外的感知力，比如在展区内放置一具恐龙头骨的复制品，邀请参观者直接触摸。“汇流博物馆”所提供的沉浸式观展模式，其目的就是希望博物馆面对最广泛的观众群：

> 个人、家庭、城市青年、(博物馆)附近的居民、弱势群体、学生、游客，(幼儿园至高中的)在校学生是优先接待对象。博物馆也努力接待那些因为身体、经济、心理，以及地域文化差异而无法经常来博物馆参观的人群，积极调动各种社会资源来满足特殊人群的需求。

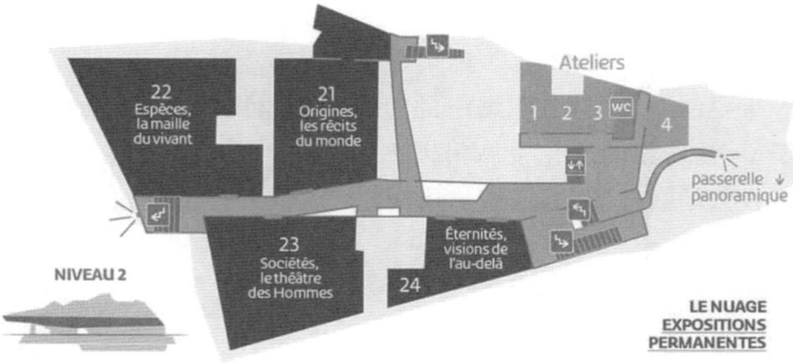

来源：“汇流博物馆”官网页面，博物馆平面图

图 7　“汇流博物馆”地面 2 平面图

“显而易见，这种将博物馆向全体民众开放的意愿，退去了博物馆的光环，并将馆藏作为确保博物馆所在地发展的工具，这听起来有些乌托邦的实践，却恰恰是‘新博物馆学’的主导力[6]35”。在多方努力下，“汇流博物馆”累积参观人数在 2015 年 6 月 26 日(开馆半年后)超过了 50 万人。近 80%的参观者来自里昂及周边地区，博物馆对所在地居民起到的社会、文化、教育效应最为直接和显著。

博物馆展览不再一味“掉书袋”，故弄玄虚、高深莫测，因为新型的博物馆是以人为本的，将参观者置于博物馆体系的中心，博物馆的职责也是“解惑”，而不是制造困惑。因此，基于“新美术馆学”理念建立起来的博物馆会更加注重参观者的感受，参观是一个互动的过程而不是单向的“填压”。如果说常年展决定了博物馆的学术定位，需要维持一个恒定的标准，那特展所表现的恰恰是博物馆兼容并蓄的多样性，可以多姿多彩，变化多端。“汇流博物馆”的特展与舞蹈家、音乐家、摄影师、画家都开展合作，让艺术成为观众通往博物馆的桥梁。这些特展运用直白的体验方式(视觉、触觉)，再加上多媒体，各种渠道的宣传手段，将更多的观众吸引到博物馆来。

3.2　徐汇滨江的艺术设施

徐汇滨江的改造开发项目的定位显然和里昂汇流区有着异曲同工的效果，都在区域内注入了以博物馆为主的重量级的文化设施。该区域最早期的规划要追溯到 2010 年世博会以前了。据著名建筑师刘亦春老师介绍：作为上海城市发展的长远战略，黄浦江沿岸的徐汇滨江段,借助于世博会建设的城市发展规划,同期也将黄浦江沿岸的一些货运码头和工厂迁出,以此启动了徐汇滨江的城市更新计划。原来的规划设计是建造一个游客服务中心,具有建筑学博士身份的时任徐汇区委书记孙继伟并不满足于简单的商业开发与设计,定名为"西岸"的徐汇滨江文化走廊的开发思路出台。徐汇区政府的愿望是将"西岸"打造成文化艺术展览、销售和文化产业中心之一。在西岸不仅有上海的两大重量级的私人美术馆:建筑面积达33000平方米的龙美术馆 西岸馆和建筑面积为9000平方米的余德耀美术馆。如此巨大的体量,其硬、软件设施可以比肩很多国立美术馆。随后,上海首家专业摄影艺术博物馆——"上海摄影艺术中心"和"上海西岸艺术中心"等重要的艺术展览场馆也陆续登陆西岸。近期,以中国最早的专业画廊之一的"香格纳画廊"为代表的一些重量级画廊也先后落户。未来,包括美国梦工厂和以"梦中心"为名的都市文化集聚区等也将入驻,届时将真正实现艺术展览、艺术销售和艺术产业三位一体全方位发展。

3.2.1 龙美术馆(西岸馆)

位于原北票码头的核心区域,龙美术馆西岸馆(图8)的公共性体现在它不再是封闭内向型的美术馆空间模式,而更多地容纳了艺术品研究、艺术品商店、艺术培训、书店、图书馆、小音乐厅、餐厅、咖啡厅等更具开放性、更具公众参与性的公共空间,使艺术不再远离大众,而是参与到公众的日常休闲生活中来。从龙美术馆的设计上也不难看出这是一座以"新博物馆学"为理论基础的美术馆,它的目标是吸引和服务于更大数量的人群,而不再仅仅是局限在艺术界这个小而封闭的象牙塔内。这点也可以从博物馆举办的展览上看出,受博物馆创办人刘益谦、王薇夫妇不同的收藏风格影响,龙美术馆(西岸馆)的展览围绕着三大板块组织:一方面邀请了世界上炙手可热的当代艺术家前来举办展览;也会举办"红色经典"主题的展览;同时也会组织传统艺术方面的展览。龙美术馆(西岸馆)充分利用其场地空间的优势,同时组织2~3场不同类型的展览来满足各种类型观众的需求。而在国外艺术家的选择上也比较慎重,不会选择那些作品晦涩难懂的艺术家。前段时间在龙美术馆举办个展的詹姆斯·特瑞尔是一位以"空间"和"光线"为创作素材的当代艺术家,其作品视觉效果强烈,展览期间也成为当时上海著名的"网红"展览,吸引了各个年龄层的大量观众参观,起到很好的艺术普及和文化普及的社会效应。

3.2.2 余德耀美术馆

余德耀美术馆能够落户徐汇滨江也得益于区委书记孙继伟的支持,余先生也在一篇采访中提到,他在参观了原上海飞机厂的机库之后就被这个独特的空间所吸引,再加上徐汇区领导的支持,让他的美术馆很顺利地就落户西岸。余德耀先生之所以会爱上这个场地,也与他收藏艺术作品的类型有一定的关系,他是以收藏大型装置著称的,所以机库的层高和空间很适合安置大型的装置作品(图9)。

和龙美术馆(西岸馆)一样,余德耀美术馆展览的组织也尽量做到亲民和有吸引力,其展览一方面是围绕着余先生的藏品展开的,就像图10上呈现的美术馆开幕展"天际之间"中展览的华裔法国艺术家黄永砯的装置作品;2015年引进的兰登国际的作品"雨屋";与瑞士贾科梅蒂基金会合作的"阿尔贝托·贾科梅蒂回顾展"都取得了很大的成功,尤其是150平方米的互动装置"雨屋"的引入成为当时非常受欢迎的展览,这也得益于余德耀美术馆的空间结构,否则如此大型的装置也很难落户。

这两家重量级的私人美术馆落户徐汇滨江后,使这段黄浦江畔成为上海艺术、尤其是当代艺术的圣地之一，几乎每个月都会有艺术活动在这里开幕，每年春季和秋季还会组织露天的音乐会。同时，住宅项目的同步开发，也为该地块集聚了人气。现在的徐汇滨江已成为上海市民重要的文化休闲场所之一。

虽然，在中法两国的城市区域更新项目中都通过地产项目来保证地块上的“人气”，但真正起到为区域引流作用的还是落户区域的重要的文化设施，尤其是赋予了博物馆、美术馆等文化设施重要的社会责任，使之成为服务市民、吸引市民的关键环节，通过这些文化场馆为区域集聚人气，为区域带来活力和生命力。除了文化设施，在改造中引入的便于市民休闲的公共空间起到的作用也非常重要，也是这两个区域成为市民生活休闲场所的关键。当然里昂汇流区被赋予的功能更为全面，罗纳大区政府办公楼的建设和里昂天主教大学的入驻又为该区域附加了行政、教育等重要的功能，同时也带来了可观的、有活力的年轻人群。汇流区的目标是等到2030年项目完全建成后，区域内的居民数从现在的7000人增加到16000人。[4]

图8　龙美术馆(西岸馆)

图9　余德耀美术馆外观

4 转型中的困惑

4.1 地产泡沫的产物?

上海徐汇滨江和里昂汇流区,这两个分处两国的地块有着类似的历史、采取相近的定位和规划措施:通过文化设施的植入来带动城市的转型。在两国的规划中都安置了不少的住宅项目,但引起争议的也正是这些商业地产项目,在上海和里昂都受到了居民对地区内住宅价格虚高,房地产泡沫的质疑。

目前汇流区的房屋均价为5000～6000欧元/平方米,远高于里昂的平均水平,比如与汇流区毗邻的圣·布朗蒂娜区的房价在3200～3800欧元/平方米。因为汇流区的建设带动了附近房地产价格的水涨船高,圣·布朗蒂娜区的房产价格在十年内上涨了124%。

来源:https://artouch.com/artouch2/

图10 余德耀美术馆内部空间

此外,虽然里昂市政府致力于各阶层居民的融合,但是要实现这个美好的愿望仿佛困难重重。自2009年汇流区的第一批居民入住后,由区域内居民自发组织的协会都反映新居民对协会工作漠不关心,投入的人力和精力都不多,远没有老居民积极。因为房价的关系,能够入住汇流区的一定是经济实力不菲的高收入人群,所以他们的工作繁忙,而闲暇时间则有限。这与以退休居民为主的原居民的状况明显不同,这也是新居民不能更多投入社区人文环境建设的原因。让原居民不安的是:因为汇流区新居民的社会、职业构成,所以他们通常只在晚上才回到自己的住宅,慢慢地该区域会变成一座巨大的“宿舍”。也有居民抱怨汇流区的新住宅项目就是房地产泡沫的产物,价高而施工质量不能保证,房屋漏水,门窗设施不合规,配套设施不完善等现象严重,最终导致了他们搬离了汇流区。

说到房地产泡沫,上海徐汇滨江也有类似的情况,介于余德耀美术馆和龙美术馆(西岸馆)之间的地块上,已建成了一些高档的住宅小区,其中一个住宅项目售楼处的工作人员说在2013年的时候,他工作的住宅项目的均价是70000元/平方米,几乎所有的住宅都已售

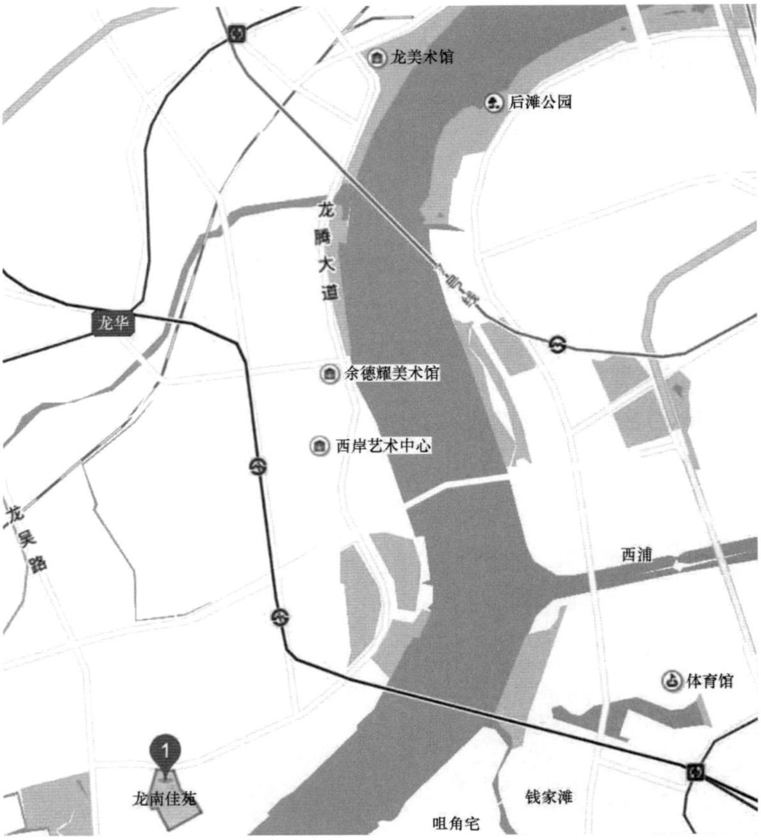

来源：百度地图

图 11　上海龙南佳苑的地理位置

出，价格几乎是当时上海市住宅的均价的 3 倍（23 000 元/平方米）[7]，这两年房价又一直持续上扬，单位面积超过 10 万元的已经不在少数了。

4.2　公共交通配套不到位

从图 11 上不难看出，虽然有两条地铁线分别经过“西岸”的附近，但是出了地铁站后还有比较长的一段路需要步行，从距龙美术馆（西岸馆）最近的地铁 12 号线龙华中路站到美术馆需步行 1 公里左右，而从距余德耀美术馆最近的 11 号线云锦路站到美术馆需步行约 800 米，而这之间没有公共交通可以选择，而且这两座美术馆之间也没有公共交通直接相连，不过最近出现的共享单车较好地解决了这最后一公里出行的问题，但是其实政府在做区域规划的时候也应该把这些配套的公共交通设施都考虑进去。图 12 摄于 2016 年 1 月 15 日，可以看到，当时只有一名观众在欣赏奈良美智的作品，也从一个侧面反映除了在工作日徐汇滨江的人流数量。而里昂的汇流区或多或少也存在同样的问题，虽然在规划时延伸了有轨电车 1 号线，来方便居民的出行，但是 1 号线是从区域的中央贯穿汇流区，所以要到达风光秀丽的河岸边也是只能依靠步行。

图 12　龙美术馆(西岸馆)内部及观众

5　结语

通过对上海徐汇滨江和法国里昂汇流区改造项目的分析,我们不难看出,随着城市工业、经济结构转型的深入、城市化进程的加剧和城市生态环境保护的需求,城市中的旧工业区被赋予了新的使命。这两个区域类似的地理位置和原先的功能定位,造成随后选择的改造方法和措施都有很多相似之处。双方都选择将改造后的区域定位成集文化、商业、休闲、居住为一体的城市滨水地带。因此,区域内被引入了重量级的公共文化设施和艺术品经营场所,以及相当数量的文化传媒企业。这些文化、艺术机构,传媒、新闻企业的入驻也为区域的定位注入了鲜明的文化色彩,使之成为地区的最大特色,是带动该区域转型的重要力量。如果说媒体、企业的入驻在工作日带来了上班族、职业人群,而真正能为区域带来稳定、持续人群的则是奉行"新博物馆学"理念的公共文化机构,当然区域的公共休闲空间的设计也起到了不小的积极作用。

虽然文化机构和企业成为带动两座城市的不同地块的原动力,但是区域的定位也会有一定的差异。这主要是因为上海徐汇滨江"西岸艺术走廊"的定位相对简单,而里昂汇流区被赋予的功能则更为丰富,它不但要通过在新开发的商业住宅中融入社会住宅来实现各社会阶层的融合,也需要通过区域内市民自发组织的各种民间协会来完成新老居民间的相互交流;其次,随着罗纳大区政府办公楼的落成,汇流区也被赋予了一定的行政使命;最后汇流区还成为法国节能住宅项目的试验场,区域内的住宅项目尽量做到最低能耗,甚至能够做到能源自给自足,不但自给自足还能将多余的能源贡献给周边。

诚然,两个区域通过文化机构的带动,从原来无人涉足的工业区变成了宜居的市民文化、休闲的中心,但是两个地块又同时面临着房地产泡沫,交通相对闭塞的问题,如果能够更好地解决最后一公里的出行,会为区域未来的繁荣起到更大的作用。

作者简介

汪弘枫,独立研究者,法国历史与文明博士,法国 DNSEP 造型艺术硕士。

参考文献

[1] MOULIN R，COSTA P. L'artiste，l'institution et le marché [M]. Paris：Flammarion，1992.

[2] Ministère de la culture et des communications. 2016 Projet de Loi de Finances[R]. Paris，2015.

[3] Ecole normale supérieure de Lyon. Sylvain Genevois，La France：des territoires en mutation Lyon-Confluence，un exemple de r novation urbaine [EB/OL]. Lyon：Ecole normale sup rieure de Lyon，2005.

[4] Société publique locale d'am nagement. La confluence Lyon，dossier de Presse [EB/OL]. Lyon：Société publique locale d'aménagement，Lyon Confluence，2012-10.

[5] WANG Hongfeng. Être artiste à Shanghai au début du XXIe siècle，entre institutions publiques et marché [D]. Pairs ：Université Paris Ⅶ，2014.

[6] François Mairesse. La belle histoire，aux origines de la nouvelle muséologie [J]，Publics et Musées，n° 17-18. L'écomusée ：rêve ou réalité (sous la direction de André Desvallées)，2000.

[7] 朱绍杰. 国内频建私人美术馆:中国收藏家重塑艺术格局[N]. 广州:羊城晚报，2014-7-26.

移民融入与包容发展

“商业城堡镇”中的日裔巴西人社区:滨松市的多元文化导向[①]

水上徹男

摘　要　在日本,有些地区被称为“商业城堡镇”。“城堡镇”一词源于日本战国时期的城市结构特点。当城市中心区的核心还是封建领主的城堡时,他们就从中心向周边发展。“城堡镇”有两个基本功能:一个是军事基地,另一个是商业区。日本的“商业城堡镇”中的商业区、房地产和其他城市设施的发展是依托一些公司进行的。著名的“城堡镇”之一滨松市,是由雅马哈音乐公司和铃木汽车公司等集团开发建设的。这个城市也以巴西人的集中而闻名,其中绝大多数都是之前日本赴巴移民们的后代。从日本到巴西的官方劳工移民早在20世纪初就开始回流,并持续到了二战后。与此同时,集体移民又重新开始,许多日本人移民到巴西作为农业劳动者。由于1990年日本移民法案的修订,来自南美和中美洲的外国人口,尤其是来自巴西的回流移民迅速增加。为了应对外国人口,包括许多非法移民的增加,1989年日本政府修改移民法,在第二年引入对非熟练劳动力迁移的限制,同时为巴西、秘鲁、玻利维亚和阿根廷等中美洲国家的日本后裔打开了大门。现在,许多不讲日语的日本人已经在一些日本的商业城堡镇里建立了自己的社区,因为商业公司的所在地已经为他们提供了制造业的工作。我的研究目的是描述滨松市的情况。滨松市一直在倡导创意城市政策,具有一定的多元文化特色。其中一些政策要求地方政府与地方非政府组织之间合作。虽然这些中美洲迁来的日本后裔拥有在日本生活的官方权利,但由于语言障碍和文化差异,这些居民遇到了各种各样的困难。因此,许多民间组织,无论是公共的还是私人的,都在应对这些新居民所遇到的困难。

关键词　商业城堡镇;日裔巴西人;滨松市;多元文化导向

Japanese Brazilian Communities in “Business Castle Towns”: Hamamatsu City’s Multicultural Directions

Tetsuo Mizukami

Abstract　In Japan, there have been some areas designated as “business castle towns.” The term “castle town” comes originally from the characteristics of Japan’s urban structure in the Age of Warring States. When the core of city areas was the feudal lord’s castle, they have henceforth developed from the center towards its periphery. The “castle town” has two basic functions: it serves as a military base and also as a commercial zone. Japan’s “business castle towns” have been developed by certain companies’ contribution to the growth of commercial zones, housing estates, and other city amenities. One of the well-known business castle towns is Hamamatsu city for Yamaha music and Suzuki motor vehicle companies and the like. That city is also famous for its

① 本文根据水上徹男教授在2017"城市与社会"国际学术论坛上的发言整理、翻译。文稿编辑:邓世碧,上海同济城市规划设计研究院助理研究员;校对:钟晓华,同济大学社会学系副教授。

Brazilian concentration, the vast majority of whom are the descendants of previous emigrants from Japan. The official Japanese labor migration from Japan to Brazil started back in early twentieth century, and even after the Second World War, group migration re-started and many Japanese migrated to Brazil as farm laborers. A rapid increase in foreign population from South and Central America, including returnees from Brazil, took place as a consequence of the amendment of Japan's Immigration Act of 1990. In response to the increasing foreign population, who included many undocumented migrants, the Japanese government amended Immigration Act in 1989 and in the following year, introduced restrictions on unskilled labor migration, while at the same time opening the door for people of Japanese descent from South and Central American countries, namely, Brazil, Peru, Bolivia, and Argentina. Now many Japanese Brazilians, who do not speak the Japanese language, have formed their community in some Japanese business castle towns since the location of business firms have offered manufacturing work. My aim is to describe the situation in Hamamatsu, which has been initiating creative city policies, with some definite multicultural characteristics. Some of these policies require cooperation between prefecture and city council governments with local non-governmental organizations. Although they have official rights to live in Japan, these residents encounter various difficulties, because of the language barrier and pervasive cultural differences. Consequently, many civic organizations, both public and private, are forming in responding to the difficulties of newcomers.

Keywords business castle town; Japanese Brazilians; Hamamatsu City; multicultural directions

本篇论文由三个部分组成。首先简单介绍一下日本的商业城堡镇,然后会侧重讲一下形成于制造业工厂所在的城市中的日裔巴西人社区,最后介绍滨松市政厅的一些政策,以及致力于在城市生活中深化这种多元文化特征的非政府的组织所进行的活动。

1 日本的商业城堡镇

在日本,有一些特定的商业城堡,就是所谓的"城堡镇"(城下町),是一种源于 15 世纪中期到 17 世纪初(战国时代)的日本城市结构。那个时代,所有的城市地区都是封建领主的城堡,城市从中心向外发展。"城堡镇"有两个基本功能:它既是军事基地,又是商业区。

在日本,从 1970 年开始就可以在报纸上看到"商业城堡镇"(企業城下町)这个术语,尽管在那之前它很可能还是其他的用途[1]。经历了 1973—1974 年的石油危机后,日本经济的高速增长停止了,亟需重新起步,依赖于组装—节能电器和机动车辆的制造业变得越来越重要。经历了 20 世纪 70 年代末的第二次石油危机之后,"商业城堡镇"这一术语在大众媒体中生根发芽。

可以用"制造企业形成的工业城堡"来描述日本的商业城堡镇。一些日本学者在把自己的作品翻译成英文的时候,将"商业城堡镇"(business castle towns)翻译为"公司城镇"(company towns)。而这种翻译并没有充分表达出原先位于城市中央的封建领主城堡是如何被大企业所取代的。

一些主要的商业城堡镇已经发展出自己独特的气质,并在其城市环境中表现出独特层级架构:在金字塔顶端是一座非常大的建筑,有各种不同的中小型零售商铺,还有一些坐落在城市近郊的分包公司——它们很多都是为大公司生产零部件。

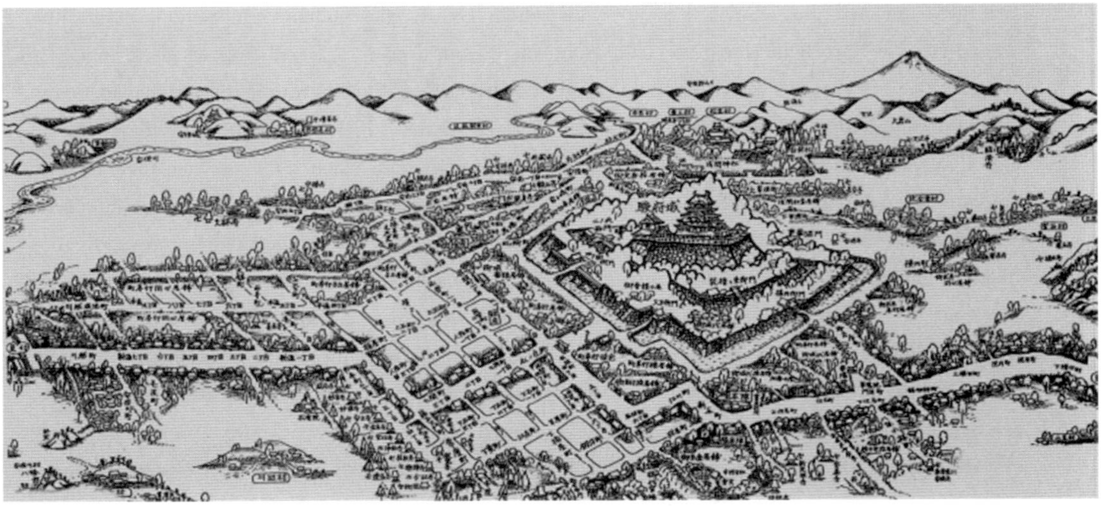

来源：http://www.city.shizuoka.jp/076_000010.html.

图 1　江户时代的松浦(静冈县)

2　移民史与日裔巴西人社区

全国有好几个城市中心从 20 世纪 80 年代中后期就吸引了一些新的外国移民群体，他们进入了日本的制造业和服务行业，现在成为日本公共经济成长的重要助力。伴随外国人口(包括很多未登记的移民)的增加，国家在 1990 年出台了《移民法案》。它严格限制低素质的非技术劳工的涌入，同时向来自中美洲国家(例如巴西、秘鲁、玻利维亚和阿根廷)的、能够取得合法就业机会的日本人后裔(尽管他们或许曾经是非技术劳工)敞开了大门，使他们可以回到日本本土。这反过来又促成了移民政策当中一个向基于血缘(由于日本人的血统观念)、而非基于土地(个体因为出生在某个国家领土内而成为其公民)的日本后裔开放的法律条款[2]。《移民法案》的出台，直接导致了来自美洲中部和南部的移民激增。

有官方记录的巴西和日本的移民往来可以追溯到二十世纪初。从 1908—1941 年的第一次移民潮开始，大概有 19 万日本人从日本移民到了巴西。《移民法案》的修订给那些移民的后代回到日本带来了可能性，但是这些大部分都不会讲日语了。在日本，1988 年时官方登记在册的巴西籍人口只有 4000 人，到 1989 年增加到了 14000 人，而到了 1990 年，就增加到大约 56400 人。此后，尽管 1998—1999 年之间有短暂的回落，到 2007 年为止，这一人口数还是增长到超过 31 万人。2008 年金融危机爆发之后，由于雷曼兄弟的破产，巴西人的数量逐渐下降。

表 1 是日本的巴西人数量排名前五的城市。其中一个著名的例子是丰田城。这个城市长期以来都驻扎着汽车企业，有很多巴西移民在这里工作，从而形成了巴西社区。滨松市位于京都和东京之间，靠近新干线。这个城市是以技术为驱动的基础企业聚集地，是由雅马哈音乐公司和铃木汽车公司等集团开发建设的。其中的巴西人口大概有 9000 人左右，占当地外国移民人口的半数以上。

表 1　巴西人数量排名前五的城市

城市名	巴西人数量	人口	面积（km^2）	所属县
滨松	9165	796114	1558.07	静冈
丰桥	6937	377431	261.86	爱知
丰田	5984	425718	918.32	爱知
大泉	4340	41462	18.03	群马
盘田	4100	170523	163.45	静冈

注：巴西人人口数截至 2016 年 3 月，总人口数来自 2017 年 10 月的数据。

3　创意城市政策与多元文化导向

滨松市是国家制造业的生产基地城市，主要产业包括交通、设备、发动机等，也生产乐器，移民的工作就与这些产业有关。这个城市同时也建立了一些鼓励产业发展的相关城市政策，也通过一些基本政策来打造创意城市。尽管创意城市政策的计划涉及方方面面，但其中最主要的还是通过组织包括国际音乐比赛在内的各种市民和国际层面的活动，致力于将城市打造为音乐之都。目前已经建立起乐器博物馆和音乐相关的文化设施。2014 年 12 月 1 日，滨松市成为联合国教科文组织创意城市网络的成员之一，这也是亚洲第一个以音乐为主题加入联合国教科文组织创意城市网络当中的城市。

来源：https://www.google.co.jp/search? q=%E3%83%A4%E3%83%9E%E3%83%8F%E3%80%80%E6%B5%9C%E6%9D%BE&source=lnms&tbm=isch&sa=X&ved=0ahUKEwjd7N7wiZHXAhUP57wKHaoHBBkQ_AUICygC&biw=1466&bih=929#imgrc=qkQmi_3b4kSSUM.

图 2　雅马哈的乐器展览

滨松市的很多产业不见得与创意城市定位直接相关，有很多其他的领域，有一些项目支持不会日语的移民，给他们机会深造学习。政府会提供外语服务，帮助外来移民：市政府办公室为不会讲日语的居民提供了关于基本日常生活的外语信息，包括葡萄牙和西班牙语，这样的话他们可以在自己居住的社区获得很好的服务和工作安排；一些医院雇佣葡萄牙语和西班牙语口译员，病人因此可以与医生进行无障碍的交流。2008 年 4 月，滨松外国居民委员会成立，其董事会成员就选自当地的外国居民。“这个委员会探讨城市关于外国居民的举措，并为‘如何改善社区中外国居民和日本居民之间的关系’提供一个讨论平台。董事会成员巩固讨论结果，并向市长提出建议”。

4 结语

总结而言，当日裔移民再次回到日本的时候，面临着种种语言障碍带来的困难。政府考虑到了这些问题，并与包括国际交流协会在内的相关组织进行合作，更好的应对日裔外来移民的生活困难问题，同时制定了相关政策，鼓励文化多元化的发展。

滨松市是介绍文化多元化导向政策的一个很好的例子。2010 年的时候，滨松市长正式建议在日本设立一个外国居民事务部[3]，这是一个需要中央政府和其他的组织共同推动的事情。2008 年雷曼兄弟破产之后，很多巴西移民又回到了巴西，但是从那之后，一些当地协会开始了更深层的合作。国际交流组织协会与日本的公共就业安全部进行合作，帮助失业的外国人找工作。滨松的城堡镇当中的这些民族社区进入了一个新的发展阶段，各种合作促进了外国移民在东道国社区中的定居。

演讲者简介

水上徹男(Mizukami Tetsuo)，日本立教大学社会学部教授。

参考文献

［1］ Hamamatsu Foreign Residents Council. Canal Hamamatsu. Hamamatsu city[EB/OL]. [2017-10-18]. https://www. city. hamamatsu. shizuoka. jp/hamaeng/topics/council. html.

［2］ Mizukami, Tetsuo. The Myth of Cultural Homogeneity and Living Together: Studies of Assimilation and Australian Multiculturalism[J]. Hyogokyoikudaigaku kenkyukiyo (Hyogo University of Teacher Education Journal), 2000, 20: 105-116.

［3］ Hori, Hisano. Tabunkakyosei nisisuru chiiki no torikumi Hamamatsu no jirei (Local activities for making for multicultural living together: A case of Hamamatsu) [M]// C. Mita. Gurobaruka nonakade ikirutowa nikkeiburajirujin no toransunashonaruna kurashi (Meaning of living in globalization: Japanese Brazilians' transnational lives). Sophia University Press, 2011: 87-137.

［4］ Green, Hardy. The Company Town: The Industrial Edens and Satanic Mills That Shaped the American Economy[M]. New York: Basic Books, 2010.

［5］ Hamamatsu-shi kikaku chosei-bu kikaku-ka (Hamamatsu City Planning and Coordination section Planning Division). 'Sozo toshi Hamamatsu' suishinnotameno kihonhoshin (Fundamental Policies for promoting 'Creative city Hamamatsu') [R/OL]. 2013.

[6] Hamamatsu shi. Hamamatsu city [EB/OL]. [2017-10-15]. https://www. city. hamamatsu. shizuoka. jp.

[7] Hamamatsu shi. Hamamatsu shi no jinko (Population in Hamamatsu) [EB/OL]. [2017-10-15]. http://www. city. hamamatsu. shizuoka. jp/index. html.

[8] SUZUKI. [EB/OL]. [2017-10-15]. http://www. suzuki. co. jp/release/d/d050323. html.

[9] Kanarinyokyoshitsu (Canarinho classrooms). Yamada zemi ISFJ ryugakuhanyo wiki [EB/OL]. [2017-10-18]. https://www31. atwiki. jp/reikozemi/pages/98. html.

[10] Matsuishi, Yasuhiko. Kigyojyokamachi eno siza (A Perspective on Company Towns) [J]. Iwatekenritsudaigaku Miyakotankidaigakubu kenkyukiyo (Journal of Iwate Prefectural University Miyako College), 2005, 16(1): 19-30.

[11] Mita, Chiyoko. Burajirujin no dhiasupora to nihon no birajirujin (Brazilian Diaspora and Brazilians in Japan) [M]// C. Mita. Gurobaruka nonakade ikirutowa nikkeiburajirujin no toransunashonaruna kurashi (Meaning of living in globalization: Japanese Brazilians' transnational lives). Sophia University Press, 2011: 3-28.

[12] Suzuki motor corporations. Gaikokujinjido no kyoiku ni engun (Support for forign children's education) [EB/OL]. [2017-10-18].

城乡接合部社区生态变迁与功能转变

王雪梅

摘　要　本文以城市社会生态学为理论基础，将城乡接合部转型社区看作是社会生态系统，探寻新社会生态的形成机制以及组织特点，即社区转变和功能变迁。首先，以北京市海淀区肖社区为个案，进行实地研究。研究发现，聚居区当地农民与流动人口共同形成租房市场、消费市场，进而建构起完整的社区经济系统，实现社区功能替代与生态变迁。从城市社会学的视角来看，流动人口聚居区是在侵入-接替的城市社会生态运动下、社区变迁的表现——社区内部的人口、空间、社会、经济等结构与功能已经发生变化，并形成新社会生态，侵入-竞争-替代的社区变迁模式可以修正为侵入-迎合-替代模式。进而，基于北京市流动人口聚居区百社区问卷调查，探究社区独特的人口结构、职住关系结构、经济结构，及其对流动人口居住与生活发挥的支持性功能。

关键词　城乡接合部；流动人口聚居区；社区变迁模式；新社会生态

Community Ecological Changes and Functional Changes in Urban and Rural Areas

Wang Xuemei

Abstract　In this paper, we regard transforming communities in urban fringe areas as social ecosystems and aim at exploring the formation mechanism and organizational characteristics of this new social ecology, or in other words, the community transformations and function changes, based on urban social ecology theories. First of all, we take Xiao community in Haidian District, Beijing City as a case to carry on field research. The research result shows that local farmers and floating population in the settlement area jointly formed the rental market and the consumer market, and then constructed a complete community economic system, and in this way, the function substitution and ecological change of the community are realized. From a perspective of urban sociology, floating population community is the result of community change under the invasion and succession urban social ecological movement — the structures and functions of population, space, society and economy in communities have changed and new social ecology have been formed, the invasion-competition-replacement model can be modified to the invasion-ingratiation-replacement model. And then, based on the questionnaire carried out in hundreds of floating population communities in Beijing, we explored the unique demographic structure, occupation - residence structure and economic structure of these communities, and the supporting function of these communities to the residence and life of floating population.

Keywords　urban and rural areas; floating population communities; community change model; new social ecology

1 引言

从20世纪90年代以来,流动人口聚集在大都市边缘(城乡接合部)城中村并形成聚居区的社会空间现象,持续地激发了人类学、社会学、人口学、地理学、规划学、管理学等多学科学者的研究兴趣。为什么聚居区的空间指向是大都市边缘区即城乡接合部?社区变迁、型构的机理是什么?是否可以用既有的理论加以解释?学者们尝试对这些问题做出回应。

关于聚居区的形成,大致有以下几种观点:城市化论[1-3]、类贫民窟论[4,5]以及生态过程论[6]——流动人口聚落在大城市的形成和发展经历了三个生态阶段:入侵、竞争、同化或隔离。

关于聚居区内部结构与功能,有的学者借助系统-功能分析法,区分了社区横向模式分析与纵向模式分析[7]。有的学者注重类型比较研究,比如根据社区内部结构的不同,区分缘聚型和混居型(或者同质型与异质型)社区;根据聚集地存在的行业依托情况将聚集地分为三种类型:完全依托型、半依托型和无依托型,完全依托型内部又细分为依托工地型和依托市场型两种。还有些学者聚焦社会互动关系,得出一系列结论:流动人口聚居社区的内聚性与聚合性特点、流动人口聚居区形成亚社会结构、社区产业导致同质性社区流动人口的分化和异质性;流动人口聚居区内本地人与外地人的隔离与分层[8]。学者们运用多学科理论知识,提出的有关流动人口聚居区形成的六种论断,大大丰富了我们对聚居区现象的发生学的理解,特别是生态过程论和城市空间分异论,颇具启发性。然而,对于聚居区形成以后,自身的发展、变动、变迁的规律,探讨不深、成果甚少,以致社区变迁对于我们来说,依然是一个"盲点"。对于聚居区内部的研究,学者们聚焦在两种互动及其结果方面,一是流动人口群体内部的互动,二是流动人口群体与本地人群体的互动,由于学者们不约而同地采用社区个案研究方法,又由于个案本身的独特性、差异性,以及个案所处时空背景的变化性和多样性,以致学者们的研究发现是千姿百态,而缺乏承续性和共识性。另外,社区互动关系的研究与社区结构功能的考察又是断裂的。以致我们难于形成有关聚居区这种特定类型社区的一般性的认识。

本文以人类生态学为理论基础,将城乡接合部转型社区看作是由流动人口在此聚居、为适应环境而建构的具有地域性和地方化的功能关系系统,即社区社会生态系统。以北京市海淀区肖社区为个案,实地研究社区转变和功能变迁,探寻新社会生态的形成机制以及组织特点。进而,基于北京市流动人口聚居百社区问卷调查,探究社区独特的人口结构、职住关系结构、经济结构,及其对流动人口居住与生活发挥的支持性功能。

2 城乡接合部社区转型——新社会生态的个案考察

在大都市快速城市化背景下,大量流动人口进入城市,逐渐聚集到城市内部特定的空间区域城乡接合部,形成流动人口聚居区。流动人口聚居区在北京已有近二十年的历史。2000年以来,首都处在空间快速扩张阶段,城乡接合部亦具有很强的时段性,形成的流动人口聚居区最近位于三环周边,最远位于六环周边,大部分处于绿化隔离带地区,呈现了与以往不同的特点:流动人口聚居引致城乡接合部地区原有社区发生结构与功能上的转变,即社区转型。

2.1 肖社区个案概况

北京市海淀区肖社区，位于马连洼街道最南端，南临五环路、小清河，西临中央党校家属区，北临中国农业大学。原有 10 个自然村，以圆明园西路这条线路为中间轴，在东西方向上分布，分别为河北新营、桥东、东正黄旗、西正黄旗、龙背村、上河沿、王庄、东村、羊场和穆家坟；原面积约 2.3 平方公里，社区内有户籍人口 4 000 多人，外来人口近 4 万。传统上，当地村民均以黄瓜、茄子、西红柿、玉米等蔬菜种植为主。1993 年，当地开始实行居民农转非，大量农民在失去土地的同时获得了城市户口和 1.5 万～3 万元不等的自谋职业费。2001 年，这里撤村并街，这部分非农业人口归入居委会管理。20 世纪 90 年代，肖社区(简称肖)就已经开始出现外来人口，但当时数量极少，散住在农民家里。自 1999 年开始，社区内的村庄陆续因被征做他用而面临拆迁。其中，农大路以西的自然村被北京大学征用，以东的自然村成了圆明园花园别墅开发商的代征地。2000 年以后，肖周围的一些流动人口集聚区陆续开始拆迁，其中，万家庄、六郎庄及南边的万柳地区整个地被拆迁，居住在这些地区的流动人口流向了北边的其他地区。肖就因其优越的交通位置和丰富的出租房屋存量而在短时间内吸收了大量流动人口涌入。同时，当地居民迫于生活的压力，也由原来的种菜变为后来的“种房”，逐渐成为远近闻名的流动人口聚居区。如今，仅有东村、王庄两个自然村暂未拆迁，两村内的户籍人口还有 2037 户，其中，人户分离达到 1 800 户，大多为居民租房在外周转三年时间等待回迁楼的建设；而外来人口仍有 1.2 万之多。

来源：马连洼街道绘制社区地图，2015 年

图 1　肖社区东村、王庄两自然村近景概貌

2.2 征地改变社区：城乡接合部的“衰落区”

肖社区的变化始于 20 世纪 80 年代末。1989—1994 年，中央党校征地，征用集体土地。实行“农转非”，所有的户籍农民转成居民户口。

所谓“农转非”是指，由农业人口转为非农业人口，或由农业户口转为非农业户口，并由国家按照市镇粮食定量供应办法供应口粮的一项重大的社会经济政策。自20世纪70年代开始，北京近郊就有征地和招工“农转非”，只是规模不大，涉及面小；20世纪80年代以来，随着北京城市建设速度加快，“农转非”规模不断扩大；自20世纪90年代开始，建设征地“农转非”逐渐成为主渠道，建设征地“农转非”以1993年市政府16号令为标志，分为前后两个阶段。16号令以前，建设征地实行“谁征地、谁安置”的原则，征地单位负责转非、转工以及超转人员，“农转非”人员基本都能得到妥善安置。16号令以后，虽然“谁征地、谁安置”的原则没有变，但允许征地单位委托乡镇政府安置，还允许符合转工条件的人员自愿选择自谋职业，并给予3万元的安置费。16号令的执行一方面减轻了建设征地单位的安置压力；另一方面则出现了许多意想不到的问题，这就是大批当年选择自谋职业的人员，失去了就业和社会保障。肖社区的征地、安置以及农转非，正是执行了16号令。每人给3万元的安置费，当时存款利率非常高，还有利息附加的钱给居民，当时大多数村民认为这3万元拿到手里，每月就能有几百元的利息钱，这是他们一笔相当不错的收入，所以90%的人选择了“自谋职业”的安置方式，也就是说，他们在失去农业生产资料、失去原本赖以为生的“菜农”职业身份的同时，“主动失业了”。

我家原来也是种植蔬菜，中央党校把我们的地给占了，1994年那会儿实行农转非，我爱人本身就是居民，我和我孩子都从农转为了居民，跟大队那边就完全脱离了关系。之后，那块地全部被占了，我们也不再种蔬菜。我们填那表就是自谋职业，我们就如同没有职业了。（当地农民访谈1）

我原来是河北人，搁这儿找的媳妇，户口就转来北京了，我今年50，来这儿也30年了。我爱人是农转非，之前是种菜地，征地占了以后，这不是都没活儿了嘛，就在家待着。我家里有一个男孩一个女孩，小的上学大的上班了。（当地农民访谈2）

我原来就在这儿，生到这儿的，也长在这儿，大约住了有三十一二年了，原来都有生产队都有房子都有地，它以前归我们。农转非前后，对我的影响肯定还是有的。在没转之前，我在村集体企业上班，每月工资应该300多元。可是，想到转了以后给3万元的安置费，光吃利息每个月也能得不少钱呢，还不受上班限制——天天早起上班晚上下班回来，挺好！（当地农民访谈3）

在此后的二十年里，肖社区又有多次征地，农大路以西的自然村被北京大学征用，以东的自然村是圆明园花园别墅开发商的代征地，通过陆续征地，集体用地逐渐减少直至完全被占用，仅保留宅基地。肖社区的土地利用方式发生了根本的变化，社区逐渐丧失了农业种植的关键功能。

随着社区居民职业身份转变和社区主导功能式微，社区组织及其功能也发生了更替，大约在20世纪90年代末，肖成立社区居委会。作为拥有城市户口的城市市民，他们与原来的生产大队脱离了关系，转而隶属于居委会管理。

然而，随着经济体制改革、物价上涨，“钱越来越毛了”（居委会主任访谈1），到2000年后，他们拿到的农转非的安置费自谋职业费所剩已寥寥无几。但是生活压力增大，像子女上学，老人看病，家庭生活等等都需要钱，大家陆续意识到了危机。但是“居委会呢，作用有限……”

影响大的那阵呢没人管，大队大队不管你，居委会它只能够管人，其他其他别的它不管。居委会想管，没有钱没有资金，大队有钱，不管这块。（当地农民访谈3）

肖社区在马连洼街道的行政管辖之下，地处海淀区城乡接合部。目前，海淀区城乡接合部集中分布在海淀乡、东升乡、四季青镇、西北旺镇以及与其紧邻的街道（青龙桥街道、香山街道、西三旗街道、马连洼街道、清河街道、学院路街道、上地街道、田村街道、八里庄街道），总面积为204.46平方千米，占海淀全区的47.4%。

城市扩张需要占用城乡接合部的土地，土地征用是城乡接合部转型的初始动力。在空间和土地使用转变的同时，也伴随着经济、社会、人口、制度等等的转型，而它们往往和空间的再生产交织在一起。肖社区是城市微观层面的一个社会生态系统。按照人类生态学理论，生态系统中，在人类聚居适应环境的过程中某些单位总会比其他单位执行了更为重要的功能。在每个有着多种功能的关系系统中，系统与其环境的联系主要是通过一个或相对较少几个功能来调节的。如果一个系统缺乏关键功能，系统就会变得脆弱和不稳定，在极端的情况下，系统不可能存在。在首都城市扩张、城乡接合部变动的背景下，随着征地-农转非的进程，肖社区逐渐衰落，甚至岌岌可危。

2.3　本地居民适应衰落的社区环境、翻建房屋出租“大窝风”

2000年，对于肖社区来说是另一个重要的变化时点。经过多次征地后，辖区仅剩东村、王庄两个自然村，面积2平方千米，户籍人口2220户、4221人，其中人户分离910人，也就是说实际居住在本地的人口约3000人。从2000年开始，大家陆续意识到自己的生活有了危机，而应对危机仅有的出路就是在自家的宅基地上打主意：

2000年前外地人还少，租房的人也特别少，那时我只有两间房出租，一开始房租也很便宜，两间房就200块钱，租不上什么价钱，也不知道怎么租，不过那时候钱还值钱呢，也算可以。

我们的宅基地是1981年批的，1999年我又翻建房屋的时候就是为了出租，就是在自家的宅基地上建房，在原来的平房上加两层。当时往外出租的时候就是在门口挂一牌，写着“房屋出租”，然后就会有人过来问，合适的就租，不合适的就走人。（当地农民访谈3）

肖租房市场形成有一个重要的机遇：2000年时海淀区城乡接合部的万家庄、六郎庄及南边的万柳地区整个地在拆迁，拆迁引发流动人口迁移潮，当时居住在这些地区的流动人口被轰向了北边的其他地区。当大量地流动人口向北寻找新的居住地时，肖因其优越的交通位置和成片的可出租平房吸引了他们：从区位图上可以看出，肖位于马连洼街道最南端，四面环路、交通便利：南邻五环路，距离中关村中心区20～30分钟车程；北有农大南路；随着2000年圆明园西路扩张、上河沿修建地铁总站，肖左近圆明园西路，可通西苑交通枢纽站和上河沿地铁站。这里公交线路密集，有15到20条线，且公交、地铁之间的换乘也较为方便，西部为京藏高速，交通位置可谓优越。

突然涌入的大量“客源”，刺激了肖居民翻建房屋出租的热情。

开始租的时候，他们都是自己找来的，也不用挂牌子宣传，在这儿一盖房就是出租，不用说做什么广告啊。不愁租，反正有前脚走的后脚就有住的，租房的人太多。（当地农民访谈2）

于是，在2000—2003年，本地居民人人参与、户户行动，刮起了一股热火朝天的翻建房屋的“大窝风”：

2003年我家又从原来的一排房翻盖成两排房，那时候全部都是租房的。我建房的那个资金，自个儿有一半，再跟亲戚借一半。

我是从2003年开始盖房的，那会儿我的房子都是土坯房，只有半层砖，翻盖的时候还捡半成砖用。那时候家家都在盖房子，可是有盖得好一点的，有盖得次一点的就得再翻盖。我就是在原有的基础上往上加层、没往前扩，我盖了30间房，出租的是24间。（当地农民访谈2）

2.4 外来人口理性选择、新型社区渐成

在经济学上，一般假定每一个做出选择的人都是理性人，他的选择是使他的利益最大化。学者的研究普遍认同这一点，认为外来人口考虑在京住所时，通常会围绕其就业状况，权衡租金、房源供应、交通条件、管理状况等因素，最终做出一个使其利益最大化的决定。我们在肖外来人口中所进行的问卷调查也支持这一观点。我们的问题是：“您选择在此居住的原因？”答案是可以多选的。按照选择人数的多少，统计出来的结果表明，排在前5位的影响居住选择的因素依次为：房租便宜、离工作单位（或经营场所）近、有亲戚朋友或熟人在附近居住、交通便利、便于孩子上学。

房租便宜是打工者对落脚之地的首选条件：

我们外地人到外面打工，经常顾不上自己，这里是脏，人一多它就脏。有利就有害，图这块房子便宜，有更好的，那得多少钱，是不是。在外面打工，不管怎样我都能承受，能租得起，那就能生存；如果受不了（环境），也是生存不下去。我在这边干活，能保证维持生活。（租房户访谈1）

相关研究也表明，亲缘和友缘影响外来人口的聚居——介绍工作和住房都要依靠由乡土、亲友关系结成的社会网络，特别有趣的是老房客往往成为求租房屋者的“预审员”——他们往往会向房东推荐自己的亲戚或朋友、老乡，也由于多了这层关系，房东-房客之间更容易沟通。

在我们的调查对象中，有相当比例的家庭或个人是在肖长期租住的。67.8%的人在此居住了三年（含三年）的，45%以上的人居住了五年，三分之一以上的人已在此居住了十年（32.4%），一成以上的人（13.4%）在此居住十年以上；住满十四年的长期住户的比例（4.7%）超过了居住不满一年的新住户的比例（3.8%）。牛瑞花是我们的访谈对象，她家已在肖居住了八年：

我们在这儿租房，就是离孩子上学近，再说在这儿住时间长了，人不都熟悉了嘛，也不愿意再换一个生的环境了。（租房户访谈2）

就这样，起初肖吸引了几个或者一批的外来人口来此地区居住，而后如同滚雪球一般，通过地缘、亲缘、友缘、业缘的引带作用越聚越多，仅仅几年时间，在此居住的外来人口已达3万多人，是本地居民的7倍多①。

① 据肖社区居委会2003年统计，社区本地户籍人口2234户、4198人，流动人口超过3万人，本地居民与外地人口的比例严重倒挂。

肖社区的实证个案研究表明，城市以“征地”手段向城乡接合部扩张，导致传统农业社区原有土地利用方式转变、农业种植的主导经济功能丧失，社区趋于衰落。在当地农民基于生存选择与外来流动人口基于剩余选择的共同行动之下，形成租房市场、消费市场，进而建构起完整的社区经济系统，实现社区功能替代与生态变迁。

社区变迁的实际过程不同于人类生态学的理论想象：外来流动人口是在社区虚位以待的背景下侵入的，社区关键功能与分化功能的更替，并不存在与原有功能的竞争与冲突，侵入-竞争-替代的社区变迁模式可以修正为侵入-迎合-替代模式。

3　城乡接合部社区现状调查：结构与功能

2016 年，北京市人口研究所组织了对城乡接合部 100 个流动人口聚居区(村)的问卷调查。调查结果：截至 2016 年 6 月 30 日，城乡接合部地区 100 个流动人口聚居区(村)实有人口 121.6 万人，其中户籍人口有 21.6 万人，占总人口的 17.8%；流动人口有 100 万人，占总人口的 82.2%。本次调查还根据北京城乡接合部地理空间区位和流动人口聚集特点，从 100 个社区村中选取了五个典型村进行深入调研，以期总结概括出流动人口聚居区主要结构特征和社区功能。

来源：《北京城乡接合部重点地区流动人口情况调查分析报告》，2016 年

图 2　典型五村(社区)分布

3.1　本地人-外地人数量倒挂的人口结构

从流动人口与本地户籍人口的相对数量看，大多数聚居村(社区)的人口倒挂现象严重。在 100 个村(社区)中，88 个村(社区)存在本地户籍人口与流动人口数量倒挂现象，其中人口倒挂比例最高的村庄是昌平区北七家镇东三旗村，户籍人口 2190 人，流动人口 58000 人，流

动人口是户籍人口的26.48倍。人口倒挂2倍以上的村(社区)75个,人口倒挂5倍以上的村(社区)35个,人口倒挂10倍以上的村(社区)12个。

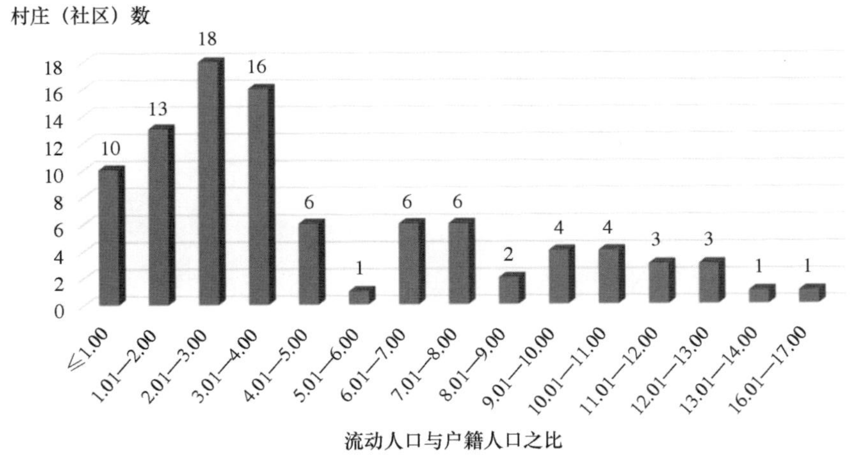

来源:《北京城乡接合部重点地区流动人口情况调查分析报告》,2016年

图3　2016年100个聚居村(社区)流动人口与户籍人口之比

3.2　四种类型的职住关系结构

从职住关系看,聚居村(社区)流动人口的就业形态以职住分离为主。在100个聚居村83.7万就业流动人口中,17.0%的人在本村(社区)内就业,19.7%的人在本乡(镇、街道)内就业,63.4%的流动人口在本乡(镇、街道)外就业。

根据各村(社区)流动人口的职住关系比例,我们可以将100个聚居村(社区)区分为四大类型:职住一体型(流动人口本村或社区内就业比例超过50%)、周边就业型(流动人口在本乡镇街道内就业比例超过50%)、职住分离型(流动人口在本乡镇街道外就业比例超过50%)、混合型(上述三类比例均不超过50%)。

分析结果显示,在100个聚居村(社区)中,流动人口职住一体型的村(社区)共16个,周边就业型的村(社区)11个,职住分离型的村(社区)最多,共56个,混合型的村(社区)17个。

3.3　社区经济"瓦片依赖型"结构

3.3.1　集体经济高度依赖土地出租和房屋出租

大多数聚居村的集体经济收入主要来源于土地出租和房屋出租。在100个聚居村(社区)中,回答有集体经济的村(社区)共54个。

在这54个村集体经济的收入来源中,土地出租和房屋出租收入占总收入的平均比例为77.8%,其中土地出租占总收入的平均比例为57.4%,房屋出租占总收入的平均比例为20.4%。其中,土地和房屋出租收入占村集体总收入的占比超过50%的村集体有45个,占比超过90%的村集体有32个。

3.3.2　私房出租是本地村民和居民支柱性收入来源

私房出租是大多数聚居村(社区)本地村民和居民的重要收入来源。调查数据显示,房

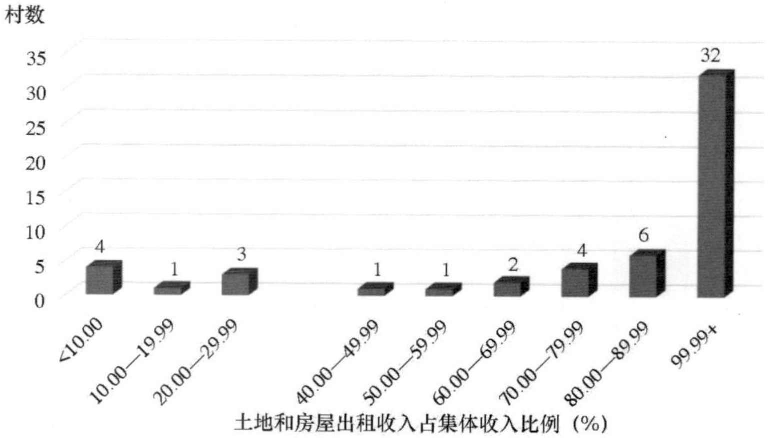

来源:《北京城乡接合部重点地区流动人口情况调查分析报告》,2016 年

图 4　土地和房屋出租占集体收入比例构成情况

屋出租收入占村民收入比例超过 60%的村(社区)有 53 个,其中,比例超过 80%以上的村(社区)53 个;房屋出租收入占居民收入比例超过 60%的村(社区)21 个,比例超过 80%的村(社区)9 个。

对五个聚居村的典型调查,也支持了这个发现,对丰台区黄土岗村、海淀区福缘门社区、昌平区兰各庄村、朝阳区东辛店村以及通州区小周易村的 5 位房东进行了访谈,房屋出租费用占据他们家庭总收入的比例分别为 60%、85%、80%、75%以及 80%。

对集体土地出租和瓦片经济的高度依赖,是村集体和农民为追求经济利益最大化而做出的一种理性选择。“瓦片经济”实质上是农民维持生计的一种经济方式。在城乡接合部,本地农民最大的问题就是失去土地后的出路问题。由于村集体土地多数被征用,对农民再就业、居住和集体资产的分配等方面产生很大影响。由于农民就业条件有限,进城打工收益小,多数从事回报丰厚的房屋出租产业。部分村以村民委员会或村民小组的名义将农村集体土地使用权出租给第三方,用于建设厂房、经营用房或出租房,所得收入用于维持村里的基本公共服务开支。

3.3.3　瓦片经济衍生社区内经营商户数量庞大

调查数据显示,100 个聚居村(社区)中,共有不同类型的商户 4.06 万户,其中门店经营 2.22 万户,市场固定摊位经营 1.22 万户,其他场所经营 0.62 万户。

从各村(社区)的分布情况看,商户数 100 个以下的村(社区)34 个, 100～199 个商户的村(社区)21 个,200 个商户的村(社区)45 个,其中 500 个商户以上的村(社区)19 个。

城乡接合部租赁经济非常发达,吸引着无数的流动人口进入。这种租赁经济使房主成为本地人的职业身份,房租成为他们的主要收入来源,使房客成为外地人的消费身份,住房成为他们的最大消费内容,本地人与外地人之间因而变得休戚相关,成为利益共同体。

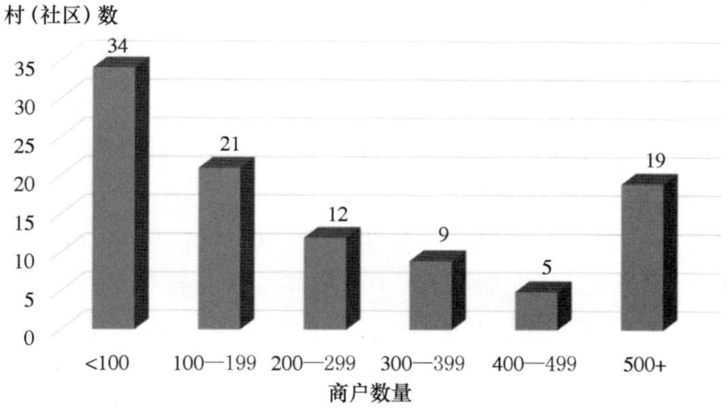

来源:《北京城乡接合部重点地区流动人口情况调查分析报告》,2016 年

图 5　聚居村(社区)域内的商户总数量

3.4　社区支持性功能——流动人口居住与生活[①]

3.4.1　流动人口居村(社区)时间普遍较长

八成以上流动人口在所在村(社区)居住时间在半年以上。从居住时间看,聚居村(社区)流动人口在所在村(社区)的居住时间普遍较长。居住半年以上的占 83.4%,居住三年及以上的占 38.1%。

3.4.2　大多数流动人口与家庭成员共同居住

在家庭结构分布上,夫妻家庭、带子女家庭和联合家庭占比分别为 30.12%、7.61%、24.45%,三项合计是 62.18%,表明大多数流动人口与家庭成员共同居住。

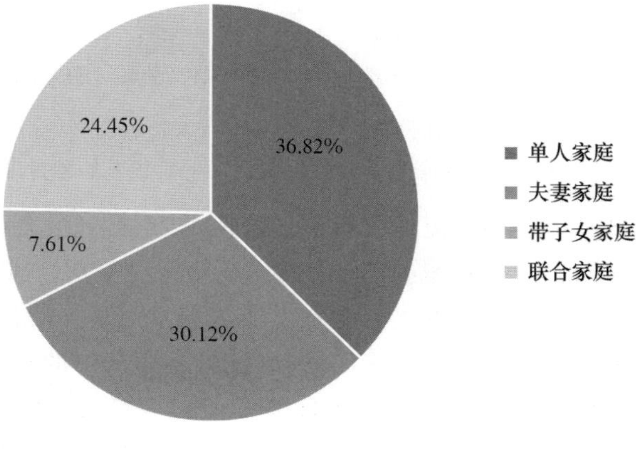

来源:《北京城乡结合部重点地区流动人口情况调查分析报告》,2016 年

图 6　典型村流动人口家庭类型

3.4.3　流动人口以租住平房为主

从住房来源来看,租房占九成,是流动人口最主要的住房来源。另外,单位提供免费住房和住在工作场所分别占 3.72%和 3.24%。从住房类型来看,大多数流动人口居住在平房(院)中,比例高达 62.74%。其次,住在公寓楼的比例也较高,约占 28%。由调查数据计算

① 本节数据来源:《北京城乡结合部重点地区流动人口情况调查分析报告》,2016 年.

出流动人口的平均住房面积约为11.73平方米。

3.4.4 生活“低消费、高积累”特征明显

流动人口家庭月平均收入6330.94元，月平均支出为2960.64元，家庭月平均收入与支出的差，即家庭月净结余约为3373元，呈现出“低消费与高积累”的特点。

3.4.5 多数流动人口有长期居住倾向

近六成流动人口打算在本村(社区)长期居住。在村(社区)居留意愿方面，有57.57%的流动人口打算在本村(社区)长期居住，其中65.47%的人打算居住1年以上；有13.26%的人不打算在本村(社区)长期居留，其中35.42%的人打算直接离开北京，13.28%的人打算去北京市内其他地方，32.47%的人表示没有想好、犹豫不决或处于观望状态。

3.4.6 流动人口对于其在北京的生活普遍比较满意。

调查数据显示，对于在北京的生活，27.53%的流动人口感到很满意，33.9%的流动人口比较满意，31.77%的流动人口感觉一般，而仅有4.63%和2.17%的流动人口感到不太满意或者很不满意。

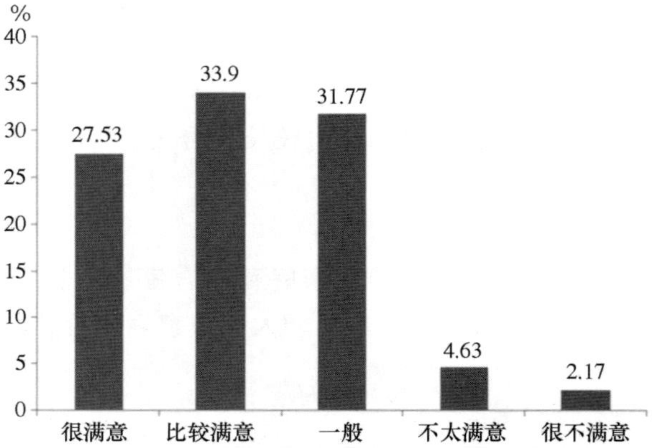

来源:《北京城乡结合部重点地区流动人口情况调查分析报告》,2016年

图7 典型村流动人口对于在北京生活状况的满意度

可见，城乡接合部社区转型为流动人口聚居社区，转型社区的功能之一是为流动人口提供缓冲性生存空间。流动人口对聚居区的依赖程度不同。聚居区或者为他们提供了住房，或者提供了自雇劳动的机会，或者提供了基本生活与关系网络。对他们而言，聚居区不仅是一堆住宅而已，其中的居民形成繁复紧密的联系，并且利用其中的空间做生意并经营非正式企业，借此在社会上得以向上流动。城乡接合部流动人口聚居区的主要功能是作为他们迁徙过程的落脚，是外来人口融入城市的跳板。在相当长时期内城乡接合部仍将且必须承担为流动人口提供重要的生存空间和融入城市的跳板的功能。

项目资助

北京市哲学社会科学规划2017年基金项目(项目编号17JDSRB002)。

作者简介

王雪梅，中共北京市委党校、北京人口与社会发展研究中心 博士、副教授、硕士生导师。

致谢

北京市综治委沈光雄先生、北京市人口研究所洪小良教授。

参考文献

[1] 顾朝林，陈田，丁金宏，等.中国大城市边缘区特性研究[J].地理学报，1993(04)：317-328.
[2] 千庆兰，陈颖彪.我国大城市流动人口聚居区初步研究——以北京浙江村和广州石牌地区为例[J].城市规划，2003(11)：60-64.
[3] 宋迎昌，武伟.北京市外来人口空间集聚特点、形成机制及其调控对策[J].经济地理，1997(04)：71-75.
[4] 蓝宇蕴.城中村流动人口聚居区的功能分析——基于城中村空间改造的思考[J].中共福建省委党校学报，2008(12)：30-35.
[5] 袁媛，许学强，薛德升.广州市1990—2000年外来人口空间分布、演变和影响因素[J].经济地理，2007(02)：250-255.
[6] 刘海泳，顾朝林.北京流动人口聚落的形态、结构与功能[J].地理科学，1999(06)：497-503.
[7] 吴晓.城市中的农村社区——流动人口聚居区的现状与整合研究[J].城市规划，2001(12)：25-29.
[8] 张展新.城中村、外来人口与城市发展——关于北京城中村改造的思考[J].北京规划建设，2005(03)：8-10.

多元中的共生:近代上海穆斯林群体的发展与融入

洪 伟

摘 要 自上海开埠后,江南、华中、华北等地回族移居上海,在经济、文教、教务、慈善与宗教对话等方面取得了一定成就。这得益于上海开放包容的社会环境和回族群体主动融入城市的意愿与实践。中华人民共和国成立后,这些移民的后代,逐渐被同化,回族-伊斯兰教文化式微。近代旅沪回族先辈扎根申城,发展自我的历史经验,对今日穆斯林群体在保存自我、传统继承、社会融入等方面,有深刻的借鉴意义。

关键词 近代上海回族穆斯林;城市融入;流动穆斯林

Symbiosis in Multiculture: The Development and Urban Integration of Muslims in Modern Shanghai

Hong Wei

Abstract Since Shanghai open its port, the Hui groups from the southern Yangtze River area, central and North China moved to Shanghai, and made some achievements in their economy, culture and education, religious affairs, charity and inter-religious communication, which benefited from the open and tolerant social environment of Shanghai, and actively positive intention and practice of Hui community to Shanghai involvement. After the founding of the People's Republic of China, the descendants of these immigrants gradually assimilated and the Hui Muslim culture declined. The historical self-development experiences of modern Hui predecessors in Shanghai shows a great significance to the contemporary Muslim communities in the perspectives of self-preservation, tradition inheritance and social integration.

Keywords Modern Shanghai; the Hui Muslim; urban integration; floating Muslim

1 近代上海穆斯林来源概述

北宋时期,上海地区已有穆斯林商人开展贸易活动。但伊斯兰教真正的传入、扎根,是元代西域与中亚地区的穆斯林随蒙古铁骑在华亭一带定居,并在元至正年间建造上海地区第一座清真寺,即云间白鹤寺(真教寺)。1840 年前,尽管上海还先后出现了几座清真寺,但整体上,伊斯兰教发展缓慢,回族(穆斯林)群体始终维持在数百人的规模,影响甚小。

上海开埠后,大量外来人口涌入,上海人口增长迅速。近代第一次回族大量迁入是因为自然灾害与社会局势的动荡。1849 年江南水灾,南京难民涌入上海,暂居南市草鞋湾一带,因此,此地又称"南京街"。这其中就有不少回民。1852 年,为了宗教生活的需要,逐步稳定下来的南京籍回民，赁地搭建棚屋三间，供礼拜、沐浴与教长起居。1853 年太平天国定都南京，南京、镇江、扬州一带回族再次成规模地进入上海。

宣统年间，上海清真董事会编《清真董事会志》记，穿心街清真寺“平日礼晚拜者约百余人。主目日三四百人不等。斋月每日约五六百人。圣忌开斋节大典约千余人”。穿心街清真寺即现在的福佑路清真寺。同治二年，南京籍回族逐渐在老北门一代聚居，并租借两间平房作临时礼拜场所。福佑路毗邻城隍庙，是老上海著名的商界区。稍有资本的古玩珠玉商人和清真餐饮从业者，都选择在此创业经营，经济活动促使此地回民人口增加，逐渐取代草鞋湾成为上海回民聚居区。加上当时上海还有另外 3 座清真寺，可预计当时上海回族大约有 3000～4000 人。

1911 年始，上海沪西苏州河沿岸，多家日资纺织厂投产。在回族富商的介绍联系下，先后有 400 余来自湖北、山东、安徽、河南等地的回族进厂务工。加之 30 年代，黄淮流域水灾，一批河南、山东、安徽回族逃荒而来，集中在沪西药水弄一带。至此，此地成为上海另一个重要的回族聚居区域。而位于美英公共租界边缘的今虹口区景星路一带，主要聚居了清末民国初数次苏北洪水而来此的苏北籍回族。

1927 年，上海特别市政府秘书处统计《上海特别市户口分类统计简表》，上海共有伊斯兰教徒 4938 人[1]44。数据仅统计了华界，未涵盖租界内的人口，加之当时的统计方法局限，实际回族人口肯定多于这个数字。

1953 年，上海市人民政府统计上海少数民族人口，上海共有回民 28166 人[2]。1959 年，上海再次进行人口普查，全市回民人口 33238 人。尽管回族人口在上海总人口中只是很小的一部分，但延续百年，回族人口增长了近百倍，也是上海人口最多少数民族。至今日，回族-伊斯兰教文化仍然在国际化大都市的上海延续，它的百年发展脉络，是本文要关注的。

2 近代上海伊斯兰教的发展

2.1 宗教场所的修建与宗教活动的兴盛

上海开埠前，松江、青浦、七宝等地区都曾修建过清真寺，但由于穆斯林人口较少，宗教活动规模有限。1840 年后，各地穆斯林涌入，上海迎来了清真寺修建的黄金时期，宗教活动日益活跃兴盛。至 1950 年的百年间，先后修建清真寺 20 余座。相当部分清真寺还经历多次重修扩大。

清末至辛亥革命前后，主要出资修建清真寺并维持日常运作的是南京籍回族。他们是近代早期回族移民的主体，不乏古玩珠宝业、餐饮业等行当的大商人，财力相对丰裕。1920 年后，逐渐站稳脚跟的湖北、山东、河南、苏北籍回族，先租房设立简易礼拜场所开展宗教活动，后在包括南京籍回族等的辅助下，创建清真寺。另外，约建于 1870 年的浙江路清真寺，是由印度穆斯林购置的坟地发展而来，首任教长为印度人，宗教活动者中也有不少外籍穆斯林，遂俗称外国寺。清真寺的修建，反映了当时回族人口的迅速增加和宗教活动的需求，也反映了当时回族经济、文化的情况。

2.2 城市商业的融入与回族经济的发展

近代上海回族发挥善经商的传统，发展传统行当的同时，迅速融入上海特殊的商业环境，使得民族经济得到一定发展。回族素有“识宝回回”的称呼，从一开始的摆地摊、做掮客，到占据上海古玩市场的半壁江山，哈少夫、马晋卿、马鹤卿等回商成为行业里的头面人物。清真餐饮业是回族传统行当，江南回族主营鸡鸭、茶食，河南回族主营牛羊肉餐馆，京津回族主营涮锅、京式糕点，加之清真酱菜、西餐厅，鼎盛时期的上海有清真餐饮店铺300家余，不仅满足了回族群众的饮食需求，洪长兴、青梅居、杨同兴等“教门馆”，也是当时上海著名的餐馆。除此之外，有一定规模的，还有皮毛业、毛纺业、西药业、进出口业、五金业、百货业、印刷业等。可以说，既有民族传统、家族传承，又有白手起家、创业经商，但凡与回族习俗不相违背的产业，都有回族经营者。

上海回族经济一大特点是“同乡同业”，即来源同一地区的回族基本从事同一行业。例如南京籍回族主要从事古玩珠玉业、鸡鸭业、西药业，镇江籍回族主要从事五金业，安徽和县籍回族主要从事印刷业，湖北籍回族主要从事棉花业。这样既能较好的保留原有的商业传统，又可在商会、行会中互保互助[3]162。

2.3 社团组织的发展与回族内部的团结

近代社会改良思潮涌动，创团体、设学校、办报刊等热潮逐渐散播。思想与社会发展最前沿的上海，其回族社团组织方面，在全国回族中起了示范作用。上海回族社团之始是成立于1905年的“务本堂”，其主要任务是开展清真寺管理、从事慈善活动、参与婚丧嫁娶事务等。① 而最有影响力的是1909年成立的清真董事会和1925年成立的中国伊斯兰教学会。清真董事会的成立，正是为应对伊斯兰教发展带来的各种新问题，“教中集会、兴学、培茔，整规，暨一切兴利除弊诸要务”。董事会突破原有伊斯兰教组织的组成形式，以董事制代替同乡会，当时上海各籍贯伊斯兰教大老悉数加入，开中国伊斯兰教组织之先河。之后因时局变化，领导者辞世等原因，清真董事会经历了数次更名、改组，但其在兴建、管理上海清真寺与公共墓地，兴办回民文教事业，发展慈善公益事业，对外交流与维权等方面起到了至关重要的作用。

1925年，哈德成大阿訇联合达浦生、马坚、伍特公、沙善余等阿訇、学者，发起成立中国伊斯兰教学会，组织翻译《古兰经》、编辑学术刊物、创办学校，享有极高的声誉，成为“近代中国伊斯兰教徒第一次自觉发动的文化运动”（顾颉刚语）中最有影响力的学术组织之一。

新中国成立前的百年，上海先后涌现了大大小小的回族社团数十个，其中有文化社团、慈善社团、经济社团，亦有中国第一个穆斯林妇女社团-上海伊斯兰妇女协会、第一个穆斯林宣教组织-中国伊斯兰教宣传所。这些社团的出现，体现了当时回族社团在发展到一定水平和规模后，逐渐实现规范化，进一步加强了回族群体的凝聚力。

2.4 文教事业的发展与文化传统的延续

文教事业的发展是民国时期上海伊斯兰教发展最为显要的特点之一。上海是近代中国

① “务本堂成立于1905年”的说法被绝大部分有关上海伊斯兰教史的研究所接收。但笔者在1879年11月19日出版的《申报》刊载的《建寺谕禁滋扰示》一文发现，“同治年间在老北门内穿心街地方公同捐资置买房屋建为清真寺供奉龙牌併设立务本堂清真义学”。可见，“务本堂”恐早于1905年所创建。但两个“务本堂”是否为同一组织，是否都具有社团组织的性质（可能是家族堂号），还需要研究。遂本文仍沿用“务本堂成立于1905年”。

伊斯兰教文教事业重镇之一。

在延续传统清真寺经堂教育的同时,倡导中、阿并授,经、汉兼重的新型伊斯兰教育的出现,培养了一批具有影响力的回族人才。创办于1928年的上海伊斯兰师范学校是民国时期最有影响力的回族学校之一。从这里走出的马坚等,成为中国高等阿拉伯语教育和伊斯兰教研究的先驱。

《上海清真董事会志》中记载学董马树周论:“德法之战,俾士麦宰相归功于小学。诚以小学即为强国之根。小学若办得好,则忠臣孝子胥出其中。小学若办不好,亦乱臣贼子出其中也”。上海伊斯兰教上层人士将基础教育提升到民族兴盛、国家兴旺的高度,教育改革也着重在从基础教育开始。自1909年马乙棠、哈少夫、金星伯等回族富商以“注重国民教育,兼重天方经文教育”为宗旨,创办的“上海清真两等小学堂”始,上海回族相继兴办回民中小学十余所。国民教育的兴起,提高了普通回民群众的文化水平,促进了他们融入上海社会,寻求新的发展空间。

中国回教经书局、上海穆民经书社、上海协兴公司售经处、上海伊斯兰文化供应社等多家出版机构,大量印刷、进口宗教书籍,所印出版物行销全国。上海回族知识界、社会活动界所创办的《中国回教月刊》《回教青年》《人道》《绿旗》《伊斯兰学生》等十余种报刊,在阐述教义、提倡教育、普及文化方面发挥了作用。特别是在国难之时,这些刊物由单纯的宗教宣传向鼓舞伊斯兰教同胞救国抗战转变,表现出了极高的爱国热情。

翻译、出版《古兰经》是民国伊斯兰教文化事业的一件大事。马复初阿訇汉译《古兰经》5卷本,哈同主持汉译《古兰经》、伍特公《汉译〈古兰经〉第一章详解》、王静斋《古兰经译解》等先后在上海印刷出版。现行最为通用的汉译《古兰经》版本——马坚译本,也是上海伊斯兰师范学校毕业生马坚(后为北京大学教授)主要在上海完成的。

2.5 社会活动的活跃与慈善事业的影响

正是因为近代上海是移民构建的“新世界”,为回族群体与外界社会、其他民族与宗教信仰者的接触创造了更频繁、深入的机会。近代上海回族的社会活动颇为活跃,文化界、出版界、文艺界、书画界、武术界、慈善界等方面都有回族参与。

最有影响力的是上海回族慈善活动。上海伊斯兰教界知名人士哈少夫先后参与战区难民救济会执行委员等多个慈善救济组织,组织难民救济,筹募救济经费,在上海慈善界颇有威望。另一位回族商人杨叔平多次参与发起组织难民救济处,并个人出资设立“回教灾民救济处”,救援回族难民,开展民族自救。回族大富商蒋星阶则动员子媳、女儿赶制丝棉背心及慰问品送抗日战士,其妻杨氏更是变卖金饰以助军用。敦化小学、云生小学、崇本小学、伊光第一小学等多座回民学校,招收汉族学生,并给予经济资助。这些善举不仅赢得教内的赞誉,也赢得教外社会的好评,从而提高了伊斯兰教界的社会声誉。

2.6 宗教对话的兴起与宣教活动的开展

浙江路清真寺教长的哈德成阿訇知晓“中华基督教青年会全国协会干事、新闻记者、美人胡籁明”在中国“考察伊斯兰教状态”之行,最终目的是宣教,特别是对伊斯兰教开展宣教,但他仍然亲笔撰写介绍信,希望各地清真寺“教长、乡老予以招待、指示为荷”。哈德成阿訇是民国四大阿訇之一,在国外求学工作多年,精通阿拉伯语、波斯语、乌尔都语、英语。见多识广的哈德成阿訇之所以愿意帮助传教士，除了其宽广的胸怀，开放的思想，也在于他深厚的学识与自信。1940 年 7 月，受冯炳南先生之邀请，哈德成阿訇赴上海基督教青年会，参加五教演讲活动之第四讲，做了题为“伊斯兰教之要旨与道德”的演讲，并受邀审定活动组织者刊印的《回教入门》一书并作序。不仅仅有哈德成这样的专业宗教人士，熟谙宗教、热心社会活动的上海回教界上层，也对开展宗教对话颇为积极。回教大老哈少夫应邀作为回教代表参加美国基督教传教士李佳白发起的尚贤堂。《上海清真寺成立董事会志》收录了哈少夫在尚贤堂发布的《应尚贤堂民教相安论》。哈少夫还担任尚贤堂主席一职，邀请各大宗教领袖、学者开讲，促进宗教对话。[4] 作为大商人、慈善家、金石鉴赏家的哈少夫，“积极主张各宗教间的相互尊重和理解，争取做到和平相处和友善为邻，这的确表现了上海伊斯兰教界人士崇高的思想境界和世界观”[5]69 。

1933 年成立的中国回教宣传所和 1939 年成立的中国回教宣教所是近代回族组织中极少有的两个宣教组织。一些阿訇、学者，还利用广播、传统、宣教会等方式开展宣传活动。打破宗教传承一般仅限于民族、家庭内部的中国伊斯兰教传统，主动对外宣教，显然这也是受到上海开放积极的宗教氛围的影响。宗教对话与宣教活动的最终目的，纵然有发展教徒之意图，但从实际效果上看，是通过主动的对话与交流，消除外界社会对穆斯林群体的误解，加强不同族群的认识与理解，提高社会影响，扩展生存空间。

3 旅沪回族城市融入的成因分析

近代上海是典型的移民城市，回族群体只是移民大军的少数。这一群体能在政治、社会、经济、文化等都明显区别于原籍的上海，不仅站稳脚跟，而且在宗教、经济、文化等事业上取得一定的发展成就，取决于其独特的主客观条件。

得益于上海相对稳定的政治环境、枕江滨海的地理位置和商业发达的经济基础，近代上海吸引了国内外大量人口的流入。人口的流动，也是文化的流动。华洋混杂的上海文化，因其人口构成的复杂，而具有“极大的融摄性”，高度开放与包容的社会环境，进一步增强了对移民的吸引力，并为各种文化的发展提供了较为平等、自由的空间。

“同乡共教敬恭，笃桑梓之情，异地一心合力，收大同之效。”回族移民的不断融入，回族群体的不断发展，也得益于近代上海回族社会开放、包容的环境与氛围。伊斯兰教文化虽然落户上海历史悠远，但人口数量及影响力始终有限。近代上海国内外文化多元共存，既带来了生存发展的机遇，也有诸多挑战。从外界来看，辱教事件时有发生，文化隔阂难以消除，而假冒清真、强迁墓地等侵犯回族利益事件亦有发生。从内部看，繁华大都市中，回族群体的信仰危机，文化危机，引发内部深度忧虑。所以，上海伊斯兰教界展现了独有的团结奋进气质，虽处世俗尘世，宗教意识不减，民族感情高涨。最显著特点之一，是宗教内部各教派的和谐及与其他宗教的和平共处。处于上海伊斯兰教领导地位的南京籍回族遵格底目(老教)教统为主，而苏北地区回族主要遵哲合忍耶教派。20 世纪 20 年代开始，旅沪河南回族给上海伊斯兰教最大的影响，莫过于河南阿訇为首的中原阿訇给上海伊斯兰教带来了伊赫瓦尼(新教)。被誉为“河南伊赫瓦尼五大阿訇”中，马儆吾、刘志三曾在上海开学，注入宗教发展的新潮流。与西北等穆斯林聚居区教派冲突频发不同，上海伊斯兰教界各教派之间的关系是团结、和谐的，基本没有大的教派纷争，更未发生教派冲突。各教派阿訇、教民之间来往频繁，经济、文化、教务、日常生活互动、合作颇多。寺内执事，遵一派而不言其他，寺外传承，怀大同而博采众长。例如，遵新教的买俊三阿訇的中国回教经书局自创世之初，所印制、发行的书籍，就突破传统与教派藩篱，除经销埃及哈勒比书局原版《古兰经》、圣训经及各类阿拉伯文书籍外，还重印明清回儒大家王岱舆、张中、伍遵契、马注、刘智、马德新、马联元以及现代学者杨仲明、王静斋、马坚、金吉堂等重要著译。上海伊斯兰师范学校成立，校长达浦生阿訇，邀请各派阿訇、学者任教、讲学，买俊三阿訇也应邀，教授认主学、修辞学和音韵学，贡献颇多。

近代上海伊斯兰教界社会结构，以“教”“乡”“行”为序。即首先以宗教为纽带，团结各地回族穆斯林大众，再以同乡为基础，加强内部关系，最后以行业为补充，加深经济联系。近代上海畸形膨胀的消费经济，为回族群体提供了生存发展的经济条件。如前所述，近代上海伊斯兰教发展中兴力量是南京籍回族。南京本是江南伊斯兰教重镇，因地理优势进入上海较早，人口较多，且多有富商家族。使得从事古玩珠玉等消费行业的南京籍回族富商不断积累财富，加之重文尚教传统，热心社会事务，不少人逐渐步入上海上流社会。其他地区较早进入上海，从事餐饮、棉花、西药等行业的回族也具有较为殷实的经济条件。他们中不乏热心教门事业、积极投身慈善者，对于上海回族社会事务投入巨大。普通回民在此扎根、生存，首先得到了他们的巨大帮助和支持，包括资助清真寺、学校、墓地等的建设、维持经费，介绍、提供就业岗位等。这对他们从融入上海回族社区这一小环境开始，进而最终融入上海大都市的大环境，提供了过渡桥梁和后盾保障。

主观上，回族展现了较强的社会适应性与主动融入社会的主观意愿。近代旅沪回族，大部分是被动迁徙的“生存型”移民。站稳脚、求温饱、图生存一直是回族群体在上海的主要诉求。“顺主、顺圣、顺社会”的传统得以充分发扬，促使回族群体能较为顺利、迅速地融入社会。

以文教事业为例，近代上海回民教育文教活动，是一种文化自觉，也是一种主动融入。回族学校课程设置中突破传统民族教育的藩篱，在保留教义、阿文等民族宗教类课程的是同时，与社会国民教育逐步接轨，并接收各方捐赠，聘请汉族老师，招收汉族学生，加强了与外界社会的接触与认识。中国回教学会宣称，“本会之唯一希望，在联合吾教优秀人才……祛除闭固拒之习，收集思广益之功”，中国回教经书局以“宣扬发展圣教，沟通回汉文化”为宗旨，这些都可见，当时的回族社会有强烈的革新意识及与外界社会沟通的意愿。

葛壮先生认为，近代上海伊斯兰教振兴的重要因素之一，是穆斯林社会中涌现出三种人构成的中坚力量，即具有丰富宗教常识、良好口碑的宗教教职人士，具有重要号召力、热心教门事务的上层人士和有深厚学识、热衷回族文化事业的学者群体。这三类人的号召力、示范性颇大，不仅仅对于上海伊斯兰教，乃至全国伊斯兰教都有一定影响力。他们之间较强的凝聚力和长期合作共事的经历，以及在上海政治、经济、文化、宗教等领域主流社会发展的经验，使得多元组成的上海穆斯林群体能够保持团结、稳定的发展态势，始终在社会融合、坚持传承的大浪淘沙中不迷失前进方向。20 世纪 30 年代中期始，哈少夫、金子云、蒋星阶、马刚侯等伊斯兰教大老相继归真，达浦生、哈德成等离开上海避难，伍特公等不愿与敌伪为伍而隐身。一时间，上海伊斯兰教界群龙无首，回族各项事务活动皆遭受打击。

当然，这种融入过程，并非毫无隔阂，观念、传统的碰撞，难以彻底消除。例如，20 世纪 30 年代，上海伊斯兰教大坊小桃园清真寺聘请了一位河南阿訇。初到繁华大都市的阿訇，对一些上海穆斯林妇女不穿长袖衣服、不戴盖头的装束颇为不满，甚至认为在上海开学已久的哈德成、达浦生阿訇对此情况负有责任[6]30。同时，民国时期多次发生的辱教事件，仍然说明当时的上海社会对于穆斯林群体的认知仍有不足。

4 当代上海回族-伊斯兰教文化的式微

1937年抗战爆发，上海回族政治、经济、文教事业受到冲击，社团组织相继关闭，教育机构停止办学，一批伊斯兰教大老或离世，或离开上海避难。抗战后期，逐渐恢复元气。新中国成立后，作为上海人数最多的少数民族，回族的生活发生了巨大变化。

4.1 回族聚居区的解体与宗教活动的式微

由于城市化进程、旧城拆迁改造等诸多因素的影响，中国城市的居住格局已发生巨大变化。东部城市中原本“围寺而居”的传统教坊式回族社区几乎都已消失。今天的上海，各清真寺周围已无成规模的回族聚居区，原本在空间上与精神上作为回族生活中心的清真寺被边缘化，同乡、同教、同业之间的纽带联系也随之断裂。

1949年至1959年，上海关闭清真寺3座，1958年宗教改革期间，关闭清真寺8座，1966年“文化大革命”开始，关闭其他的10座清真寺，仅保留小桃园清真寺，供在沪的领事馆外籍人士使用。回族的饮食、婚嫁（族内通婚）、丧葬（土葬）等具有鲜明宗教特色的传统习俗，被视为守旧落后、封建迷信，普通穆斯林的宗教生活与宗教习俗，无法延续。直到1979年，逐步开放沪西清真寺、小桃园清真寺等（大部分再未恢复），宗教活动逐渐恢复。但一代人甚至两代人的宗教习俗传统已经断代，民族传统的传承已经举步维艰。今天来上海清真寺参加宗教活动的穆斯林中，近代回族移民的后裔屈指可数，除丧葬习俗外，坚持其他习俗传统者寥寥无几。

4.2 文教机构关闭转型与文化传统的艰难

1937年，伊斯兰文化供应社的业务因抗战而停止，但上海穆民经书社、中国回教书局等出版机构直到建国初期还在编印回族-伊斯兰文化的书籍，并行销全国各地。仅1956年至1958年期间，上海穆民经书社就印刷发行各类书籍223800余册，对建国初期的伊斯兰文化交流传播起到了一定作用。但1956年公私合营后，中国回教书局业务结束。1958年宗教改革后，上海穆民经书社也关张停业。

现在上海市共有杨浦区回民小学（前身为伊光第二小学）、黄浦区回民小学（前身为敦化小学与崇本小学）、普陀区回民小学（前身为云升小学）等三座回民小学，以及回民中学（前身为大化中学与敦化小学），皆为民国时期回族人士创办的回族教育机构发展而来。根据政策法规，所以这些学校虽然名为“回民”，但在日常教学中，并无系统的民族文化知识课程，更不可能有民国时期回民学校开设的教义、阿拉伯文等课程。

4.3 民族经济的瓦解与职业选择的多元化

中华人民共和国成立后，上海过度发展的消费经济逐渐消失，社会主义改造、公私合营后，回族小商铺、小作坊数量急剧减少，回族群体逐渐脱离传统行业，就业更加多元。例如，

1958 年 4 月,中国古物商场与中国古玩市场合并为公私合营上海古玩市场,市场从业人员 175 人,其中回族 76 人。回族从业人口比 1946 年时,少了 200 余人,比 1956 年社会主义改造时,少了 85 人。

中华人民共和国成立后,教育事业的发展,普通回族群众受教育机会的增加,促使从民族特色的劳动密集型就业向大众型技能密集型、知识密集型就业转变。中华人民共和国成立后,上海涌现了中国科学院院士、大学教授等回族知识分子,更多人成为工人等普通劳动者,走上了社会主义国家建设之路。

具有鲜明民族特色的经济,是回族发展的重要纽带。古玩珠玉、清真餐饮、皮毛业等行当多是回族传统经济行当,与回族的历史风俗传统有密切相关。可以说,职业决定了回族始终与本民族群体、本民族的传统保持密切联系。直至今日,一座城市回族文化保存相对传统、完整,那么肯定保留了一定规模的回族经济,例如清真餐饮等回族传统行当。

中华人民共和国成立后,上海城市回族-伊斯兰教文化的式微并不是个案。这种融入,是以一个群体的风俗习惯、文化传统的消亡为代价的,是以"同化"为结果的。这一历史过程,伴随着回族群体在经济方式、生活方式等方面的变化,更是因为特殊年代,无法选择的命运。

5 结语

中华人民共和国成立后至改革开放,上海伊斯兰教发展曲折波折,近代上海回族社会结构已不复存在。今日之上海,近代旅沪回族之后代,已经成为上海"土著",城市融入不断加深,民族与宗教的特征已不明显。但今日之上海,穆斯林群体的规模远超旧时,群体构成更加复杂。而近代旅沪回族先辈扎根申城,发展自我的历史经验,对今日穆斯林群体在保存自我、传统继承、社会融入等各项事业发展,有深刻的借鉴意义。

百年以来,回族都是上海人口最多的少数民族。回族也是除了汉族外,分布最为广泛的少数民族。这与回族的形成过程,与回族先民元朝色目人的广泛分布,"元时回回遍天下"的历史有关,与明初南京等江南回族受命迁徙各地有关。更与回族先民为生计(如东北回族多为华北各地闯关东,运河沿岸回族随运河贸易而迁徙),为生存(如清末回民起义大量回民迁徙新疆)等有关。回族-伊斯兰教文化,在思想观念、礼仪规范、生活习俗等方面本与汉族(及其他民族)有较大差别,但迁徙之路从未停止,文化传统从未停滞,与各地文化的互动互融从未停顿。应该说,回族在与汉族及其他民族的接触中,为生计生存,形成了一套成熟的生存哲学与处世方式。

相比近代上海穆斯林群体主要是由江南、华北、华中等地回族组成,今天流动穆斯林的构成更加多元。国内群体中,青海、甘肃等地来沪经营清真餐饮的回族(也包括撒拉族、东乡族等)人口最多。云南、华北、东北等地回族亦有一定数量。新疆籍的维吾尔、哈萨克民族也主要从事餐饮业。来自全国各地在沪各高校求学、企事业单位工作的穆斯林也是重要组成部分。而外籍穆斯林组成更加复杂,留学生、领事馆工作人员、求职者来自全世界。

民国初年,穿心街清真寺"平日礼晚拜者约百余人"的盛况已经不复存在。随着清真寺周边回族聚居区的消失,现在流动穆斯林分散在整个城市中,各清真寺每天五次的礼拜活动参加者已不多。但每到周五主麻日聚礼日时,上海所有的清真寺都处于饱和状态。开斋节、古尔邦节等伊斯兰教大型节日中，甚至要采取清真寺周边街区暂时性封闭的措施，方能满足穆斯林进行宗教活动。格致路、浙江中路一带有新疆、青海、河南、甘肃等地口味的清真菜馆及清真牛羊肉铺、点心店、馕饼等近 20 家，形成一定数量规模的清真食品街区。其中心与源头，就是曾经的浙江中路清真寺。但整体上来看，上海穆斯林在空间上的“哲麻体”（穆斯林社区）已经不复存在，更多是精神上的“哲麻体”，流动的“哲麻体”。

学术界与民族宗教管理部门，更多用“流动穆斯林”来表述现在城市外来穆斯林群体。相比近代旅沪穆斯林，现在的流动穆斯林群体有明显的差异。首先，主要来自西北地区（亦包括外籍人士），相比民国时期江南、华中、华北地区的回族，民族宗教传统更加浓厚，在价值观念、生活习俗等方面，与其他地区差异更大。第二，之所以被称为“流动”，是因为他们最终的归属地还是家乡，他们感知、体验、融入城市的意愿并不强烈。第三，职业选择相对单一，由于受教育水平、工作机会等原因，大部分来自西北的穆斯林主要从事清真餐饮等行业。同时，通过求学、求职，最终留在上海的白领、蓝领穆斯林群体也在不断壮大。第四，尽管同乡间的经济、亲友互动较为密切，但相比近代回族社会，文教、公益、社团等方面的互动较少。

民国时期的上海，各文化在多元并存的同时，又相对独立发展。不同群体的交往互动，亦不如今日之频繁便捷深入。特别是网络发展条件下，突破了时空界限，今天的穆斯林群体，还期许在一个相对封闭、独立的空间内，坚持价值观、生活方式，不被外界关注与审视，或完全被外界接纳，恐怕已不可能。特别是当前“伊斯兰”成为国际热点，打着伊斯兰旗号的恐怖主义活动成为热门新闻，欧洲穆斯林移民问题也屡现报端。原本陌生而神秘的穆斯林群体，被肆意解读，流动穆斯林不再只是职能部门的管理服务对象，而成了大众的“外来问题”。

有学者提出，从城市社会结构转型所导致的制度性障碍来看，流动人口面临的相似的困境是“就业隔阂、岗位隔阂、居住隔阂、交往隔阂”。对于当前穆斯林移民，甚至还包括语言隔阂、文化隔阂。近代回族移民最终被同化的命运，使得当前流动穆斯林倾向做“过客”。但越来越多的接受过高等教育的知识群体，选择留在上海等大城市中，在面对与其他外来人口在就业、住房、劳动保障等相同问题的同时，他们希望传播民族宗教文化，便利的清真餐饮，求职、生活中避免民族宗教歧视等诉求，也是最为关心的问题。

作者简介

洪伟，南京晓庄学院商学院讲师。

参考文献

[1] 上海特别市政府秘书处. 上海特别市户口分类统计简表. 上海特别市市政统计概要中华民国十六年度[M]. 上海，1927：44.

[2] 上海档案馆. 上海市少数民族人口统计表[Z]. 上海，1953：B21-1-7-1.

[3] 上海民族志编撰委员会. 上海民族志[M]. 上海：上海社会科学院出版社，1997：162.

[4] 佚名. 尚贤堂演讲佛耶两教[N]. 申报(增刊)，1926-1-30.

[5] 王建平. 近代上海伊斯兰文化存照[M]. 上海：上海古籍出版社，2008：69.

[6] 樊前锋，哈德成. 德学昭远谦谦君子[J]. 我们. 2015(3)：30.

存量更新与多元协同

多方协同、共建共治理念引导的老旧住区更新规划实践与机制探索

——以上海江浦社区为例

陆勇峰

摘　要　上海在城市更新转型发展和创新社会治理的时代背景下，中心城区的老旧社区更新成为改善人居环境、实现社会公平与社会包容及提高社区自治能力的重要载体。本文以笔者参与的上海杨浦区江浦社区辽源西路睦邻中心周边老旧住区综合更新为具体案例，探讨“多方协同、共建共治”理念引导下的社区更新规划实践。基于客观分析该老旧住区更新存在问题与面临瓶颈的基础上，创新提出具有针对性的更新规划理念与空间更新策略，并探索了社区规划如何与既有的基层社会治理体系相结合、社区规划如何引导社区居民公众参与等工作方法与机制。

关键词　多方协同；老旧住区；社区更新；上海

Planning Practice and Mechanism Exploration of Old Residential District Renewal Guided by the Concept of Collaboration、Co-Construction and Co-Governance

— Taking Jiangpu Community, Shanghai as a Case

Lu Yongfeng

Abstract　At the background of development of urban regeneration transformation and innovation of social governance in Shanghai. The old residential community in the central of the city has become a vital carrier which helps improving inhabited environment、realizing social equity and social inclusion and improving community autonomy. This paper taking a case which we are engaged in the community renewal project near Mulin center in Liaoyuan Road, Pujiang community, Yangpu district in Shanghai. Based on the concept of collaboration、co-construction and co-governance, we try to do a practice of community renewal planning. After analyzing problems and bottlenecks in this project, we propose creative renewal planning concepts and space renewal strategies. On the other hand, we explore how to combine community planning with the system of basic social governance, and how to encourage residents to participate in the planning process.

Keywords　collaboration; old residential district; community renewal; Shanghai

1 上海城市转型发展与社会治理的时代背景

1.1 上海城市转型发展进入城市更新阶段

上海在《上海市城市总体规划(2015—2040年)纲要》(简称《纲要》)中率先提出要转变城市发展理念,明确提出建设用地"零增长"甚至"负增长",做到建设用地只减不增。上海的城市发展进入了以城市更新为主线的阶段,即推动城市更新,转向存量规划:以提高城市活力和品质为目标,积极探索渐进式、可持续的有机更新模式,以存量用地的更新利用来满足城市未来发展的空间需求,同时做好城市文化的保护与传承,倒逼土地利用方式由外延粗放式扩张向内涵增长效益提升转变,促进空间利用向集约紧凑、功能复合、低碳高效转变。同时在《纲要》中也明确提出,"灵活推进建成社区的有机更新","探索建立多方参与的机制"。上海有机更新的内涵主要包括三个方面:①有机更新是城市成长过程,也是短板修补和问题治理过程;②有机更新强调历史人文和自然生态传承,也强调城市品质和功能创造;③有机更新更关注公众参与的过程,强调多方合作共建、共治、共享过程。

中心城区大量的老旧住区则是这些存量用地中的主角,以往大规模拆除式的旧城改造已不再符合上海城市转型发展的要求。然而,建于20世纪八九十年代左右的老旧住宅小区,因为缺乏经济利益的驱动,成为城市更新中的痛点,普遍存在着基础设施老化、建筑年久失修、生命通道堵塞、交通组织不畅、停车矛盾突出、小区环境差、物业管理欠缺等诸多问题,严重影响了居民最基本的日常生活,老旧住区的更新诉求强烈。

1.2 上海创新社会治理的时代要求

2015年1月5日,中共上海市委、上海市人民政府发布《关于进一步创新社会治理加强基层建设的意见》(简称《意见》)和《上海市加强住宅小区综合治理三年行动计划(2015—2017年)》,将大力推进基层协商民主,引导和组织群众有序政治参与。根据《意见》,上海的目标是:"经过3—5年努力,进一步完善基层社会治理体系,进一步提高基层社会治理能力,使基层社会在深刻变革中既充满活力又和谐有序,为城市治理体系和治理能力现代化奠定坚实基础,为上海顺利实现'四个中心'和社会主义现代化国际大都市建设目标提供坚实保障。"《意见》中还明确,建立健全以居民区党组织为领导核心,居委会为主导,居民为主体,业委会、物业公司、驻区单位、群众团体、社会组织、群众活动团队等共同参与的居民区治理架构。

城市中的居住社区不仅是城市空间结构体系中的基本单元,更是社会治理体系中的基层载体,因而社区层面的规划可以很好地与基层社会治理相结合,社区规划将成为推动社区治理的有效方式和途径之一。

2 项目概况与更新改造问题难点

2.1 项目概况

本项目位于上海市内环线内杨浦区江浦街道辖区,东起打虎山路、西至恒阳花苑、南至辽源西路、北至昆民中学，合计占地面积约 1.2 公顷。现状涉及三个住宅小区，小区名称分别为辽源西路 190 弄、铁路工房、打虎山路 1 弄，均为 20 世纪 80 年代左右建成。其中打虎山路 1 弄有 2 栋 6 层住宅楼，建筑面积 6520 平方米，住户 90 户；辽源西路 190 弄有两栋 6 层住宅楼和 1 栋 2 层公共建筑（辽源西路睦邻中心），建筑面积 6619 平方米，住户 81 户；铁路工房小区有 5 栋 6 层住宅楼、建筑面积 11821 平方米、住户 256 户。三个小区合计户数 427 户，人口约 1280 人，其中年龄在 60 岁以上的占比超 50%。其中打虎山路 1 弄与另外两个小区中间有围墙相隔，其出入口位于打虎山路；辽源西路 190 弄和铁路工房小区共用出入口，出入口位于辽源西路上，两小区内部空间以睦邻中心东侧、北侧围墙为界，无绝对意义上的分割；睦邻中心，是为周边社区居民提供生活配套服务的公共活动中心，内有阅览室、舞蹈房、乒乓室、儿童活动房、社区卫生站等（图 1、图 2、表 1）。

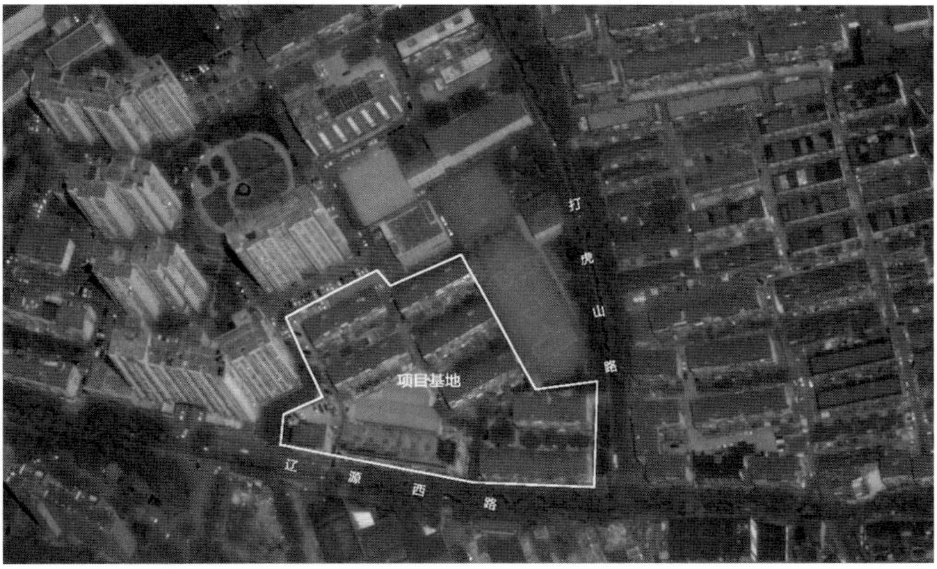

图 1　本项目及周边地区影像图

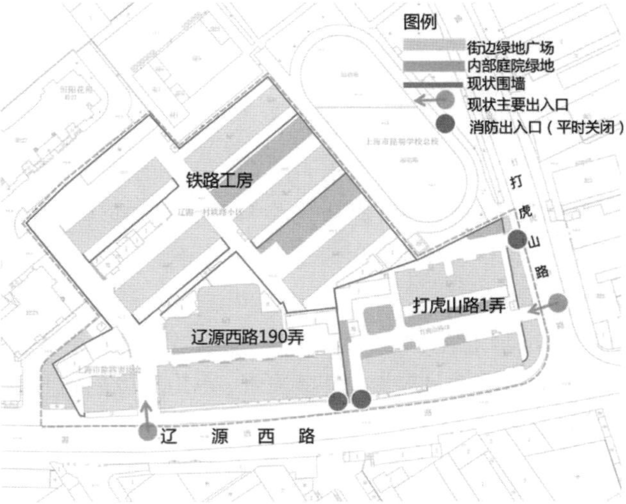

图 2　三个小区现状空间格局图

表 1　　小区现状基本情况一览表

小区名称	占地面积（m^2）	建筑面积（m^2）	户数（户）	物业标准情况	老龄化程度
辽源西路 190 弄	3600	6619	81	无	50%（按大于 60 岁计）
铁路工房	5978	11821	256	0.18 元/平方米/月	
打虎山路 1 弄	2800	6521	90	0.8 元/平方米/月	
合计	12378	24961	427		

同时，与周边城市环境相比，临近小区周边住宅区多为配套设施和内部环境较好的商品房小区以及未来待开发用地，因此本次涉及的三个老旧小区所呈现的特征是上海在快速城市化进程中遗留下来的一个典型缩影，同时也是当前上海城市更新和基层社会治理必须要面对的难点所在。其特征具体表现为：①小区面积小、建筑密度高、活动空间少；②按照规划，三个小区为保留地块，基本无二次开发的可能；③房龄老、建筑旧、整体环境差；④老龄化比重高，对社区环境健康适老性需求大；⑤小区居民整体的经济水平条件有限，其中不乏一些困难家庭；⑥与周边商品房小区相比，社区居民心理落差大。

2.2　主要问题

2.2.1　物质空间环境层面

(1) 安全及基础设施问题

老旧小区的安全问题是首要问题，也是居民最为关注的焦点。比如调研中发现小区出入口道闸缺失或损坏、缺少监控系统；同时小区内有对外开放的睦邻中心，因此人员进出较为随意；路面破损，坑洼现象较多；非机动车棚内缺少充电设备或者私自拉接充电线路，存在安全隐患；小区底层单元入户防盗门门禁损坏；下水道管网堵塞等。

(2) 交通组织及停车问题

老旧小区原先配置的机动车车位数量远远满足不了居民当下与日俱增的停车需求，机动车占用小区道路、占绿毁绿等已成普遍现象，甚至导致生命通道堵塞，危及了居民的财产和生命安全。

(3) 环境卫生及绿化问题

小区缺少绿化、环卫的日常养护和保洁，小区内仅有的几个庭院绿地内杂草丛生、绿化种植单一、景观效果差；垃圾箱房破损、周边卫生环境差、缺少建筑垃圾堆放点；部分大树常年缺少修剪，遮阳挡风，对部分居民生活也造成一定影响。

(4) 建筑本体功能性问题

老旧小区因建造早、房龄老，虽然相关部门也有做个诸如“平改坡”等工程改造，但是很多建筑还是出现了墙体涂料或饰材脱落、屋顶漏水、公共部位门窗损坏、公共楼道管线杂乱、自行车棚破旧等现象。

2.2.2　社会心理属性层面

由于老旧住区年久失修，物质空间环境的衰败和基础设施的坏损，加之与周边商品房住宅小区的对比，从最初仅仅是物质空间层面的影响慢慢扩展到居民们的社会心理层面。他

图 3　小区现状环境系列照片

们中的大多数盼望着拆迁，盼望着早日搬离，不再关心共有的住区环境，更有甚者私自搭建，破坏公共环境，久而久之对社区的归属感慢慢消失，更谈不上获得感和幸福感。幸好近年来杨浦区推进的睦邻中心建设，让本次涉及的三个小区有了改善的趋势。

2.2.3　配套政策机制层面

长期以来上海城市的发展是以增量扩张为主，诸多规划和配套政策的制定也更关注于增量土地的开发建设，存量、尤其是老旧住区的更新改造往往面临着很多政策和机制的约束或缺失。比如老旧住区，停车矛盾是较为突出的，小区改造中的增加停车位和减少绿化面积之间的矛盾仍待处理。另外以物业管理为例，老旧小区普遍面临物业管理难的问题，如本项目中的辽源西路 190 弄小区，因为规模小，物业缺位；部分小区物业费用低，本项目中的铁路工房物业标准只有 0.18 元/平方米/月，不足以满足支付物业管理、绿化保洁的费用，导致小区整体物业管理水平和服务质量较低。

2.3　更新改造面临难点

2.3.1　固有围墙分割的空间权属打破，难度大

三个小区长期以来空间分割，如今要打破围墙进行空间整合，需要小区居民在思想上的统一。尤其是打虎山路 1 弄小区有围墙与辽源西路 190 弄、铁路工房分隔，其规模虽然小，但有独立物业，小区也较为安全和安静。按照改造方案，中间围墙拆除后，三个小区将成为一个整体，且打虎山路 1 弄将贡献出大部分场地作为整合后的小区公共空间使用。因此在改造方案制定之初，我们将此问题预设为本次改造最大的难点，也是事关小区改造后品质提升的关键所在。

2.3.2　居民个体间的利益协调，难度大

正因为是存量更新，老旧住区改造的直接对象虽然是物质空间环境，但涉及的利益主体本质上是使用这些环境的社区居民，尤其是更新改造方案必然会涉及不同利益主体间的冲突和矛盾。比如我们在改造方案里，提出了拆除内部围墙实现三小区合并后，将原先位于图 1辽源西路上的分属于两个小区的两个消防出入口合并调整为一个主要的出入口，并增设相应道路，就有一楼和二楼居民表示随之而来的机动车和行人的频繁通行会对其原先生活环境造成干扰。其他包括停车位设置、垃圾厢房设置等具有“邻避现象”的矛盾，在小区改造中也是很大的协调难点。

2.3.3 更新改造资金筹集,难度大

由于三个小区规模小,且只有两个小区缴纳物业费,缴费标准又较低,合计维修资金也仅有60万元;同时小区内超过60岁的老年人口占到50%以上,总体经济条件一般,因此小区居民只能象征性地自筹小部分改造费用;改造的主体费用,主要依靠区政府财政统筹。当然少数几个小区开展此项工作,资金依靠政府财政解决尚还可以,但是若铺开到量大面广的老旧住区改造,政府财政也会有压力。

3 更新规划目标理念与主要内容

3.1 更新规划目标、原则、理念

3.1.1 明确"以人为本"的更新改造价值目标

老旧住区的更新改造应结合老旧住区的客观条件,以解决居民百姓最为关心的小区中存在的"急、难、愁"问题为重点,提倡以"安全、整洁、文明、有序"的居住环境营造为更新目标,建立以人为本、以提高居民获得感为价值导向。在本项目更新中,作为社区规划师,我们联同政府部门(街道办事处)、居委会、业委会、居民代表、物业等召开多次前期方案讨论会议,在尊重居民反映的现实问题和客观条件基础上,坚定统一了更新改造的价值导向和改造目标,并对推进中可能遇到的困难做好了充分的心理准备和相关预案工作。

3.1.2 建立"自下而上、上下统筹"的更新改造原则

老旧住区的更新改造应坚持"拆、建、管"并举,拆违方案、建设方案和综合治理方案三案合一,做到统筹谋划、综合施策、建管并举、群众满意。在此基础上,强调"自下而上、上下统筹"的原则,尊重居民意愿,在方案讨论、方案公示、方案表决等各环节,突出社区居民在改造过程中的主体地位,体现空间正义。

3.1.3 运用先进理念,提升更新改造效果

老旧住区的更新改造要秉承"共谋、共建、共治、共享"的基本思想,在此基础上结合不同小区的实际情况,因地制宜提出针对性的更新理念和改造方案。结合老旧住区的特征,笔者将其主要理念总结为十个:安全性、生态性、活力性、健康性、人文性、友好性、适老性、特色性、参与性、智慧性。比如在本项目中,结合睦邻中心等资源,在改造方案中更多关注"共享、活力、生态、健康"等理念的落实。

3.2 更新规划主要内容

针对本项目的实际情况,结合前期的调研基础,以目标导向和问题导向相结合,其物质空间更新改造内容可以概括为"安全维护、交通组织、环境提升、建筑修缮"四个方面。

3.2.1 安全维护更新

主要指对小区内的安全设施进行统筹规划,通过增设或维护,实现住区安全全覆盖,主要包括:对小区出入口的门卫岗亭、智能化道闸、安全技防等设施进行综合改造;对小区内的路面、二次供水、排水管网、户外照明等基础设施改造、疏通和维修,从而提高住区的安全性和归属感。

3.2.2 交通组织更新

以确保生命通道和消防通道畅通为主要目标，针对现状存在的行车路线不合理、机动车停车矛盾突出、非机动车停车无序等问题，在“三区合一、资源整合”大的思路指导下，方案提出了较大的交通组织优化策略。打破既有的围墙分割和空间限定，结合辽源西路机动车单行道（自东向西）的交通管制要求，将现有辽源西路上的消防出入口改造为小区新的主入口，将原先辽源西路190弄出入口作为机动车出口考虑，将打虎山路1弄出入口调整为以人行进出为主、机动车进出为辅。在出入口处实现人车分流，内部机动车以单向交通组织为主，提高小区内部的交通安全性。

3.2.3 环境提升更新

重点从景观功能性、针对性、适用性以及美观性四个方面，对小区内绿地和活动空间改造，规划通过“三区合一，校区联动”实现资源共享，重塑小区公共景观活动空间。规划构筑“一脉三园”的景观结构体系，一脉即健康活力脉，设置1.5米宽的健康步道，东联昆明中学运动场（条件限制型对外开放）、中接睦邻中心、西至恒阳花苑小区街角广场；三园，即东侧的健康活力园、中间的睦邻文化园、西侧的社区休闲园。拆除睦邻中心东、北两侧现有围墙，将单一的灰色硬质场地改造为“灰绿结合”共享开放的社区绿地，同时睦邻中心及周边场地将成为改造后小区内部的主要公共活动空间。

3.2.4 建筑修缮更新

针对诸如屋顶漏水、墙面渗水、楼道整治等建筑本身存在的问题，需进行综合梳理，并由专业部门予以落实解决，从而解决居住建筑的功能性与美观性问题。尤其是在空间允许的情况下，针对老旧住区老龄化现象，应尽可能通过改造，增加适老性设施和无障碍设施。

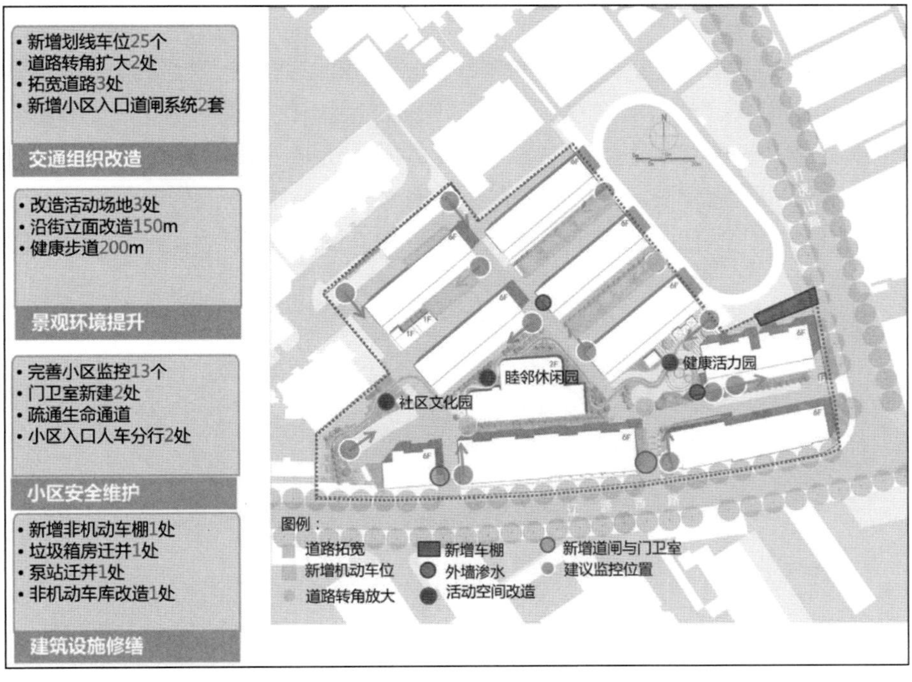

图4 更新改造项目汇总图

图 5　局部节点改造方案

4　老旧住区更新中的机制探索

4.1　建立社区规划引领的住区更新模式

老旧住区的更新改造并非是近年来的新词，全国各地也都有各自的成功经验，上海也同样经历过“平改坡”等单一的工程改造。这些改造虽然从硬件上改善了居民的居住条件，但传统的老旧住区改造，更多是以政府主导、房修类工程导向的改造建设为主，社区居民处于被动从属的状态，对改造方案缺少了解，更新过程参与度极低甚至缺位。因此，在当前创新社会治理背景下，社区规划和社区规划师综合作用机制引领的住区改造模式更为行之有效，建议在相关部门的联动下，比如规土局、房管局等达成共识，建立社区规划引领的老旧住区更新模式，并建立相应机制，倡导从单一的空间改造转向多元的社区营造，促进社会治理，从而推动老旧社区的综合复兴。

4.2　构建老旧住区更新的多方协同机制

老旧住区的社区更新，其整个过程涉及的角色主要包括四大类，分别为：政府部门、社区居民（居委会、业委会、物业、居民构成三会一代理平台）、社区规划师、工程建设单位。因此在当前创新社会治理的背景下，老旧社区更新必须要建立一套完善、可行实施机制，明确各参与主体的职责和角色定位，制定清晰的操作流程和实施路径。政府部门（街道）以搭建平台、做好配套保障为主，比如确定设计单位、落实改造资金等；居委、业委、物业三方，构成小

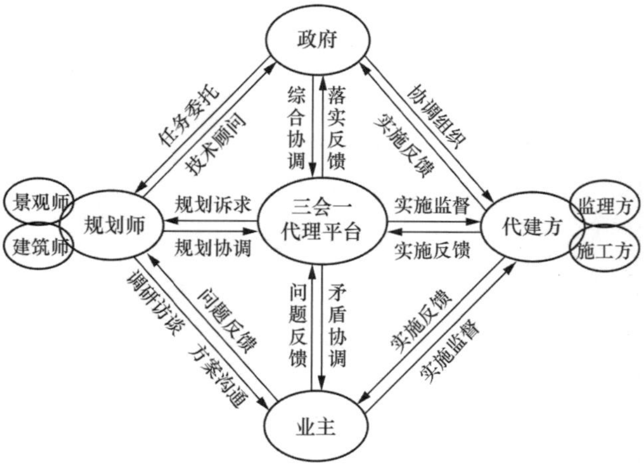

图 6　社区更新多方协同模式框图

区改造和推进工作的主体，应积极组织社区居民开展问题汇总、方案讨论、意见反馈、矛盾协调、实施监督等；社区规划师，提供专业的技术改造方案，强调全过程的参与，尤其是做好与社区居民的方案解释、沟通交流、空间利益协调等工作；代建方（实施方）组织好监理单位、施工单位具体的工程建设，并做好与政府、社区居民、规划师之间的协调；社区居民（业主），则是整个更新改造过程中的利益主体，依托三会一代理平台，应积极表达诉求、参与方案讨论、投票表决、工程监督等。

4.3 健全社区规划与社区治理的互动机制

城市规划具有公共政策的属性，在创新社会治理的背景下，基层社区治理要充分依托社区规划的综合作用，使社区规划与社区治理相互作用。以本项目为例，依托社区规划这一平台，居委会、业委会、物业、楼组长与居民代表等逐渐探索并形成了小区更新改造的居民自治议事平台和工作机制，比如定期的例会制度、居民成立志愿者队伍等。同时社区规划师作为专业性的技术人员，全过程参与到整个社区更新的各个环节，编制和讲解社区规划方案、听取居民意见、解答居民疑问、协调居民之间的空间矛盾、指导施工单位实施建设等。可见，社区规划一方面作为专业性的规划技术支撑，为社区物质空间环境改造提供解决方案，更为重要的是与“社区治理、自治共治”相结合，成为创新社会治理背景下，有效推动基层社区治理、做实公众参与的协同平台。

4.4 倡导社区规划师常态化的工作机制

社区规划是以问题导向为主的实施性规划，其规划结果往往也具有多变性，不同于以往目标型蓝图式的规划成果，而是以渐进式、微更新的方式体现，因此需要地方政府、规划管理部门、规划设计机构及院校、社区基层单位、社会 NGO 组织等共同探索并建立一套因地制宜完整的社区规划师工作机制，包括社区规划师培训、社区规划师认定、社区规划师职责、社区规划师考核等。结合本项目规划实践，社区规划师的作用可以概括为以下六点：

（1）专业技术，易于居民信任。在正式施工前，经由社区规划师团队先提供实施方案，这样更易于和居民百姓进行沟通交流，在方案得到百姓的认可表决后再开始立项和施工程序，更容易获得居民们的理解和信任。

（2）桥梁作用，利于利益协调。通过设计方案，可以有效地协调不同居民之间的利益诉求，将问题提前暴露，避免将难题和矛盾留到实施环节，力求使整治方案利益最大化、普惠化，体现空间正义。

（3）设计表达，引导公众参与。依托社区规划师团队的专业技能，在现场调研、方案制作、方案展示、方案实施等若干环节，倡导公众参与理念，积极引导小区居民主动参与小区更新改造的全过程。

（4）创新理念，提升更新效果。社区规划师依靠其专业知识和技能，可以在老旧住区更新改造方案中，引入“绿色生态、智慧科技、节能环保、海绵城市”等当前城市发展的新理念和新技术，提升住区改造的综合效果和社会效益。

（5）成果规范，利于指导实施。每个小区通过表决的实施方案都形成一套规范的图册，便于指导进场的施工单位可以做到按图施工，力争实施效果与设计方案保持一致。

（6）实施跟踪，便于后续服务。在后续实施环节，若方案与施工出现矛盾或需要协调，社区规划师也会同步跟进并及时对节点进行设计变更，满足具体实施需求。

4.5 完善优化相关配套政策保障机制

调研发现老旧住区因当年建造的社会经济和时代背景的差异，当时的诸多建设和配套标准也已跟不上人们现代生活的需求。比如老旧住区中机动车位严重不足已成为主要矛盾，导致占道停车、占绿停车等现象成为常态，严重情况下导致生命通道受阻，这也成为小区突发事件时进行有效施救的最大障碍。而道路拓宽或车位增加势必又侵占一定的绿化空间，在这样的矛盾局面下，如何平衡和破题成为难点。假设更新方案在居民表决通过的前提下，老旧住区是否可以通过增加垂直绿化、屋顶绿化、绿色植栽等方式平衡少量的平面绿化用地的减少，尝试采用增加“综合绿量”指标代替“绿化率”的指标，对应的则是需要相关部门主动积极的完善和优化相关配套政策。其他包括原有小区权属边界调整后的地籍信息变更机制、老旧住区更新改造资金的保障机制、老旧住区更新改造专项条例或规范等一系列配套政策都需要进一步研究和完善。

5 结语

我国的城镇化水平逐年递增，目前已近57%，北、上、广、深等一线大城市提前进入了以存量更新为主线的转型发展阶段，老旧社区的更新也已成为城市更新中的热点和难点。同时存量居住社区，尤其是诸多老旧住区的空间问题与社会问题也尤为突出。作为社会治理的基本单元，老旧住区更新改造已成为很多城市补短板的重点和抓手。上海面对城市转型发展和社会治理的时代要求，近年来相关区、街道开展了若干老旧住区更新改造的积极探索和实践。在本项目中，我们除了为老旧住区提供专业的空间更新改造方案，更为具有积极意义的是，我们探索了社区规划如何与社区治理相结合，推动了社区规划师从之前理论层面的倡导走向了真实的规划实践，为上海社区规划师制度的建立起到了积极的试点作用，这同样也显现出了与时代发展、社会发展、现代社会治理相符的理念与价值导向。

作者简介

陆勇峰，上海同济城市规划设计研究院二所副总工程师，注册规划师、高级工程师。

参考文献

[1] 中共上海市委.关于进一步创新社会治理加强基层建设的意见[R]. 沪委[2014]14号.上海，2014.

[2] 上海同济城市规划设计研究院. 上海杨浦区辽源西路睦邻中心周边住宅小区社区更新规划[R]. 上海，2017.

[3] 匡晓明，陆勇峰.存量背景下上海社区规划实践与探索.中国城市规划年会论文集[C].北京：中国建筑工业出版社，2016.

[4] 赵民，孙忆敏，杜宁，等.我国城市旧住区渐进式更新研究——理论、实践与策略[J]. 国际城市规划，2010(1)：24-32.

[5] 黄瓴，许剑峰.城市社区规划师制度的价值基础和角色建构研究[J]. 规划师，2013(9)：11-15.

成都市小街区更新思路与“1+N”机制的协同思考及延伸问题

谭露露

摘　要　每座城市都有其独特的肌理，如若都是如法炮制的对各个城市进行“穿衣戴帽”与“综合整治”，城市将会渐渐地失去其城市肌理、历史韵味与人文情怀。在过年几十年间城市更新的学术探讨和项目实践经历从早期的效仿欧美实行大推大建，到2016年国家城市会议所提出的中医疗法“街区制”-小规模、渐进式的城市更新。同时，研究视角也逐渐拓宽，从建筑或规划的单一学科研究与实践到社会、经济、环境、城市设计的多学科融合探讨，城市更新不仅仅是城市建设问题，而更多的是城市断面、可持续发展、社会公平、城市管理系统等综合性问题。因此文章将基于文献研究、案例学习、实际城市更新项目的参与及政策分析来阐述成都市城市更新的新探索——小街区规制，并基于实际应用中对机制的思考，提出“1+N”机制与小街区理念的配合，旨在协助成都市“小街区规制”的更新思路能够形成系统，并促使“小街区”更新形成良性循环。

关键词　小街区规制；1+N机制；协同机制；城市更新

The Coordination Process of “1+N” and Extension Problem of Chengdu Smaller-Scale District

Tan Lulu

Abstract　Every city has its unique texture, if modeled on the “dressing up” and “comprehensive regulation” of each city, then cities will gradually lose its own texture, historical charm and humanity. Over the decades of city renewal of academic study and project practice experienced from the early implementation of imitating the western rough way, and until to the 2016 National City conference proposed Chinese medicine “small-scale district”　it's a way through small and gradual to renewal cities. At the same time, the research perspective is gradually widened, from the single subject research and practice to multidisciplinary society economy and environment of city design, construction or merge of planning, city renewal is not only the city construction, and more is the comprehensive city section, sustainable development, social justice, city management system etc. Therefore, the article will be based on the literature research, case study, the participation of the actual urban renewal project and the policy analysis to explain the new exploration of urban renewal in Chengdu - small-scale districts of regulation, and with reconsider to the mechanism of the practical application, put forward “1 + N” mechanism and small-scale districts concept matching, to help Chengdu city small-scale districts regulation update ideas to form a system, and to promote the“small-scale districts ”regeneration form a virtuous circle.

Keywords　regulation of smaller-scale district; the mechanism of 1 + N; the mechanism of coordination; urban renewal

1 引言

所有生机勃勃的城市都具有一个共同的必备因素，那就是城市结构不但高度复杂，而且各有规律。而城市这个有机体只有不断调整其复杂性和条理性才能够跟上人类的发展及需求。因为城市的进化也是人类思维的进化[1]14，这也就是说明社会在不断地发展中，经济、政策、环境等人为或非人为因素都会促使社会结构发生改变，居住人群的思维跟着调整，相对应的城市结构也都需要进行调整。外界冲击会不断打破空间、时间、交流、意义的平衡。因此，城市更新的意义便在于找回城市结构的平衡。但是谁来找回？怎么找回？找回的平衡是新的还是旧的？这些都是值得每一个从事城市更新人员思考和研究的。

我国早期的城市更新处于学习和探索阶段，不管是在城市更新方面的研究，还是城市更新项目的实施都仅仅关注在短期内的效益，比如“推倒重建”或“穿衣戴帽”。但经过时间的验证，这些进行短时间内的物质更新区域所耗费的人力、物力和财力所得到的不过是五年左右的城市“脸面”，并没有从根本上解决城市问题。这样的阶段，其实不仅是中国城市发展的困境，更是全世界城市发展的问题。“城市更新的实际成效仍有待检查……当前城市政府在政治上欢迎城市更新，更多的只是城市的一种表态而不是事实。随着越来越多的人开始明白城市更新的本质后，人们对城市更新的支持就会萎缩，甚至敌对……”[2]125-126

也正是在这样的一个不断尝试与探索的过程中逐渐意识到，城市是像大脑一样运作，而不是电脑，因此强行拆除配件、替换配件这种方式不可取。成都城市更新也开始脱离简单粗暴的更新方式，走向对城市空间的关注。“针灸式”的中医疗法——以街区为单元，鼓励社会参与、放宽市场准入[3]等方式，来促进城市复杂性和城市活力的恢复。不管是阿莫斯·拉布普特(Amos Rapport)或是尼克斯·A·萨林加罗斯(Nikos Salingaros)，他们的研究成果都表明城市环境的成功与意义是在于人们在生活中对环境线索地收集、领会，当这些环境信息是积极的，有机的，基于这些的行动也就会与城市环境成为一体，这就是一个活着的城市。

2 反观历史——成都城市更新历程、模式、成效及其存在的问题

2.1 成都城市更新历程及模式

2.1.1 反观成都城市更新历程

成都是一座具有4500年以上城市文明发展历史、是具有“城不改址三千载，址不改名二千五”特征的历史文化名城[4]，其文史价值不言而喻。成都的城市更新之初以中华人民共和国成立之后起，期间历经几次城市规划，都以原清贡院为中心，向四周进行外延式发展。2014年，天府新区地获批，成都城市在新总规的基础上构建“双核共兴、一城多市”的网络城市群，形成破解成都圈层式结构和“大城市病”的新的发展路径[5]。这一系列城市规划策略的转变都与城市更新息息相关，也展现城市规划概念的改变和城市更新概念的发展、转变过程。

1994年府南河改造；而后的2001—2006年，成都东郊成片工业区约40万平方米的土地进行整体搬迁置换；2002年，成都市对二环路以内20世纪80年代前的近410万平方米危旧

房屋进行拆除重建；2002 年，文殊院历史街区进行了更新改造；2003 年，成都市政府对少城区域的宽窄巷子进行保护性改造；2009 年，大慈寺片区内用地作为商业地产用地被公开拍卖、改造；2012 年成都市启动北部城区老旧城市形态和生产力布局（城市业态）改造工程。反观近三十年的更新历程，以上大部分更新工程已竣工多时，有的区域仍旧破败，有的区域欣欣向荣，这些经验和教训就是我们继续前进的基石。

1.1.2　成都城市更新机制

更新机制就一直是争议点，公务员、规划师、公益企业、文化部门、居民之间究竟如何协调？更新决策如何作出？这些都是城市更新机制所包含的内容。在成都或者国内大多数城市，更新机制基本与住建部在第三次联合国住房和城市可持续发展大会上的国家报告中所述相差无几。

在大规模实施棚户区更新改造中意见中提到，棚户区改造采取由政府主导、市场运作、住户参与的方式，中央政府在财政上投入，建设用地、税费和信贷等当面给予支持，引导地方政府实行财政补贴、税费减免、从土地出让净收益中安排一定资金等支持政策，允许棚户区改造项目配套建设一定比例的商业服务设施和商品住房，吸引社会力量参与棚户区改造。在安置方面，实行食物安置与货币补偿相结合，充分尊重群众意愿[6]。因此，文章将前文所提及项目的更新机制主要分为如下两类：

（1）政府主导的更新机制

一般具有较大影响力的更新工程是由政府主导，其更新模式基本与府南河改造的模式一致，政府成立专门的小组，相关参与单位各有负责人，同时辅以相关的临时制度、政策等。这种目标管理式的方式对于项目后期的管理、维护、评估及资料的存档等造成不利。更新项目一般需要持续很长时间，更新项目在规划阶段的平均时长约为三年。从编制规划至新建筑的完工总耗时平均需要十二年左右[7]131。

（2）开发商介入的更新机制

根据“东调”工程的案例，前期为政府主导，后期为开发企业主导，也就是在特地完成熟化工作后，由成都市土地拍卖中心向社会拍卖，确定房地产开发企业。这种模式最终的效果颇具争议，如通过拆迁与建设前后的卫星地图、规划方案的对比，发现开发商期初编制的概念方案是尊重现状肌理、最大程度地保护树种和历史建筑，但最终实施方案却是大相径庭。原职工、居民迁至安置房中，腾出来的地块被开发商建成甲级写字楼、星级酒店和高档住宅等。

由此可见，两种更新模式都有其自身的弊病，同时，这两种模式也代表两种利益主体，但实际上在城市更新中所涉及的利益群体并不只有政府、开发商，还有居民、公益组织、文化部门等。优秀的开发应同时成就参与者和旁观者，使双方称为赢家[8]40。

2.2　更新成效与问题

2.2.1　更新成效的评估

如今反观成都城市更新近三十年，之前更新的模式及更新方法已经初显其成效。除却府南河改造工程、宽窄巷子报奖，其余类似于成都市二环路综合整治工程这类项目，基本都停留在项目完工的验收上，后期并未再有任何针对其后续状态的评估公布。诸如清华大学杨瑞博士提出的根据城市更新目标框架对“东调”项目进行评估的结果（表 1）。可惜该表仅为学术论文中所述，并非应用于城市管理系统中。

表1　成飞发动机厂片区更新效果评价表[9]

	更新效果评估	评估类型	详细情况
正面效果	产业结构调整	经济效益性目标	成飞发动机厂搬迁到新都工业园，实现中心区二产向三产的转化和工业向园区集中的目标
	企业经营效益	经济效益性目标	成飞发动机厂从20世纪90年代资产负债率超过90%到2007年实现销售收入13亿元，利润1.3亿元，出口创汇6700万美元，真正实现了扭亏为盈、跨越发展
	土地开发效益	经济效益性目标	2006年东调工作完成后，成都东片区腾出土地9000多亩，政府土地出让费收入超过12亿元(不含土地开发商缴纳的费用)，同时收回1500多亩土地用于道路和公服配套建设
	城市风貌提升	环境景观性目标	打通道路，引入大型商场、超市，修建现代化小区，彻底改变东郊工业重污染的形象
负面效果	基础设施承载力	经济效益性目标	整体推进带来拆迁整体安置，安置方案较为单一，对职工安置需求调查不足，导致大部分职工安置在城区，工作在郊区，职住比低，每天通勤往返，交通压力大
	城市特色	环境景观性目标	区域原有的肌理、一人的巷路尺度、多年的原生树种荡然无存，只留下千篇一律的现代都市形象
	建筑保护	文化效益性目标	具有重要保护价值和纪念意义的建构筑物没有得到有效地保护
	社会安定	社会公平性目标	完成目标任务为目的，快速推进，后续问题逐渐显现，对企业职工就业问题考虑不足，对企业升级后的职工下岗问题估计不足，造成社会不稳定因素；且整体拆迁安置异地，原厂址建设高档住宅小区，加剧社会空间的极化

2.2.2　更新过程中存在的问题

(1) 各利益主体更新目标较难定位

在这些城市更新建设的实践过程中发现，各相关参与方和利益主体对城市更新的认知有较大的偏差，如政府既有公共利益这样的目标，但是作为有具体“代言人”，其任期内的政绩与抱负对城市的发展也有着一定的影响；开发商的目标更为直接，就是实现其投资的最大回报；居民本作为一个群体，但有较大的个体差异，也不能一言概之。

（2）各参与方工作权责问题难以界定

由于成都尚未出台关于城市更新的专项法律法规，也没有针对性的实施细则和办法，更没有统一的部门进行管理和筹划。较多更新项目被拆分成多个子项，被放到相关的管理部门。诸如土地问题回归到国土局、规划问题回市规划局等等，这就造成多方决策问题。各行政管理部门又有自己独立的管理方式，且更新项目又属于一个全新的领域，相应的管理机制还不完善。不管是欧美国家还是亚洲国家，都在探索自己的更新机制来避免“各人自扫门前雪，不管他人瓦上霜”的现象继续。

（3）各类型的更新项目评估难度大

首先，没有统一的评价体系。就更新项个体差异而言，就很难以单一体系去全部归纳。因此，整体对更新项目的认知要么偏向装饰装修、要么偏向新建建筑，很难在中间找到一个平衡点，中间多层法律规范也都无从界定，存在较多的监管漏洞。

其次，项目阶段性数据收集与分析的问题。更新类项目所涉及基础数据及跟进数据的量要远超过新建项目，如包括基础地图、人口数据和标准等基础数据通常分为场地、交通、市场、经济、政策、环境、规划、历史和项目方案[10]。对这些数据的收集、保存、跟进与分析需要较多部门的数据支持，以及与数据分析机构合作。

（4）城市更新政策的缺失

成都城市尚未出台关于城市更新的相关政策，只有部分临时文件与政策，因此这对于更新项目而言，就没有规则和政策来引导。一切遵循市场和领导的意志，势必导致城市更新项目寸步难行。

3　发硎新试——成都“小街区规制”理论

3.1　成都“小街区”“小街区规制”基本概念及目标层级

3.1.1　“小街区”与“小街区规制”的基本内涵

“小街区”是指城市主干道、中小街道分割、路网密度较高、开发强度适中、土地功能复合、公共交通完善及公共服务设施就近配套的开放街区模式[11]。而“小街区规制”则是指通过制定技术标准将城市小街区模式规范化、制度化，用规制的手段进行固化，用制度的形式保障小街区规划理念落到实处[11]。“小街区规制”从微观层面贯彻落实了中央提出的“创新、协调、绿色、开放、共享”五大发展理念，将构成城市最小单元的街区作为解决“大城市病”的突破口，通过建设一个个便捷、宜居、有人情味及有特色的街区，实现城市的和谐、宜居与繁荣[12]。

3.1.2　“小街区”与更新目标层级

城市更新的目标层级与所处的阶段有着紧密联系，不同的更新阶段、项目情况所面临的问题也不同。成都市小街区的发展方向和目标是“开放便捷、尺度适宜、配套完善、邻里和睦”，应该归属于第二目标层次和第三目标层次之间，根据图1中所示发展阶段和成熟阶段，这个阶段则是尊重人文特色，促进经济可持续发展，相比其他植入性的文化，本土历史及人文更具有生命力。人文复兴是旧城复兴的重要标志。它无形但具有触动人心的吸引力，能为城市经济的发展提供新的和更为持久的动力。

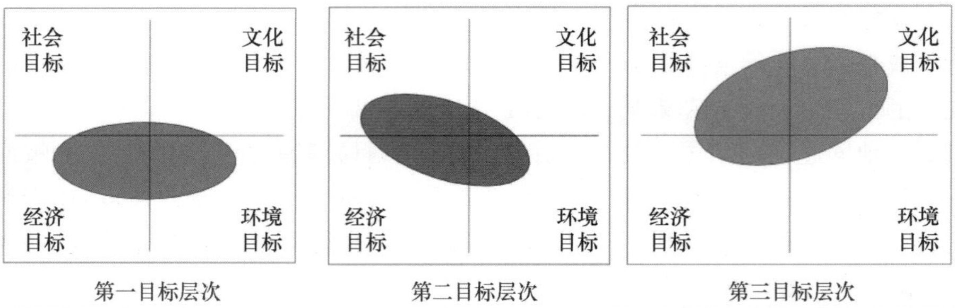

图 1　万艳华的城市更新目标层次与阶段示意图[13]

3.2　“小街区”的更新机制

更新机制与更新理念之间是相辅相成的关系，因此针对“小街区”的小尺度、渐进式更新思路，更新机制的调整也是时势使然。亚里士多德也说过：“即便是法律，也不应一成不变。随着理念而改变的机制也是如此。”第一批小街区的实践和更新机制都尚未成型，还处于多方探索阶段。比如政府出台组织编制的《小街区规制》、先行实施示范片区以及多方参与等。

根据市政府办公厅《关于加快推进“小街区规制”规划建设管理工作的通知》（成办函〔2015〕150 号）和《关于印发成都市中心城区小街区街巷加密成网行动计划的通知》（成办函〔2016〕145 号）要求，由市建委牵头、相关区政府负责、有关市级部门配合，从技术标准和具体项目建设两方面着手开展了相关工作。一是编制并发布了《成都市“小街区规制”规划管理技术规定》、《成都市“小街区规制”规划编制技术导则》和《成都市“小街区规制”建设技术导则》；二是中心城区按照小街区规制划定 100 个街区，启动了 9 个小街区规制示范片区和 18 个小街区规制街区建设工作[14]。

其次，系统性研究。“小街区规制”的建设目标不仅仅是单纯要求街区规模要“小”，其还是一项系统性强、涵盖面广的复杂目标体系。因此，成都建立了一套系统性的研究框架，对涵盖用地、交通、服务设施，以及生态、业态、文态、形态方面的 7 大项 18 小项内容进行了研究[12]。首先高新、天府新、锦江、青羊、金牛、武侯和成华七个片区分区规划小街区的示范片区，并从交通、用地、公服、生态、产业、形态和文态等角度梳理区域问题，确定小街区更新内容。

再次，多方参与。成都市建委召开了推进“小街区规制”建设任务工作会，市规划局、市国土局、市水务局、市交委、市房管局、市城管委等相关政府部门和青羊、锦江、武侯、金牛、成华、高新、天府新区成都直管区等相关区政府、以及四川省建筑设计研究院参加了会议[15]。同时，也借助外力，比如联合国人居署等专家团队。

最后，评估与考核机制。“小街区”从街区尺度、路网密度两个方面对成都现状进行评估，基于此评估，成都市规划设计院绘制成都中心城区街区平均规模分析图（图 2）、成都中心城区规划路网密度分析图（图 3）以及梳理现状问题，如通过评估发现，中心城区内以商业商务功能为主导的片区大多数无法满足“小街区” 的尺度要求；二环路以内以居住功能为主导的片区基本符合“小街区”尺度要求，二环路至绕城高速路段以居住功能为主导的、符合“小街区”尺度要求的片区，由内向外呈圈层递减趋势[12]。同时针对前期分析所提出的问题提出解决思路。

针对“小街区”更新项目，市建委将最终建设成效纳入区相关部门的绩效考核中，考核的

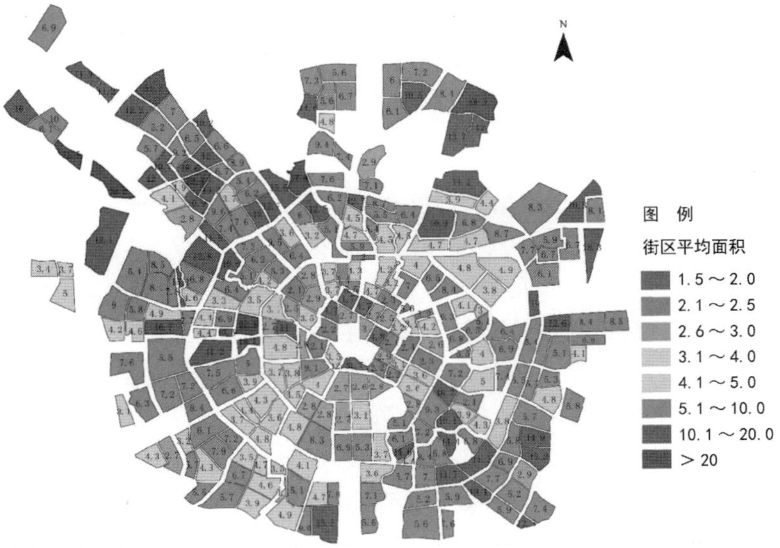

图 2　成都中心城区街区平均规模分析图[12]

图 3　成都中心城区规划路网密度分析图[12]

内容主要是以《导则》技术标准。如 2017 年末，市建委科设处比照《成都市“小街区”规划建设技术导则》技术标准对实施质量效果进行了全面考核[16]对天府新区、高新区、青羊区、武侯区、锦江区、成华区、金牛区 2017 年小街区建设工作开展情况进行了考核。具体考核情况与最终结果暂时未公布在网上。

4　案例分析——少城“小街区”更新项目

4.1　项目概况

鱼骨状路网、街巷尺度，历史格局等这些独特之处让少城区域一直以来都是成都更新建设领域的热点地块。少城片区自2004年的宽窄巷子更新完成开始，且不说其关于保护建筑部分的争议的，但是其以点带面的更新效果是有目共睹的，宽窄巷子向四周延伸的街巷都开始发生转变，从单纯的成都街巷生活转为街巷生活掺有部分文创、艺术空间。与宽窄巷子单纯的商业为主的街巷相比，奎星楼街、小通巷、泡桐树街这些街巷空间高度复杂，充满活力。

表面上，这里看起来缺乏秩序，但这些街道融合了杨·盖尔所说公共空间中的户外活动的三种类型，自发性活动、必要性活动和社会性活动，其背后有一种神奇的秩序在维持着街道的安全与城市的自由。单元门口晒太阳的老人家长里短的摆龙门阵，同时他们也在关注着街道上的每一个人；一些存在十几年的成都风味的美食店老板也早已是街道的一部分，还有不定期的文创活动。这种秩序充满着运动和变化，正如雅各布斯所说，尽管这些是生活，不是艺术，但是若我们发挥想象力，这就是少城街区的“芭蕾舞”。

4.2　项目机制

少城项目的推进过程，实际上已经打破之前的临时更新机制，在更新过程中尝试将参与方都纳入机制中(图4)，比如社区居民、专家、策划、设计等等。这是在成都之前的政府主导的更新项目所未出现的，但是也有一些尚未成熟，比如专家团队的建设、策划与设计方的配合等。

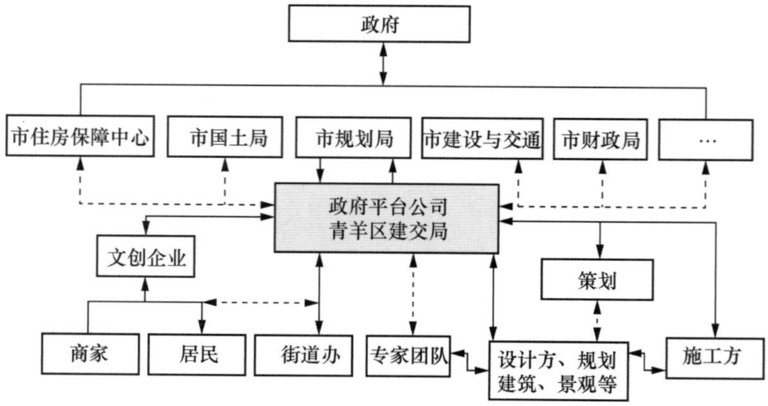

图4　成都少城“小街区”更新机制

(1) 策划

项目的前期策划往往决定项目的成败，因此在项目前期，策划的介入与作用至关重要。在该阶段，首先是基于少城历史人、文、物、地四个方面进行挖掘，承接历史，对应未来，文实相融，落地构建；其次是基于少城现状的分析，如范围、道路、业态等，形成以“四门两广场六街两环”作为区域文态提升的核心内容。最后，政策分析，比如政府意见、发展规划等，提出成都区域更新的思路“传承文化、改善人居、奠定产业”的产城一体。最终提出整改区域的定位“千年老成都，活力新少城”。

（2）规划

基于前期成都市规划设计院对成都市的评估、《导则》这类技术文件与政策，项目前期策划的区域定位，青羊区的少城片区在原有规划基础上进行深化。最终形成成都“小街区规制”示范片区（少城片区）规划图（图 5）与规划实施项目一览表（表 2）。

表 2　　规划实施项目一览表[12]

分类	建设项目	建设内容	投资估算/万元
交通	打通通道	按规划疏通市政道路 3 条（东二道街、上半截街、长富新城东侧道路），长 300 米	500
		在西郊河岸东侧新增 2 条横向车行通道，长 400 米	600
	增强公交服务能力	沿长顺街、同仁路新增 6 个港湾式停靠站	450
	道路断面改造	对小通巷等 11 条街道进行道路断面改造，共计约 4192 米	2100
	地下公共空间	延伸地铁 4 号线宽窄巷子东北角出口至同仁路东侧	800
公服	新增社区养老服务设施、文化活动中心各 1 处	建筑面积共计约 2000 平方米	1200
生态	井巷子改造	建筑面积共计 800 平方米	1000
	增加公园绿地及广场	井巷子增设垂直绿化和创意树池	300
		按原规划落实 9 处公园绿地	1200
		新增位于同仁路的 2 个小型街角公园、广场	400
	打造特色树种街道	桂花巷种植桂花，街道长度约 330 米	15
		长顺街种植银杏树，街道长度约 1450 米	60
	西郊河沿岸改造	东城根街、金河路种植樟树，街道长度约 3000 米	80
产业	新增 6 条特色产业街道	吉祥街、奎星楼街	6000
	明堂 2 期建设	用地面积约 1390 平方米	1000
	鼎鑫地块建设	用地面积约 10500 平方米	1000
	水表厂地块建设	用地面积约 6200 平方米	6000
文态	井巷子增设互动式文化墙	文化墙长度约 178 米	15
	民生里街道景观提升	街道长约 292 米	300
	城门景观	共打造城门景观 4 处（西门、东门、北门、南门）	240
形态	商业街片区立面综合整治	对商业街两侧建筑进行立面整治和底商整治	2800
	部分居住片区立面综合整治	对奎星楼街、小通巷两侧建筑进行立面整治和底商整治	4500

图 5　成都“小街区规制”示范片区（少城片区）规划图[12]

（3）专家

清华同衡规划设计研究院四川分院常务副院长何兵提议组建专家团队的建议（表 3），来解决公众参与、多元化利益兼顾，社会进步和人的多样化、动态化需求。并建议开展基于公共政策制定与实施的城市设计研究工作，提升该项工作的学术价值和可操作性。

表 3　组建专家团队的建议

专家团队	文化产业家	文化学者	历史学家	社会学家	城市设计专家	规划专家	社区规划师
	周莉 于侃	李作民	袁庭栋	罗家德	何兵	袁牧	刘佳燕

注：这只是最初的建议稿，此处作为思路的参考。

来源：根据何兵副院长建议书所绘

青羊区政府与联合国人居署合作开展少城片区有机更新项目，并前后有过3次实地调研，结合《新城市议程》《公共空间手册》等城市与区域规划国际准则，对少城片区城市有机更新和规划导则提出系统性意见建议。

（4）设计方

当策划、规划都确定，最终落实到城市空间中可观的部分则是城市空间设计方案。然而，由于项目前期并未形成引导后期空间设计的成果，设计方在进行方案设计的过程中比较被动。同时，设计方还需考虑资金、建筑现状、居民情况等多方问题进行方案设计。

4.3 小结

首先，项目前期的策划、规划过程并未形成结论与任务书，与实施阶段并不存在较多的协同。因此项目前期策划与规划阶段对实施阶段的指导性不强，导致规划与策划落地性不高。其次，在少城“小街区”实施过程中，实施阶段的牵头方与前期的牵头方存在一定变动。因此项目在实施过程中就变成两个牵头单位和两个设计单位，且设计范围、内容都重复，虽大的设计方向一致，但对于小空间的处理还是有一定的差异。最后，此次方案设计并未涉及居民居住空间的优化和调整，同时，对底部商业的处理也是依据现有的商业业态进行考虑，并未以项目前期策划阶段的业态调整为依据，不具备长远性。

5 创新机制——“1+N”机制

5.1 “1+N”的模式的基本概念

协同理念最早出现在管理学领域，如美国管理学家伊戈·安索夫提出，在项目管理、运营、投资等环节通过合理组织，可以有效地分配生产要素和环境资源等条件，形成资源互补，达成1+1>2的协同效应。在城市更新项目中，项目的进展情况往往都是“1+1+1+1+1+…<1”，而不能真正实现协同效应。由于城市更新项目的持续时间较长，并涉及各类型的利益相关者利益[17]。因此，基于更新项目的复杂性，更新模式不应局限于简单的“1+1”式的协同方式，而更应该是基于不同的项目阶段、项目目标等来调整协同方式与对象。“1+N”模式就是综合所有资源，不同阶段进行不同的资源配置，通过统筹资源，达到最优的城市活力。

5.1.1 固定值——“1”

前文所述的项目中，不管是政府主导还是开发商主导，这个主导方的如果是利益相关者，很难出现大公无私的情况，因此在“1+ N”的协同模式中，根据不同项目及项目的不同阶段，其“1”所代表的是应该是类似于城市更新局或更加中立的平台，应具有专业知识背景，对城市更新理论具有一定的基础，对项目的认知与定位准确，并能够辅助或实行决策，把握整体方向。

5.1.2 可变值——“N”

由于项目的每个阶段都有不同的关键实施者，在适当的时间建立适当的组织结构对项目的成功实现是至关重要的[18]。不同的阶段，参与方不同，同一参与方的角色也有可能发生变化。

表 4　　前期阶段参与者

前期阶段	经济		文化			社会		环境			
	区域经济学家	社区经济学家	文化产业家	文化学者	历史学家	社会学家	居民代表	城市设计专家	规划专家	社区规划师	建筑策划师

注：项目前期主要是项目立项决策部分，因此参与的多数为专家、教授级高工或者资深从业者。

表 4 所示的是项目前期验证阶段，主要分为经济、文化、社会和环境四个方面所需要参与的专家，在这个部分则还包含数据收集，为进行项目立项决策时提供充分的数据支撑。只有通过科学的决策，项目的根基才会扎实，多方利益群体都能接受的项目方案才能够真正得到推进与实施。因此，这个阶段所形成的文件及最终决策是项目推进的基础，同时也指导下一步项目方案的设计和实施。

在项目前期阶段，项目决策是至关重要的，如何避免决策失误是小街区机制中的重要环节。为了处理这种复杂的决策过程，多准则决策（MCDA）方法和工具已经开发了越来越多的应用在不同的领域，其优先次序工具是基于可持续发展框架，同时 MCDA 也允许从不同的观点来评估，尊重多元利益相关者的需求[18]。

表 5　　实施阶段参与者

实施阶段	规划			建筑			市政			景观	社区		…
	规划师	交通设计师	街区规划师	建筑策划师	建筑设计师	结构师	工业设计师	电力工程师	给排水工程师	景观设计师	居民代表	社区管委会	…

注：阶段二参与的大多为主任项目设计师或项目设计师、工程师等实际操作级别人员。

表 5 所示的是项目实施阶段的参与方，主要是涉及规划、建筑、市政、景观、社区等。基于项目前期的定位、场地基础数据及项目初步概念方案等决策文件，实施阶段主要是将概念方案深化设计、现场调解及空间实施，较多会集中在城市实体空间中的问题，整体设计的尺度由大转小。

表 6　　评估阶段的对象

评估阶段	经济		文化			社会		环境				…
	区域 GDP 增长率	人均 GDP 增长率	文化产业增加值	文化娱乐生活质量	历史文化保护建筑的数量	人均住房使用面积	居住质量（问卷调查）	容积率	建筑高差比数值	建筑平均密度	开敞空间面积	…

注：由于阶段三的对象发生变化，不再是以人为对象，而是以空间及社会为对象。

“小街区”更新思路与可持续发展的城市发展思路是一致的，因此评估阶段可持续发展也应属于评估中的部分。

5.2　“1＋N”模式与小街区更新机制的协同

通过对少城区域“小街区”更新过程中所出现协同问题的思考，“小街区规制”是以缓慢、渐近式的理念来应对复杂的城市更新，这就要求相对应的管理机制能够承担和协调好其复杂性。如图6所示。虚线大框内的是不可变的元素，是中国的政府机构组成图示，而虚线框之外的则是属于可以建立和改变的。不变的元素与可变的元素之间的衔接和协调正是符合中国特色的“小街区”思路，同时，也可以解决项目可持续性和远瞻性考虑的问题。

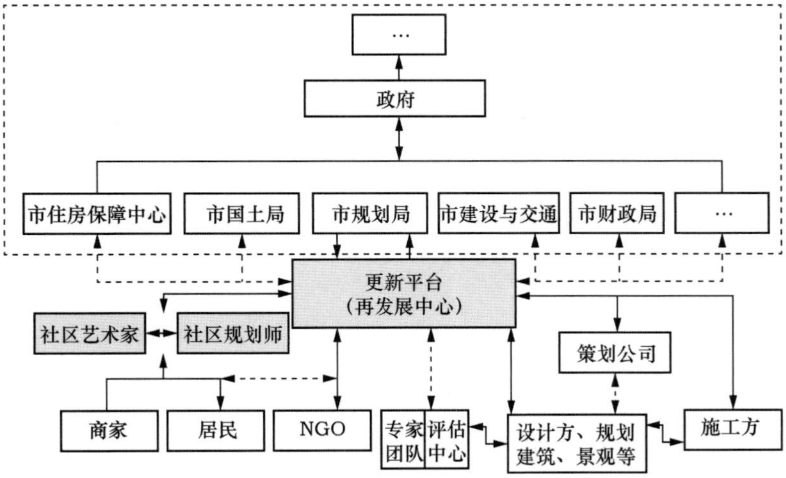

图6 “1＋N”更新机制框架

5.3 小结

“1＋N”的协同模式还尚未完善，“1”的领头非常重要，倡议成立“城市更新局”或其他统一协同的平台，一手抓，一手硬；其次则是建立相关的制度，“小街区规制”的建立已经开端，不断探索相关制度来为“小街区”更新保驾护航。“N”的灵活调整也是这个模式的特色之一，“N”方的设计、参与、实施、调整等正是权衡多方利益和优势。街道更新如果没有经济、政治、社区上的支持，更新将仅仅是一时而已。

6 更新之后

对于这次成都市少城片区的“小街区”实践，虽然只是初步试行，当中存在很多的不足与问题，但是其传递的协同意识、建筑和街道的尺度以及街区内在的运转机制是在之前项目中未出现的。这些都说明成都的城市更新不再是大拆大建，而是开始注重自身的条件与问题；不是一味地效仿，而是从内里出发，找回本质。同时也意识到少城片区的“芭蕾”并非是某个设计师的杰作，也不是在短时间内形成，而是在城市历史潮流中逐步层层叠加而成的。城市的活力取决于居民二十四小时的日常生活，也就是这些小街小巷才能够孕育出街道生活复杂性和自发性。

对于城市街区而言，前面所述的是城市更新的一个部分，还有一个很重要的部分就是更新之后的问题，这是一个值得思考的问题。虽然在更新的前部分，还有很多需要探讨，但对于城市而言，没有对更新之后的关注将会带来很多社会隐患。因此，后更新机制（post-regeneration）的考虑也应该在项目过程中逐渐形成。这样才能够让街区在政府或者更新平台撤出之后，能够启动自我循环。

作者简介

谭露露，成都市建筑设计研究院工程师。

参考文献

[1] 尼克斯·A·萨林加罗斯. 城市结构原理[M]. 阳建强，程佳佳，等译. 北京：中国建筑工业出版社，2011：14.

[2] 安德森. 美国联邦城市更新计划(1949—1962 年)[M]. 吴浩军，译. 北京：中国建筑工业出版社，2011：125-126.

[3] 中华人民共和国中央人民政府. 中共中央国务院关于进一步加强城市规划建设管理工作的若干意见[R]. 北京，2016.

[4] 王娟. 房地产档案开发与利用的现状——以成都市历史房产档案为例[J]. 档案时空，2013(12)：34.

[5] 成都规划公众平台. 围绕建设国家中心城市：全面推进新一轮城市总体规划修编工作[R]. 成都，2017.

[6] 中国人民共和国住房和城乡建设部. 第三次联合国住房和城市可持续发展大会(人居三)中国国家报告[R]. 北京，2015.

[7] 安德森. 美国联邦城市更新计划(1949—1962 年)[M]. 吴浩军，译. 北京：中国建筑工业出版社，2011：125-126.

[8] 亚历山大·加文. 规划博弈-从四座伟大城市理解城市规划[M]. 曹海军，等译. 北京：北京时代华文书局，2015(2)：40.

[9] 杨瑞. 成都城市更新管理机制研究——与深圳比较的启示[D]. 北京：清华大学，2013：23.

[10] LENNERTZ B, LUTZENHISER A. The Charrette Handbook[M]. Chicago: American Planning Association, 2006.

[11] 成都市城乡建设委员会. 成都市小街区规制规划管理技术规定[R]. 成都，2017.

[12] 沈莉芳，陈诚. 小街区规制——街区制的成都实践[J]. 规划师，2017(7)：26-30.

[13] 万艳芳. 向度与选择——旧城更新目标新论[J]. 城市发展研究，2010(7)：103.

[14] 成都市城乡建设委员会. 成都市城乡建设委员会关于《关于进一步优化小街区规制有机更新中心城区的建议》答复的函[R]. 成都，2017.

[15] 成都市城乡建设委员会. 市建委召开推进小街区规制建设任务工作会[R]. 成都，2016.

[16] 成都市城乡建设委员会. 市建委开展小街区建设情况考核工作[R]. 成都，2017.

[17] 王廷魁，邓兢兢. 城市更新项目方案决策专家系统框架研究[J]. 城市发展研究，2010(7)：103.

[18] Nogués S, ARROYO N L. Alternative Approach to Prioritization of Brownfield Reclamation Attending to Urban Development Potentialities: Case Study in a Depressed Industrial District Northern Spain[J]. Journal of Urban Planning and Development, 2016, 142(1).

协同机制下的大城市副中心演进策略研究

——以上海江湾-五角场副中心为例

刘　琦　邹昊阳

摘　要　大城市规模随着城市化进程的推进而扩张迅速，大城市副中心纷纷由“卫星城”向“城市圈”概念转变，在职能上也逐步脱离旧有的“商务核心区”职能而表现为复合度更高的“次级城市中心”职能。本文将大城市副中心作为协同学研究中的复杂系统对象，以上海五角场副中心为例，从经济、文化、环境、社会四个子系统研究其在协同机制下的演进策略，以期对国内大城市副中心的协同演进方法作出一定启示。

关键词　协同机制；大城市；副中心；演进；上海江湾-五角场

Researches on Development Strategies of Metropolitan Sub-CBD under Coordination Mechanism — Taking the Case of Jiangwan - Wujiaochang, Shanghai

Liu Qi　Zou Haoyang

Abstract　Large cities expand rapidly along with the urbanization steps, and the concept of Metropolitan sub-CBDs transform from “Satellite City” to “City Circle”, meanwhile their new functions of “secondary city center” has higher composite than “Central Business District”. This paper takes Metropolitan sub-CBD as complex systems in synergetics, discuss their development strategies in four subsystems of economics, cultural, environment, society under coordination mechanism, in the hope of providing enlightenment for the co-evolution methods of Metropolitan sub-CBD in our country.

Keywords　coordination mechanism; metropolis; Sub-CBD; development; Wujiaochang Shanghai

1　我国大城市副中心发展的基本问题

1.1　大城市副中心：从 Sub-CBD 到 Sub-City Center

城市副中心最初以“Sub-CBD——次级商务中心区”的概念出现：随着 20 世纪后期西方大城市中心区有限资源所承载的人口、交通、环境、产业负荷加剧，城市的人口和生产要素由中心区外溢而形成既有核心之外的新的城市核心点，这种核心点的形成带有大城市在规模扩张初期明显的区域职能诉求特征，即以商业和商务城市职能为主，作为对“CBD——中央商务区”的呼应和补充。伦敦的金丝雀码头、多伦多滨湖区等区域的建设都是大城市在这一时期发展的典型城市副中心区域，它们的建成有赖于交通、通信等社会技术环境的提升，其规划建设的目的重在“运用经济杠杆疏散城市中心地区的部分商业、商务功能，培育新的城市经济增长极”，从而以经济为出发点带动城市空间结构在文化、制度、生态等各方面的优化过程。

伴随国内外大城市在规模上的逐步扩张，大城市的空间格局从“单核”到“多核”的发展模式转变为由“单一化”到“网络化”的整体框架。城市副中心不再局限于“Sub-CBD”所表达的商务核心职能区域概念，而是部分地表现为“Sub-City Center——次级城市中心”的概念范畴。新的城市副中心理念是大城市由扩张初期逐渐进入发展成熟期的体现，指大型城市体系中能够局部分担或代替城市中心区所承担的城市发展核心效能的周边区域。次级城市中心与早期的次级商务中心区相比，前者在职能构成上更加趋向复合且更强调区域的独立城市导向，在不过分依赖中心城区的资源和服务的同时对趋向中心的人口流向起到截留作用。新型大城市副中心区域部分形成于既有副中心的演进更新，另一部分是政府基于当前的区域发展形势所作出的规划设计与政策引导下的结果。因此，这种大城市副中心在定义上带有行政区划中城镇体系的概念倾向，对其形成与发展的关注也是以多层次网络化的空间结构形态解决大城市由于规模扩张所引发的城市问题的合理途径，巴黎拉德芳斯副中心、上海嘉定新城等区域均属这一类型的大城市副中心。

1.2 我国大城市副中心更新的特征及主要问题：“蓝图式”模式的终结

大城市副中心的形成产生于快速的城市化进程为单核的城市中心区带来的压力，而其演进的过程则与区域自身的地理条件、文化基础、资源优势等要素关系紧密，也是政府、市场和社会三重系统共同作用下产生的结果。在这一涉及多方利益相关者的区域更新过程中，对公众参与度在更新机制中引入的关注有利于寻找到复杂过程中多方利益者的平衡点。当前我国的大城市副中心规划过程，仍然更多倾向于传统的以政府政策为主导的终极“蓝图式”发展模式。这种模式下所进行的城市副中心物质空间与非物质空间自我调适带有很大的被动意味，与多方主体的多元化利益诉求相违背。核心区域更新的问题终究是一个“不破不立”的城市命题，脱离既有更新机制中政府作为单一主体定制愿景的“蓝图式”模式，是解决当前大城市副中心发展中职能复合度较低、空间格局不完善、地域文化缺失等一系列问题的“破”之契机与“立”之伊始。

区域职能的复合度是影响大城市副中心演进更新的关键要素，复合度上的不足会为副中心区域发展带来交通、人口、产业、环境等各方面的问题。首先，副中心在城市职能与功能构成上的单一化直接导致交通压力的增大和核心辐射力度的降低。对单一场所建立的片面重视所导致的通勤距离增加直接加大了城市系统的交通成本，同时也使区域核心由于资源配置多样性的不足而在对周边的辐射影响上有所缺乏。金丝雀码头在功能复合性方面的发展是较为成功的案例，从1980年开始的泰晤士河两岸改造中的单一职能开发到2005年的商务、商业、居住一体化综合环境的形成，金丝雀码头在空间复合化更新上的探索过程值得借鉴。其次，由于副中心区复合程度的提升直接作用于内部人居环境的正向塑造，因此也对是否能够形成以人才流入为导向的合理化人口结构亦具有决定性的影响效应。

此外，我国大城市副中心在当前的功能转型、人口增长、资源约束、技术革新的大环境下，还面临着与动态环境因素相关联的诸多问题：大城市副中心区域仍然无法适应新的城市圈概念下的演进模式，中心城与周边层次不够明晰的连绵发展态势仍未得到有效遏制；区域内的产业结构与服务业能级有待提高，目前普遍规模较大的产业用地的集中布局与能效提高问题未得到解决；大城市副中心在注重经济增长的同时部分生态空间品质已接近城市安全底线，大而无当的负面公共空间品质提升仍是打造高质量人居环境的过程中需要直面的问题。因此，以复合化、网络化及多元化的视角应对城市核心区域发展问题，是通过对大城市副中心建设的完善实现城市总体精明增长的未来趋势。

2　城市副中心发展中的协同作用

在国内外大城市对副中心的定位纷纷脱离“卫星城”而转向“城市圈”概念导向的今天，大城市副中心在承担城市宏观共同体系构成要素职能的同时其自身的复杂性共同体特征也愈加明显。对这一独立区域的共同体来讲，其内部各部分既互相依存又是一系列竞争的个体。在副中心的发展过程中，利益的分化导致系统的失衡，为修正这种失衡需要引入与多元利益方相关的协同机制来对其系统变迁进行引导和控制。

2.1　协同机制的理论基础

协同学作为一门研究不同系统结构从无序到有序转变发生中的机理与条件的学科，对于大城市副中心区域演进更新的协同机制的形成具有理论支撑的基础性作用，因其学科特征即“用协同的视角研究系统的存在形式、运作机制和演化机制”[1]与城市区域系统中客观存在的协同研究需求是相一致的。在协同学理论下，城市副中心遵循远离平衡状态的开放系统由旧结构向新结构转换的一般规律，有序结构的获得有赖于内部子系统的协同作用。何明俊将系统与其内部参序量的关系总结为：“表征系统宏观行为有序化程度的参量为序参量，系统的结构变迁取决于系统的序参量……当序参量到达临界点时，系统的宏观形态出现有序的结构。”[2]。

2.2　城市副中心的复杂系统

协同学研究的复杂系统具有整体性、动态性、微观导致宏观变化、确定性与随机性结合四个特征，大城市副中心作为由社会、经济、文化、生态、制度等多层面复合因素构成的整体而具有协同学研究对象的相同特征，因此可采用协同学中对复杂系统的分析方法，从对区域内部要素间的相互作用关系上把握这一复杂的自适应系统的规律。

大城市副中心系统中的子系统与其发展过程中牵涉的客观因素相关，主要包括经济子系统、文化子系统、环境子系统和社会子系统。基于前文对复杂系统中序参量的表述，大城市副中心系统中每一子系统的序参量对系统变迁起到决定性作用，其中经济子系统的主要序参量是区域内产业能效、文化子系统的主要序参量是文化传承力与创新力、环境子系统的主要序参量是人居生态环境品质、社会子系统的主要序参量是多元利益维系。对于副中心区域系统整体而言，作为城市系统中划分出的相对独立的共同体单元，其主要的序参量则是区域的可持续性(图 1)。

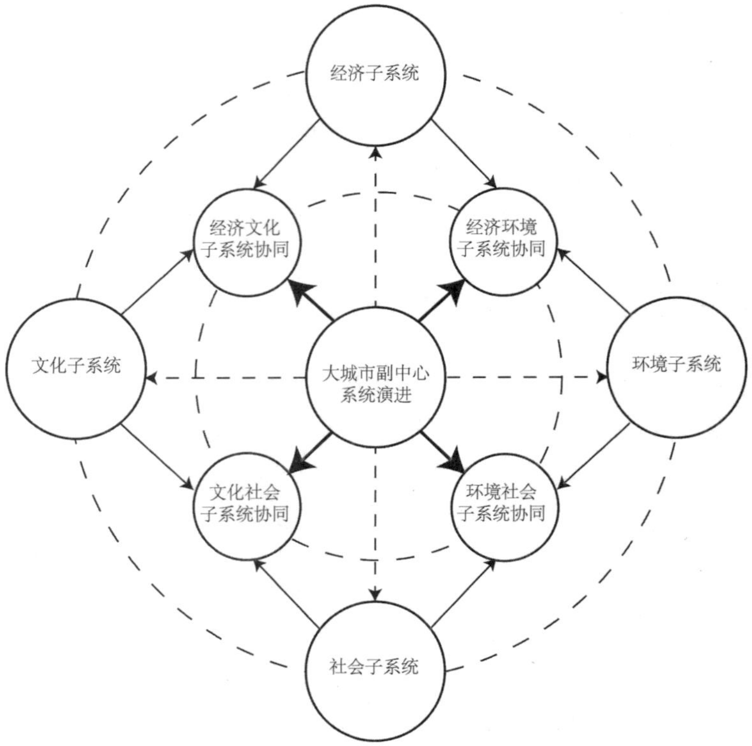

图 1　大城市副中心子系统协同演进图示

3　上海城市副中心的协同性演进更新策略

3.1　大城市副中心系统演进的协同机制

大城市副中心区域在协同机制作用下更新发展的最终目标是通过经济、文化、环境、社会各子系统在发展过程中所发生的协同作用，将资源进行最大化的有效利用，实现以土地资源利用为核心的系统整体结构有序性提升。这一目标的实现由微观到宏观分为两个过程阶段，即各个子系统内的协同性提升和子系统之间相互作用而达成的区域整体协同性提升。在具体方法上，需要针对每一子系统的实际状况和序参量制定适合该区域对象的子系统演进模式，将各子系统相对独立的利益制约关系转化成更为协作的、有机的、系统的构成关系。

3.2　上海五角场副中心的协同更新策略研究

上海五角场分区位于上海的东北角，最初规划自 1985 年开始，当时的分区范围东起黄浦江，西至逸仙路，北至闸北电厂，南临虬江、走马塘；总面积 23.8 平方千米。[3]《上海城市中体规划(1999—2020 年)》中明确提出将五角场作为上海“一主四副”的四个副中心之一，南至邯郸路-翔殷路，东至国和路-政立路-国京路(科技大道)-民京路，北至殷高路，西至国定路-政通路-国宾路，总用地面积为 2.29 平方千米。

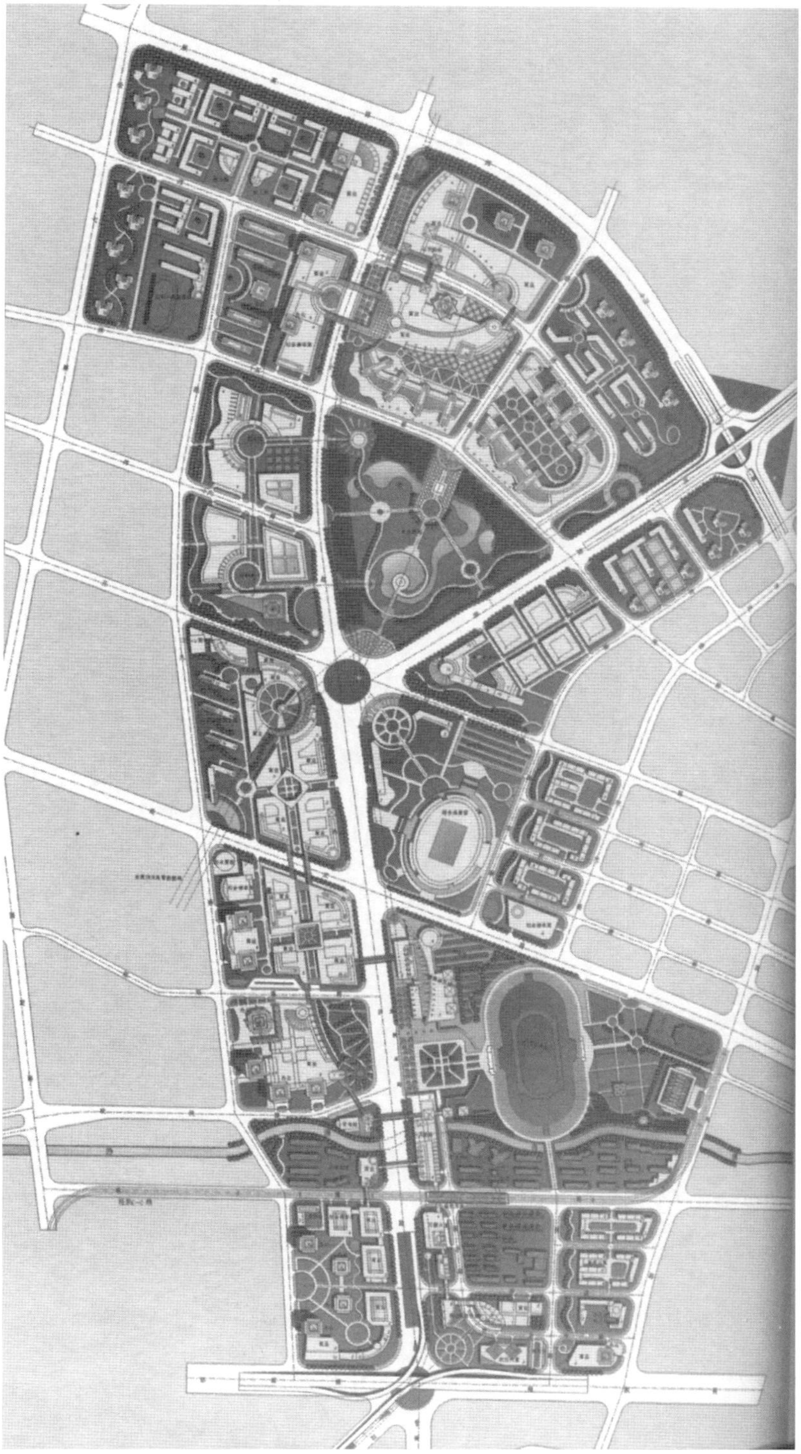

来源：上海市城市规划设计研究院，《循迹·启新：上海城市规划演进》

图 2　1998 年五角场副中心详细规划

来源：肖玲，易伟忠，《江湾-五角场城市副中心交通规划》

图3 五角场后期交通规划图

3.2.1 经济子系统：高新技术与体验经济一体化模式

从该副中心经济子系统的主要序参量产业能效方面分析，五角场副中心的产业结构发展与其“知识创新特色区”的定位关系紧密。在以五角场作为中心且以四平路和翔殷路为边界趋向北侧的不足4千米半径范围内的扇形区域中，分布有同济大学、复旦大学、上海财经大学、第二军医大学等高等院校，为五角场副中心区域的知识服务相关产业结构的设置奠定资源基础。[4]回顾其发展历程，五角场副中心所在的杨浦区曾是上海工业发源地之一，其1986年的工业总产值曾占全市的20%；而今天发展迅速的五角场商圈在很长时间内交通枢纽的城市职能远大于商业中心所起到的产业效应，“环岛商业”一度经营惨淡。在以产业能效为推动地区发展的主要序参量情况下，这一区域的产业结构优化框架存在着以知识服务业接续替代旧有工业商业的总体趋向，这一角度下土地更新利用模式与产业结构优化的方向相一致。近年日趋完善的创智天地街区已具备良好的示范效应，正在投入建设的腾讯众创空间、复旦管院、上海财经大学科技金融谷项目亦以教育服务与科技服务的产业特点成为提升五角场副中心经济子系统产能效应的重要因素。为进一步提升区域内产能效应，应以当下及未来的社会技术环境和科技理论背景为参照，在创智天地核心区域增设以高校为依托的人工智能、云计算创新产业基地，使之与既有的传统教育科技行业互为补充。同时，应在国定东路创新创业街区内部密集度与复合度达到一定标准后将其进行适当延伸，使其与五角场商圈形成交互融合的过渡带(图4)。在传统商业模式遭到网络信息技术冲击而走向衰落的时代背景下，五角场副中心的核心商业必将与周边的教育科技产业相结合，走向与科技基础密不可分的以体验经济和共享经济为核心的新型商业模式。对于向新型商业模式转型以摆脱时代困境的土地利用方式的改变上，五角场商圈具有区域性高新科技产业的技术支撑优势。在确定了以整体性思路融合五角场副中心知识服务产业与商业的土地更新模式策略下，如何有效利用教育科技产业的技术平台，激发本身带有一定非生产性特征的体验商业与共享商业的高增进性，并使二者合理协作并互为激励要素，是值得我们进一步关注的问题(图5)。

3.2.2 文化子系统：历时性多核心网络模式

文化子系统在一定程度上代表了区域的非正式制度，包含了副中心区域中的惯例、规则、风俗、历史以及长期以来形成的集体性价值认同体系，其重要的序参量是文化传承力与创新力。“五角场”的历史得名来自1923—1930年五条向心性辐射城市干道的修筑，曾在《大上海计划》制定期间因上海中心地带沦为租界而一度被归至上海东北隅新的核心区域建设中。[5]尽管这一计划随着租界的收回而夭折，在计划期间所建设的市府大厦(现属上海体育学院)、博物馆(现长海医院影像楼)、飞机楼(现上海第二军医大学校史馆)、图书馆(现改造中杨浦区图书馆)、三十六宅、江湾体育场等建筑以及包括三门路在内的核心区部分路网均为具有重要文化价值的历史遗存，也是构成区域历史文化继承体系的重要近代元素(图6—图9)。

对于大城市副中心文化子系统而言，区域文化环境的传承与创新同等重要。在五角场副中心以知识创新为核心的文化创新背景下，应当选择继承与创新相结合的多核心网络模式构建副中心的文化子系统。这里的多核心并非是以机械地将物质遗存以景点的形式开发保留，而是在空间关系上建立历史脉络与文化创新之间相互激发的网络关系，这一过程意味着多样化、历时性和交互性。文化子系统与经济子系统在演进过程中关系密切，区域产业结

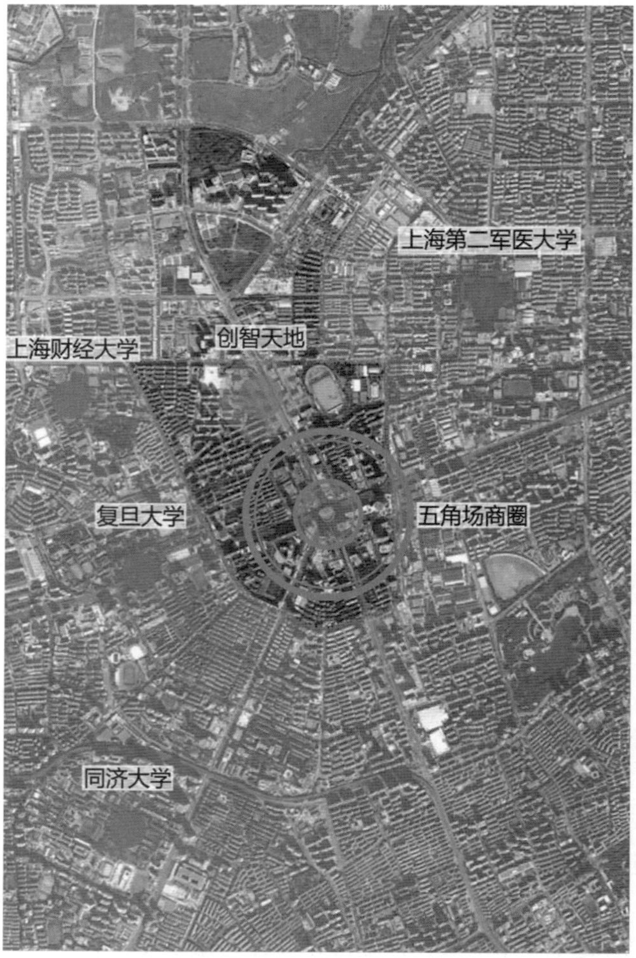

图 4　江湾-五角场副中心的经济子系统网络要素

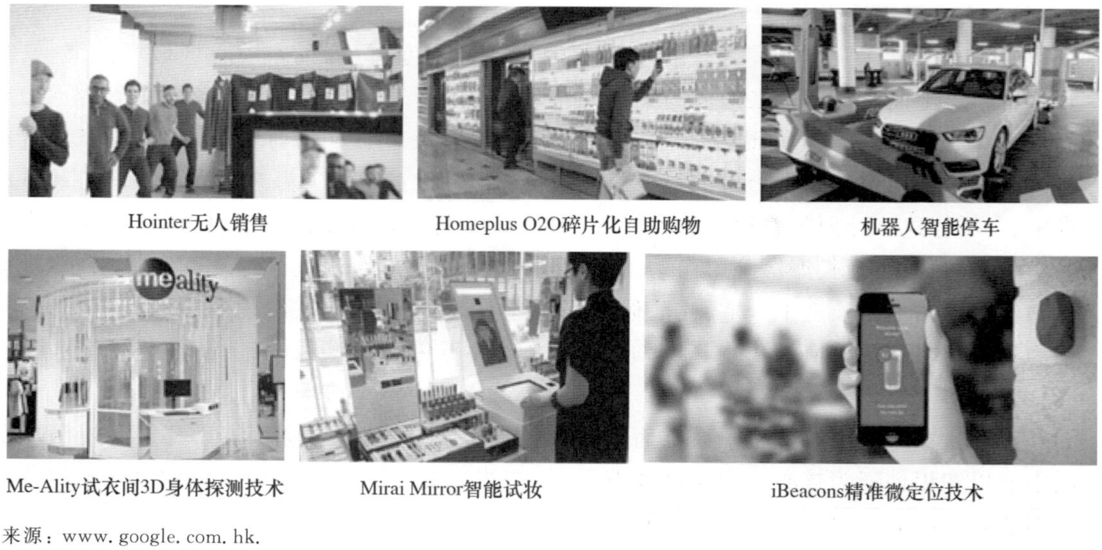

来源：www. google. com. hk.

图 5　以高新科技为依托的商业模式转型

图 6　旧市立图书馆现状

图 7　旧市立博物馆现状

图 8　旧上海市府大楼现状

图 9　旧飞机楼现状

构的发展需要一个以根植性为特点的制度环境，而文化环境正是这种根植性的基础所在。在五角场副中心内，以创智天地为代表的教育与创新产业提供了产生新产品和工艺的资源，但产业内交易行为的良性发展还需要环境中“非交易性的相互依赖”的存在，正是高度共享的文化价值观促进了“依赖性”与“根植性”的产生。因此，以历时性多核心网络模式优化五角场副中心的文化子系统结构是面对区域现状条件得出的对策，是从物质与精神双重层面对文化继承力与创新力这一序参量上升的积极引导，也是文化与经济子系统协同更新的必经路径。

3.2.3　环境子系统：多层次生态恢复模式

城市化水平较高的五角场副中心环境子系统所需面对的主要问题是生态退化和非生物环境降质所引起的系统内部无序，对系统脱离无序状态而向有序转化的序参量是人居生态环境品质，这与城市中以人作为环境质量主体的考量标准是分不开的。

五角场副中心及周边区域在 20 世纪 60 年代前属于宝山县管辖范围，当时的农田农地构成区域主要景观，与黄浦江相连通的多条河流交织纵横[6]，形成品质较高的生态网络。这一地区的城市化于 20 世纪 90 年代基本完成，目前的五角场副中心内生态环境较为优质的是位于东北角的新江湾城生态展示馆周边区域。除殷高东路附近外，主要绿地仅存于复旦校园、黄兴公园、江湾体育场及小区的公共空间中，绿化系统与建筑设施的建设节奏相比发展相对滞后，频繁的人为活动所引发的空气污染、噪声污染、水质下降、土壤板结等问题并未得到及时的解决(图 10)。对于环境子系统中人居生态环境品质这一序参量的提升，可以分两个层次逐步进行。首先是对大气环境、水环境、声环境等可感知要素的调整，将绿化系统的覆盖率、分布、结构及功能进行完善，结合景观配置形成宜居的人居生态环境体系。第二层次是对生态可持续性的实现，改变现代城市生活中“高能耗”“非循环”的负向环境运行机制，实现城市社会、经济、人口与资源的深层协调。针对五角场副中心在城市化进程中生态环境的变迁状况，环境子系统的提升可以选择多层次生态恢复模式进行实现。“多层次”既指人工、半人工、自然的多途径恢复层次，也指区域、街道、建筑的多尺度恢复层次。五角场核心区域东南侧的黄兴绿地、东北侧的共青森林公园以及北侧的江湾城生态绿地区均为重要的大型绿地，品质较高的周边点状区域共同对区域中心发生辐射作用形成覆盖区域的面状范围，以横贯该副中心区域的虬江水系作为线状的串联轴线，完成由街区层面到邻里层面的立体化生态恢复网络，实现这一区域在环境优良的初始时期与生态有待恢复的城市化时期的融合与对话。

1980年代江湾－五角场生态旧貌

江湾－五角场生态现状

来源：www. google. com. hk.

图 10　江湾-五角场 1980 年生态状况与现状对比图

3.2.4　社会子系统：公共开放空间嵌入模式

社会子系统的主要序参量是社会利益的维系，社会利益维系将大城市副中心社会子系统中的社会群体及其利益诉求以及相关的社会心理、制度、文化等因素融汇结合。其中“社会利益”所具有的“公众对促进社会发展和进步、维护社会稳定方面的需要”。[7] 内涵，也反映出社会子系统在公众心理需求方面与经济、文化、环境子系统的协同特性，即城市副中心更新相关机制制定的本质在于多元利益相关者的平衡与共赢。

在对五角场副中心更新过程中的多利益方的综合考虑中，公共性始终是最值得关注的要点。对副中心区域基础设施的策略性控制方面，在既有的空间架构中嵌入“促进剂”作用的公共空间元素，是一种尊重既有环境的渐进式更新方式。而对公共空间体系的建设和更新，也最符合城市更新中最多方利益相关者的利益诉求。公共空间嵌入方式包括点状、线状与环状，最终目标是与其他子系统共同联结形成有机体系。例如，对“大上海计划”时期上海政府旧址的保护性修复与公共性开发，是以点状的公共空间触媒激发与之相连的线性可达公共空间网络。这一公共空间嵌入设计中所涉及的历史建筑与当前状态下所属的学校、医院等利益方的经济效益、对历史遗存所持有不同利用态度而引发的文化效应以及开发利用中对政府旧址周边环境系统的改变，都需要提高公众在这一过程中的参与度来获得最大程度的利益平衡（图 11）。除置入点状空间外，线性公共空间如景观廊道、滨水步道、视线通廊等，环状公共空间如环区域慢行系统、环区自行车与公交系统等，这些被嵌入的空间可以是市政设施的，也可以是建筑物、构筑物的。例如，鉴于与环境子系统的协同作用，我们可以考虑通过人工湿地等方式对五角场副中心原有河流风貌进行适当恢复，结合东走马塘在现有的东西向虬江水系基础上丰富水系网络，以矢量线性空间的嵌入带动区域公共空间体系的完善（图 12）。以河道为依托的公共空间更新案例如布法罗河口、莱茵河等，均获得较好效果（图 13）。

来源：作者根据谷歌地图自绘

图 11　江湾-五角场副中心的社会子系统网络要素

图 12　虹江沿岸空间现状

来源：http：design. cila. cn.

图 13　法布罗河口的公共空间嵌入

3.2.5　系统整体提升：循环经济模式

对于复杂系统，各子系统的低层级序参量可以经由进一步的协同合作产生控制和决定系统整体有序进化的新的、更高层级的序参量。本文经过研究认为，区域的可持续性包含了经济子系统中的区域内产业能效、文化子系统中的文化传承力与创新力、环境子系统中的人居生态环境品质、社会子系统中的多元利益维系，可以作为系统整体的序参量。

为提升区域可持续性这一系统整体序参量值，可以采取发展循环经济的城市区域策略。从概念上讲，循环经济是以提高资源和环境效率为目标、以物质循环和资源节约为方法的一种经济模式，这种模式的运作与科技创新基础和市场机制推动密不可分，所获得的结果是在满足城市化进程推进需求的前提下使资源利用率达到最大化和环境污染破坏的最小化。发展循环经济视角下的具体的开发方式包括开发生态产业园区、生态文化旅游区、公园体验式商业等。

4　结语

大城市副中心的演进是其内部子系统不断协同的过程，当子系统序参量起主导作用时，系统的演化方向则是从无序到有序的。这种协同既有一般开放性物质系统发展特征，也与人类特有的感知方式和心理诉求休戚相关。在协同机制下发展的大城市副中心，不仅能获得有序的城市结构，还可以获得真正有机的、协调的空间利益结构，最终通过副中心区域的系统性精明增长带动大型城市的整体提升。

作者简介

刘琦，同济大学建筑设计研究院（集团）有限公司助理级工程师，建筑学硕士。

邹昊阳，同济大学建筑设计研究院（集团）有限公司助理级工程师，建筑学学士。

参考文献

[1] 曹堂哲. 公共行政执行协同机制研究的协同学途径——理论合理性和多学科基础[J]. 中共浙江省委党校学报，2009(1).

[2] 何明俊. 城市规划协同机制中的公共协商[J]. 规划师，2013(16).

[3] 上海市城市规划研究院. 循迹、启新：上海城市规划演进[M]. 上海：同济大学出版社，2007.

[4] 冯身洪. 知识服务中心——五角场地区产业发展定位初探[J]. 上海综合经济，2002(05).

[5] 陈秉钊，范军勇. 尊重历史、挖掘历史——上海五角场地区历史文化资源整合规划[J]. 城市规划学刊，2005(3).

[6] 唐仕敏，唐礼俊，李惠敏. 城市化对上海市五角场地区鸟类群落的影响[J]. 上海环境科学，2003(6).

[7] 操小娟. 土地利用中利益衡平的法律问题研究[M]. 北京：人民出版社，2006.

遗产保护与社区治理

社会价值和城市遗产的原真性:来自中国的视角①

普拉西多·冈萨雷斯·马丁内斯

摘　要　过去四十年中,中国城市在全球城市之间展开了激烈的竞争。政策制定者和规划者的目标很明确:把自己定位为投资的吸引者和文化、社会和经济发展的促进者。当代城市历史学家强调,中国城市的快速经济发展和城市建设使其失去了原本的空间结构。与此同时,大规模的拆除更凸显了城市遗产认定之于当代中国全球城市的重要性。传统城市已不再被遗忘在历史中,而被置于微妙而深刻的转变中。由此,文章围绕中国传统城市的原真性,从理论角度提出了两个主要问题:

在全球城市中,当代城市原真性的理论基础是什么,以及它们如何与中国的遗产的社会价值相关联?

中国经济发展与遗产保护合流的情况下,以经验为基础的原真性的后果是什么?

本文根据中国目前最具影响力的全球城市的更新实践之一——上海虹口区来研究这一理论问题。通过展示关于这个城市历史区域的案例研究,推进城市原真性的定义,并对产生于其中的新身份进行描述。

关键词　原真性;建成遗产;遗产的社会价值;上海的遗产;中国的遗产

Social Values and Urban Heritage Authenticity: A Perspective from China

Placido Gonzalez Martinez

Abstract　Chinese cities have entered a fierce competition in the four last decades between global cities. The aim of policy makers and planners is clear: to position themselves as attractors of investment and generators of cultural, social and economic development.

Contemporary urban historians have highlighted how economic development has meant the loss of an important share of urban fabric in Chinese cities. At the same time, extensive destruction has meant the confirmation of the heritage city as one of the main layers of contemporary Chinese global cities.

The heritage city has been is no longer set aside from the course of history, but is yet subject to subtle, profound transformations. This raises two main questions around the authenticity of the Chinese heritage city that this contribution proposes to address from a theoretical perspective:

- What are the theoretical fundaments of a contemporary urban authenticity in the Global City, and how do they relate to the social value of heritage in China?

① 本文根据马丁内斯教授在2017"城市与社会"国际学术论坛上的发言整理、翻译,英文稿经演讲者审阅。文稿编辑:邓世碧,上海同济城市规划设计研究院助理研究员;校对:钟晓华,同济大学社会学系副教授。

- What are the consequences for the definition of an experience-based authenticity of the confluence of economic development and heritage conservation in China?

The aim of this contribution is to study this theoretical question in light of current redevelopment practices in a district of China's most influential global cities: Hongkou district in Shanghai. Through the presentation of case studies in historic areas in this city we will advance towards the definition of urban authenticity, and a depiction of the new identity that emerges from it.

Keywords authenticity; built heritage; social value of heritage; heritage of Shanghai; heritage in China

1 引言

本文是一个建筑和城市遗产视角的研究，把目前上海虹口区的一个遗产的改造和转型作为一个例子，从遗产、尤其是原真性概念的角度来研究它。虹口的变迁的关键是什么？给这一城市遗产的企业化管理带来了什么影响？

从我的角度来看，旅游业以及创意产业正在成为城市发展的主要基因。本研究计划将遗产城市视为全球城市的当代产品，因为城市遗产能够吸引游客，并且使城市产生具有吸引力的国际地位。由于采用非传统遗产标准来打造，作为旅游创意之基础的意识形态话语对城市遗产有着非常重要的影响。但这也会导致巨大的损失，尤其是考虑到大规模遗产开发和对经济效益的过分关注。本文将讨论公众和私人利益相关者的新的兴趣点。上海是一座遗产城市，目前也正在进行着一系列保护城市遗产的行动。我们将看到，为了旅游业的商业成功和创意城市政策，这些行动是如何扩展了原真性的含义。

本文将界定“遗产城市”，并回顾关于其城市遗产原真性定义的一些争议。其次，本文将上海视为一座遗产城市，梳理当前发生在选定区域虹口港的变化，并研究这个工业与居住建筑混合的地区的文化经济和产业转型。在结论部分，本文将评估上海虹口港的建筑城市遗产的原真性，尤其关注在中国遗产实践背景下这一问题的复杂性。

2 遗产城市：定义

以全球城市的定义为起点，且作为这一复杂定义的附加层次，本研究将遗产城市作为一个评估遗产保护与城市发展的二元关系的概念框架，特别考虑到 2008 年经济危机的影响，以及遗产和记忆在这一全球城市的政治、文化和社会中日益增强的影响力。

实际上，取消遗产限制与一个全球性的保护主义政治项目有关，这一项目由教科文组织或非政府组织这样的利益相关者推动，呼吁环境保护[1]。这一项目的目标并非阻止经济发展，反而是促进经济发展，并在当前城市治理中培育起保护的新角色。本文中“遗产城市”的含义包括：①建筑的形象和外观对于城市竞争力非常重要[2]；②历史对于其创造新的本土和国家叙事具有重要意义，并由此强化身份认同[3]；③其文化与新传统的创造和环境的保护密切关联[4]；④在经济上依赖于遗产所产生的场所，以及这些场所对于房地产和旅游业的影响[5,6]；⑤由于大部分居民难以获得遗产商品化带来的收益，从而造成社会不平等[7]。

因此,虽然文化遗产被视为城市发展的助推器,但就像哈里森(Harrison)[1]指出的,尤其是对于中国而言,“遗产和过去的相关性不大,而实际上基本都是对未来的汇集和塑造的实践”。在中国更多的与商业相关,也就是与遗产有关的房地产业、旅游业。

由此,需要重新定义遗产的原真性,来看旅游业和创意城市原真性的定义对于当前建成遗产的认定、保护和解读到底有什么影响。

3 原真性争议:遗产和创意阶层的视角

我们的争议在于,这种现状是由遗产原真性概念的适用局限性带来的。在当前环境下,比如从联合国教科文组织的历史性城镇景观(HUL)这样的国际建议来看的话,遗产的原真性概念被视为一种发展的障碍。城市遗产正在吸引与旅游和创意城市相关的社会经济活动,而旅游业、创意城市的经验都基于对原真性的定义。这些前提使得重新关注个人体验意义重大并且很有市场潜力。决策者、规划师和设计师所制定的标准采纳了很多不同的城市遗产原真性旅游的界定。从旅游的角度来看,国际遗迹与遗址委员会和联合国教科文组织这样的国际组织旨在提出一个基于经验的原真性定义。例如,1996 年国际遗迹与遗址委员会的美国《圣安东尼奥宣言》的界定,将游客视为城市遗产原真性概念的合法的利益相关者。这一重要的概念性进步表明,要代表当前持续变化的游客群体,在方法论上是十分困难的。这通常是旅游经营者采取的,他们的概念定义往往带有怀旧的刻板印象。游客的目光也以一种盛行的全球化文化的方式延伸到真实的居民身上,这使得事情更加复杂了。再从创意城市的角度来看,正如佛罗里达在 2002 年提到的那样,根据创意阶层的经验,这种基于体验的原真性也包含了旅游的例子当中描述过的怀旧的细微感受,同时包含了一种对于社会包容性和混合社会的要求。

创意城市原真性的社会维度明显践行了国际建议,但是似乎在包容性方面带来了反效果。事实上,创意城市与城市遗产的居住或商业绅士化密切相关,它提供了新来者的外来经验,而这种经验并不总是与原住民的日常生活相互联系。这点尤其具有争议,因为创意阶层可能是社会当中很不稳定的一个组成部分,而且它也有执行的权利,其成员经常活跃地加入社会参与的过程当中。这也是城市遗产的持续过程中的矛盾之一,特别是因城市遗产网络的完全同质化,从另外一个角度讲,也会带来对城市遗产的持久性的影响,特别是城市遗产网络完全同质化,基本上永久地改变着所有社区和陈旧的工业空间。因此,我们尤其是那些将社会空间作为社会生产模式的结果的人认为,遗产原真性的新定义:①应基于确保满足当前建成环境当中人们权利的需求[7,8];②还应考虑到,为了在城市遗产区域创造原真性的“旅游”或者“创意城市”经验,谁的、什么权利正在被置于首要地位,并相应地影响着政策导向;③包括共同价值观框架下的权利问题[9],“体验”有可能会吞没被错误代表的社会阶层,即一些延伸的遗产话语中所说的那些当前被剥夺了遗产使用权和获益权的人们[10];④它还将把来自人类和自然事实的所有声音带到权力的话语中。

4 评估上海虹口港的变化(1933老场坊和国家音乐产业基地)

研究案例位于上海虹口区。这是一个具有非常丰富的历史特色的地区，工业生产结束后，新的商业和企业进驻这里、改造了陈旧的设施。这改变了周边正在经历居住和商业绅士化的里弄居住区的肌理，挑战着中国城市传统的功能混合特征。

上海的案例提供了一种新的范式，一种纯粹的表达，明确地与城市旅游业和创意产业促进结合在一起。上海音乐谷与城市的殖民历史联系在一起，是原上海公共租界的一部分。从过去几年上海采取的促进遗产、旅游和创意城市政策的举措中，我们可以看到这一区域的商业化管理中所有这些元素的交融。

虹口港位于一个非常重要的遗产地区，目前由一家名为“上海音乐谷创意与创新管理公司”的公司管理着。它主要与当前这一地区所经历的转型相关，旨在转变整个区域原有的工业基地性质。

①国家音乐产业基地；②1933老场坊（原上海市屠宰场）；③原公共卫生办公室；④半岛湾时尚文化创意产业园；⑤嘉兴剧院；⑥原上海人力车夫协会；⑦1930鑫鑫创意园；⑧老洋行1913；⑨瑞康里；⑩瑞庆里；⑪长乐里。

来源：作者根据谷歌地图自绘

图1 上海音乐谷区域(上海，虹口港)

我在这里举两个例子：一个是从前的屠宰场，一个是以前的工业生产单位及该地区的新平衡保留的转型。在这里我们会发现，虹口区内部的条例之间缺乏共识。它在2007年做出了完全拆除该地区里弄的决定。但另一方面，还有其他的利益相关者，例如同济大学建筑与城市规划学院，在2005年制定了第一个尊重现有的居住区的规划，并且随着时间的推移发生了一些变化。目前，居住单元的转型延后了，主要的转型以这些重要公共建筑的保护为导向。与遗产的结合是推销上海音乐谷这个新创业的一种方式。它同时结合了一些很有争议的想法，比如说把这附近的社区变成上海的纳什维尔①，同时改变人口的性质和特征来适应这个新的音乐空间，基本上就是以音乐人来取代本地人。

我们可以看到这个目的如何影响了工业遗产的革新。例如，以前的屠宰场，一个与我们所谓"黑暗遗产"相联系的地方，一个由鲜血等东西构筑的地方，现在已经被修缮过了，并且有工作室或俱乐部之类的高档商店坐落于此，完全忽略这个地方原来的黑暗历史，从而强化来到此地的游客和购物者的体验感。

另外还有一些以前的单位生产场所，现在已经成为中国音乐产业园区这一促进音乐产业的公共机构的所在地。如你所见，这里已经完全成为某种文物保护组织了，通过整合这些完全脱离了这一地区的本质和历史特征的命定元素，尤其是忽视这个城市与劳动相关的记忆之间的连接，这也发生在其他的工业设施当中，"更新"在某种意义上脱离了社会记忆。

5 结语

遗产保护公共机构的指导并非成功的保证，但是它被企业化管理所替代则造成了价值分布的不平衡。这些价值由那些行使权利获得商业利益的利益相关者所界定，因而扭曲了原真性的含义。城市遗产保护建立在对于原真性的特殊定义之上，包含了深刻的意识形态和经济内涵，而且是一个持续进行的创造历史的过程。中国的治理结构偏好采用以价值为基础的遗产保护手段。上海音乐谷所建立起来的遗产价值含义取决于利益相关者之间的博弈，尽管经济价值占主导地位。由此产生的原真性和权威性遗产叙事服务于旅游业的利益和创意城市的理想，与已经成为刻板印象的现代上海的形象相一致。利益相关者之间的这种不平衡的权利行使使得地区变化趋于遗产商品化和居住与商业的绅士化。

演讲者简介

普拉西多·冈萨雷斯·马丁内斯，同济大学建筑与城市规划学院副教授。

参考文献

[1] HARRISONR. Beyond Natural and Cultural Heritage: Toward an Ontological Politics of Heritage in the Age of Anthropocene[J]. Heritage and Society, 2015, 8(1): 24-42.

[2] BANDARINF, VANOERSR. The Historic Urban Landscape: Managing Heritage in an Urban Century[M]. Oxford: John Wiley & Sons, 2012.

[3] ASHWORTH G J, KAVARATZIS M. Why Brand the Future with the Past? The Role of Heritage in the Construction and Promotion of Place Brand Reputations [J]. International Place Branding Yearbook, 2011.

[4] HARVEY D. From Managerialism to Entrepreneurialism: The Transformation of Urban Governance in Late Capitalism[J]. Geografiska Annaler Series B Human Geography, 1989, 71(1): 3-17.

[5] HUTTONT. The New Economy of the Inner City[J]. Cities, 2004, 21 (2): 89-104.

① 纳什维尔(Nashville)，是美国田纳西州的首府，位于美国中南部，是医疗卫生、音乐、出版和交通运输的重要中心，是美国乡村音乐的发源地。

[6] GREFFE, X. Is Heritage an Asset or a Liability? [J]. Journal of Cultural Heritage, 2004, 5(3):301-309.
[7] HARVEY D. The Right to the City[J]. New Left Review, 2008(53): 23-40.
[8] LEFRBVRE H. The Production of Space[M]. Paris: Editions Anthropos, 1974.
[9] JOKILEHTO J. Human Rights and Cultural Heritage. Observations on the Recognition of Human Rights in the International Doctrine[J]. International Journal of Heritage Studies, 2012, 18(3): 226-230.
[10] SILBERMAN H. Heritage and Authenticity. The Palgrave Handbook of Contemporary Heritage Research[M]. London: Palgrave Mac Millan, 2015.

社区媒介对于社区社会资本的影响机制研究

——以台湾桃米社区为例

程情仪　刘佳燕

摘　要　本文概述"9·21"地震发生后，社区媒介在桃米社区发展过程中所起到的作用以及其对社区社会资本的影响。包括不同种类的社区媒介在参与社区建设的实践中，对社区社会资本重建的重要性以及社区媒介主体参与时所赋予的角色及其实质表现。在此传播过程中所形成粘合型社会资本、桥梁型社会资本、连结型社会资本亦为社区居民自主、自为的学习过程中提供了不同资源的助力。以此探索社区媒介在社会中究竟是如何运作并如何发挥其对社会资本的作用与影响。以此反思北京大栅栏社区在更新发展中社区媒介的发展，及其对于中国的社区传媒改革可以提供哪些启示。

关键词　社区媒介；社区营造；社区认同；社会资本

Impact of Community Media on Community Social Capital — Taking Taomi Community in Taiwan for Example

Cheng Chengi　Liu Jiayan

Abstract　This paper tries to explore the effect of community media on the development of Taomi Community after the earthquake which happened in 21st, September in 1999. Based on the study on the different types of community media practicing in Taomi which is important to reconstruction of local social capital. And the paper analyzes that the practical result of Taomi has been entrusted by community media's substantive manifestation. In the process of propagation, it forms bonding social capital, bridging social capital, linking social capital to help the local people to obtain external resources building the ability of self-leading life styles. Furthermore, it explores how the community media operated in the society and play its social role in community building. Reflection on the development of community media in the community of Beijing Darshilar and proposes what inspirations can community media offer to China's community media reform and community planning.

Keywords　community media; community building; community identity; social capital

1　引言

社区强调的是群体或社会层面培育和发展社会资本，是有利于群体和社会的发展。当中，"社区"(community)、"交流"(communion)、"传播"(communication) 密切关联，[1] 更被帕特南认为是重要的反潮流趋势。此外,传播(communication)一词与社区(community)一词有着共同的词根,这绝非偶然。没有传播,就不会有社区;同样,没有社区,也不会有传播。[2]“沟通和社区有相同的词根,这并非偶然。如此,社区是通过传播来动员社区成员共享资源进而创造有效的社会网络流动,社会网络建构的同时形成了社会资本储备。可是,现今媒体发展日新月异,传统人们“面对面”的传播方式逐渐被非语言文字传播所取代,其导致的负面影响是公共联络被逐步减弱。

然而,本文以台湾社区为案例的“桃米社区”却强调以社区中的“人”为主体中心。在过往这个只拥有1200人的社区 ,是埔里镇最贫穷的里之一 。桃米离著名景点日月潭只有20分钟的车程,但旅游观光却从未辐射至桃米社区。因此,在面对城市化过程中年轻人纷纷搬离社区的情况下,导致社区变成一个人口结构老化,农业经济衰退的老旧社区。[3]直到1999年“9 ·21 ”地震,桃米社区的问题引起了社会的关注和反思,成为明星灾区。为了让社区得到转机,社区在灾后重建的时候,以“人”作为媒介,为社区建立了社区邻里间的深厚且紧密联系,同时利用各种社区媒介来联系至社会甚至国家,从而引起了社会大众的热烈回响,并以此为基础来宣扬社区居民的精神文明及建设社区旅游发展。此外,在社会资本可能快速形成而产生交易或政治上偏颇的时候,却依旧把社区媒介回归到社区的根本,从而能良好地为桃米社区服务并带来长远的公共利益。因此,本文借研究”桃米社区”来思考今时的社区媒介该如何形成对社区建设产生积极促进作用,从而发挥社会资本的有效发展。

2 什么是社区媒介

社区媒介(community media)又称之为社群媒体(social media)、参与式媒介(participatory media),有别于大众所认识的“大众传播媒介(the mass media)”,其指的是“通过草根或地方级媒介形式发起,共享言论自由和参与式民主,同意促进社群关系和稳固社群团结的媒介”[4]。国际传媒与传播研究协会(IAMCR)对社区媒介的定义是:“(社区媒体)源自公民社会领域,于公民社会传播,引起公民社会回响……存在于国家和市场之外的媒介传播领域(也就是一般是非营利和非政府官方),但同时能够与国家和市场发生互动。其将社区媒体视为公民社会重要的组成部分,是国家媒体和商业媒体之外的‘第三种声音’”。[5]因此,从广义上来说,社区媒介是一种通过自愿式、平等式的对话,以此方式互相流动,从而凝聚共识及建立归属感和认同感。其本质是为了给社区成员提供一个平等参与和表达的机会,为发扬地方文化和本土精神的传播路径。在地方上,社区媒介具有地方精神文化传播,在地方文化经历一段时间后的传播和建构,感染社区成员共同响应社区营造,使其能在特定的地域上构成一个促进社区动员力量的动员机制和行动,以此进一步吸引外围关注的社群大众。

3 社会资本的意涵与类型

社会资本(social capital)由20世纪80年代以来一直受到不同学科、学派的研究者所关注,其中,由经济学家格林·洛瑞(GlennLoury)[6]在《种族收入差别的动态理论》中最早使用社会资本这个概念。社会资本被广为流行主要是受法国的社会学者布迪厄(Pierre

Bourdieu)、美国社会学家詹姆斯·科尔曼(James Coleman)、美国政治学家普特南(Robert Putnam)三位学者的影响。布迪厄认为社会资本是“实际的或潜在的资源集合体，这些资源与对某种持久性的关系网络的占有密不可分，这一关系网络是大家共同熟悉的、得到公认的，而且是一种体制化的，集体的每一个成员拥有这些资源”[7]。科尔曼[8]呼吁连结人与人之关系的社会资本，它不仅能启动社区人际的信任关系，也有助于促进其成员在追求共同的目标时，彼此会更具有合作的意愿。因此，形成社会资本的重要成因是需要依靠成员在互相频繁的沟通过程中所维系的网络关系。

所以，根据社区成员之间互动网络紧密的不同，基特尔(Gittell)和比达尔(Vidal)[9]遵循普特南人与人以及人与团体之间连结的亲疏远近的概念将社会资本分为“粘合型社会资本”(bonding social capital)与“桥梁型社会资本”(bridging social capital)，这种区分方式与格兰诺维特(Granovetter)[10]所提之社会网络的“强连结”(strong ties)与“弱连结”(weak ties)有相似之处。[11]而近几年，一些学者提出了社会资本第三种分类的概念，被称之为“连结型社会资本”(linking social capital)(Woolcock，1999[12]；世界银行，2000[13])。指的是与有权力地位的人群之间的关系，如公共代表(警察、政党)和私人机构(银行)的代表。[13]总的来说，按照成员或团体之间沟通的频率以及关系的亲疏程度，由“强连结”到“弱连结”(指范围小到范围大，当社会关系更为广泛的时候，其联系却会更为浅薄)社会资本可以分成三种：

一、粘合型社会资本(bonding social capital)：指的是家庭成员、亲密朋友或是邻居等相对同质且有紧密联系的群体之间的关系，且是具有排外性质的。普特南[14]指出如社区的兄弟组织或教堂里的女性阅读小组。

二、桥梁型社会资本(bridging social capital)：主要指由异质性的人所形成较弱、较疏远的联系，例如：工作上的同事或社区内之社会组织或宗教团体。格兰诺维特[10]指出弱连结是产生社会流动机会的重要资源。如寻找工作机会上，因为这一种关系虽然更为薄弱，但往往多样化，在扩散传播上较为广泛。

三、连结型社会资本(linking social capital)：指的人们或组织跨越层次结构中的权力、地位的连结，为一种垂直的连结。通过与不同层级的个人、组织或团体的连结来获取社区以外的资源。

4 社区媒介对社会资本的作用及其影响——以桃米社区为例

4.1 “桃米社区”的社区媒体在社区营造中的作用

1996年，桃米社区成立了社区发展协会，但社区居民多限于血缘或亲属关系间的互动，其社区网络较为疏散，社区成员之间的连结并不密切，这也使居民对于社区公共事务的参与积极性偏低、社区共同的意识与认同凝聚较为薄弱。到1999年“9·21”地震中遭逢重创，桃米社区所要面临的是如何连接社区成员之间的联系，以及重建社区建设。因此，地震后1年，在新故乡文教基金会与都市改革组织埔里工作室的协助下，组织社区重建委员会，成立了四个重建小组，其中各组的组长分别由社区人士推派选任。[15]随着重建委员会的成立，社区中积极关怀重建事务的有志之士得以施展抱负；居民的主动参与，也迅速地改变长期以来其对公共事务的冷漠态度，拉近了桃米社区居民的感情，进而建立一个彼此互助、关怀的社区。桃米社区采用了各种社区媒体(表1)扩大其知名度，吸引观光游客。记者廖嘉展亦运用个人社会资源，邀请了政府部门的官员前往桃米观光体验。在首批官员游客到来之后，加上一些媒体宣传的配合，桃米社区的知名度逐步扩大，开始迎来外地游客。过程中，世新大学观光系陈墀吉教授，带领埔里埔籽工作坊的大学生做专业的人文基础调查，并引进导览解说、领团、民宿、生态等培训课程，让当地社区民众除了增进知识之外，更从实务学习中认识环境，进而产生爱护自己周遭环境的情愫，增强了社区民众对家园的认同。

表1　桃米社区的社区媒介类型

<table>
<tr><th>社会资本类型</th><th colspan="2">社区媒介类型</th><th>营运主体</th><th>功能</th><th>范围</th></tr>
<tr><td>粘合型社会资本</td><td>社区报纸</td><td>《希望埔里报》</td><td>南投县新故乡文教基金会</td><td>媒体近用功能、社区居民认同、培训社区种子、居民培力</td><td>小</td></tr>
<tr><td rowspan="2">桥梁型社会资本</td><td>社区导览</td><td>导览解说员</td><td>本地居民</td><td>社区居民认同、培训社区种子、居民培力、宣传</td><td>中</td></tr>
<tr><td>社区音乐会</td><td>“9·21”地震10周年纪念音乐会</td><td>台湾新故乡文教基金会、台湾点灯协会、台湾音乐人协会</td><td>对外展示、宣传、社区民民认同</td><td>中</td></tr>
<tr><td rowspan="3">连结型社会资本</td><td>社区图书</td><td>《桃米生态村的未来》图书</td><td>信义房屋</td><td>支持社区建设、文化传播</td><td>大</td></tr>
<tr><td>社区杂志</td><td>《新故乡》</td><td>台湾社区营造学会</td><td>对外展示、宣传、社区民民认同</td><td>大</td></tr>
<tr><td>社区影像</td><td>《青蛙共和国》记录片</td><td>台湾点灯文化协会</td><td>对外展示、宣传、文化传播</td><td>大</td></tr>
</table>

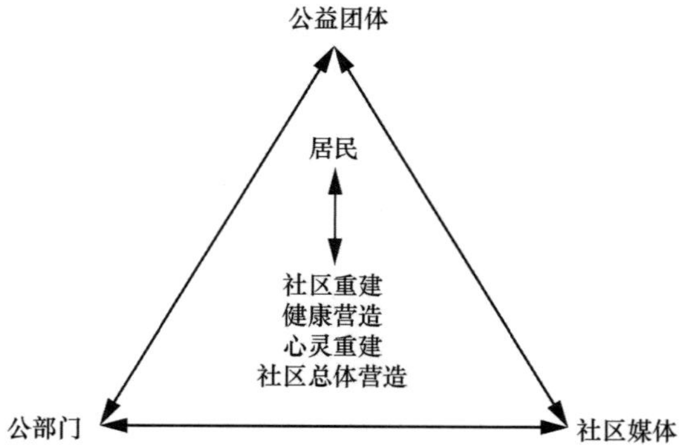

来源:蔡莺莺《"9·21"地震灾后的社区报纸与培力》

图1　地震灾区组织结构三角型互动模式示意图

由此,社区媒介在桃米社区发展中不单只形成触媒更是成为促进社区发展的主体。由图1的三角型互动模式可以看出,社区媒介是担任着促进社区成员参与行动者的组成,达到为社区发声的角色。同时,透过三个主体间双向流动互动网络,为灾民提供了资讯与资源,以此促成社区居民自助和互助。

4.2　以"小区人"为核心形成粘合型社会资本

社区营造所仰赖的是社区成员间的彼此合作与互助。在此建立的前提下,是要认知彼此在共同社群和人际网络生活,[16]以及社群成员间拥有有效的传播沟通机制。[17]在桃米社区的案例中可以看到,当面临残破的家园和死伤的亲友,当地人发起创办社区报推行灾后重建工作,以此关注社区未来发展和凝聚社区居民间的向心力。如2000年7月5日,由在地的南投县新故乡文教基金会发起《希望埔里报》,不仅实现了民众期望扮演公共论坛及意见交流的功能,同时亦加深了社区居民认同;但由于灾区社区报为免费,常常连印刷出版都出问题,因此在总共发刊了六期后停刊。虽然《希望埔里报》并不能持续地为社区服务,但其在社区艰苦时刻为建立社区成员间的信任和社区内部信息的流动产生了极为重要的作用。

同样在较小的空间传播范围里,桃米社区还实施了内围人"人学习-人"生活化的传播模式(图2),如社区居民自己培育的导览解说。其传播方式在自我学习的过程中,达到了社区人间的"强连结",以此进一步推进居民赋能达到社区互助合作和社区认同的功效,形成较深的社群意识和集体价值。对于培训社区种子及对居民的培力,亦使居民获得的社区归属感和荣誉感,形成更高的文化认同。因此,通过本土文化的自我学习,到以"我"作为精神文化传播的载体的传播与建构过程,更有利于促成一定程度的社区自立、自为乃至于实现自主的社区营造目标。同时,我们也可以发现在第一个"人"在投入传播过程中,其组织成员间的联系主要为邻居、亲近的朋友等同族群居民,成员同质性较强,由此动员社区成员参与组织形成成员之间的交流渠道更容易使成员达成共识并形成集体行动,同时形成与本土共生的意识连结。所以,此类型的传播模式更容易建立粘合型社会资本,其传播主体主要为当地居民和当地的组织 ,目的主要在于凝结社区力量和共识。因此,其更为关注社区内部居民的参与和回响,同时亦为社区居民建构一个包容性平台来迎接下一步。同时,这种传播方式所产成的社会资本更能形成实际的社区资源集合体,这些资源对于社区来说更具有持久性,以其建立的内部关系网络为其后期获取资源占有密不可分的意义和作用。

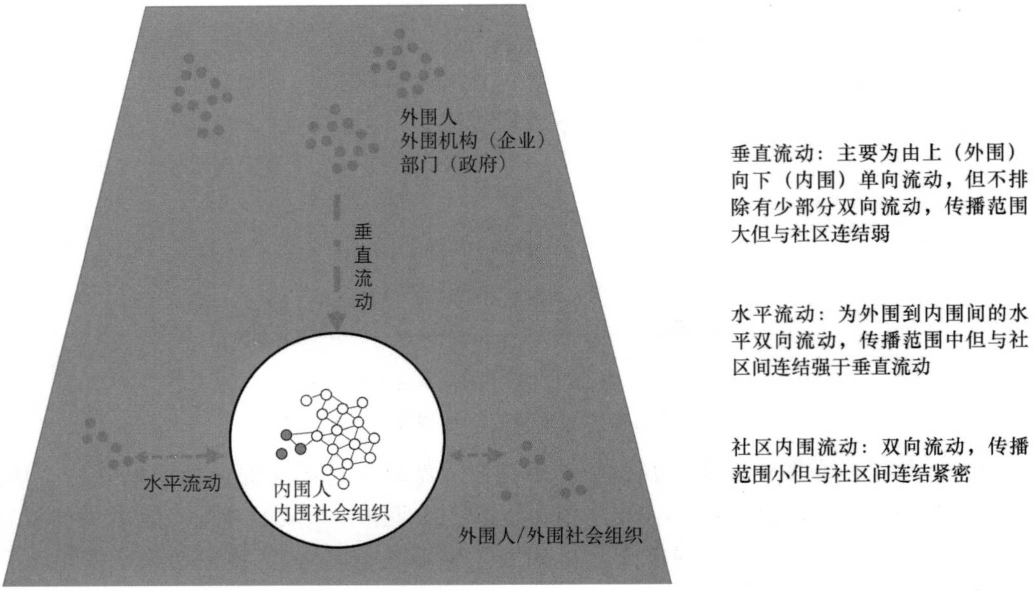

图 2　传播模式示意图

4.3　社会组织助力社区建立社区媒介从而获取外部资源建立桥梁型社会资本

在整个社区推动和重整的过程中，桃米社区亦吸引了外界的支持，其主要功能是为了帮助社区获得更多资源与信息流动，所以参与主体主要为非政府非营利组织。在此种传播模式下，社区与外部的联系对社区的地方组织起着十分积极的作用。如世新大学陈墀吉教授带领的学生成为第一支为桃米社区授课的团队。他们带领居民做调查，摸底桃米里的资源特色，为居民们讲授培养休闲产业的相关课程。另一方面，得到专业系统的培训的社区居民能提供较为优质的观光服务，从而提升观光游客的观光体验，进而保障了桃米社区的生态旅游发展模式得以持续。此外，潜移默化的知识培育还促使社区居民重新了解、认识自己所在的社区，进一步激发了社区居民作为主体参与社区发展的热情。其后，社区内部进一步凝聚共同的价值观。居民通过民宿和餐厅经营者上缴 10% 的收入、观光导览上缴 20% 的收入的方式，桃米社区设立了公积金制度，以作公共支出及社区弱势照顾之用。[9]这种由外围社会组织的进入所形成媒介，能为社区居民获取资源，其水平互动的传播方式不仅能回归到社区媒介中使社区居民参与，保有其促进社群关系和稳固社群团结的意义，亦能传递给社区居民自发、自主地建立社区内围社会组织。同时令媒体最初的报道注重以台湾本土文化的角色出发，树立了桃米社区本土特色风貌的形象，以此来开拓大众对桃米社区的视野。[18]

4.4　与大众互动的社区媒介产生连结型社会资本

为了达到与外围有更多互动和扩大受众，社区媒介不只是局限于地域上的族群圈子，同时还为了达到行销或宣传社区的目的。因此桃米社区在传播模式中的组织成员间的联系不只是邻里关系或社会组织，还有其他广泛且具有层次关系的”外围人”。因此，其减少了信息传播的排他性，能更好地连接外部的资源，有助于得到更多更广泛的效益和传播范围。此外，桃米社区营造的推动人之一廖嘉展，他协助台湾社区营造学会创办了杂志《新故乡》。作为台湾岛内第一本按照商业体系发行的社区性质刊物,《新故乡》杂志也得到了学术界人士的募款,寄托了"汇集文化界力量,营造台湾成为梦想起飞的'新故乡'"的希冀。[19]台湾点灯文化协会更是拍摄纪录片《青蛙共和国》,进一步打造青蛙名片。而飞利浦公司在"9·21"地震满两周年前夕,于台北举办"打造家园新希望"行动说明会,宣布将赞助新故乡文教基金会在埔里镇桃米里进行的生态教育工作。信义房屋也表示长期赞助桃米的发展,并出版了图书《桃米生态村的未来》支持桃米社区的生态建设。此外,桃米社区希望能使政府看到成绩愿意给社区更多的资源,邀请了政府部门参观桃米社区的建设,同时利用新闻报道的机会宣传社区。这些社区媒介都加大桃米社区在社会上、经济上的联系,形成的集体社会资本,更进一步拓展了连结型社会资本的发展。社区对外围所建立的社区媒介的根本目的都是回到对社区公共利益的建设,大多外围机构或部门都是以赞助形式来支持桃米的发展,其并非因社区而产生对机构或部门的直接利益或营利,所以社区居民拥有更多主动和自主创造社区建设的机会。

4.5　社会媒介对社会资本的影响

(1) 在社区内传播的社区媒介,其传播范围少却对社区成员间具有强连结,能够把分散的社区成员聚集起来,建立社区认同感从而集体解决社区的困境问题,其所产生的粘合型社会资本能引发成员们自发形成社会资本,如社区内的社会组织,对下一步传统的扩散效果提供了基础建设。其连接的个人社会关系网络、信任和社区声望在促进信息流动的同时增强了社会资本的累积。

(2) 由外围社会组织进入社区传播的社区媒介,其传播范围中同时对社区成员间能产生良好的连结,社区成员通过与外围社会组织的长期合作所形成的信任,为人们获取教育和就业等提供更多的机会,对社区资本再生产有着积极作用。

(3) 与国家和市场发生互动的社区媒介,其传播范围十分广泛且能达到快速的传播。但对社区成员间能产生的连结却较为浅薄。能够促进在经济上的资本累积,这种社会资本给居民带来一定的资源和利益,有利于增加居民收入,提高居民的福利水平,如在生活保障、经济支持方面。

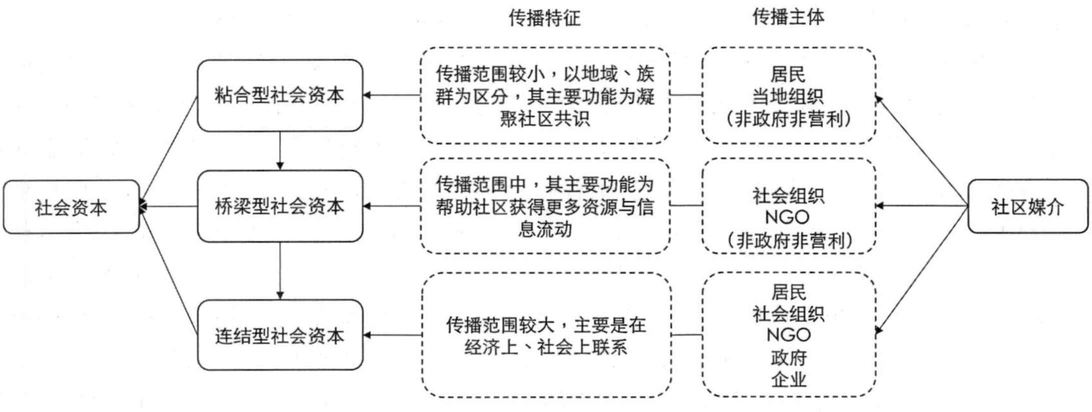

图 3　本文分析框架

5 社区媒介促进地方文化再生产到空间的再生产

桃米社区借由重新挖掘当地文化资源，用社区人“讲社区事”，解说员作为文化传播策略。希望借此以原生社区居民为解说员述说社区故事和文化，并在说与听故事等亲身文化传播过程中建构地方文化与社区感。不仅呈现“桃米社区”的集体精神与共同历史叙事，也将“人”视为地方文化新建构，以此造就更形象化的“桃米社区”，进而繁衍出社区共同归属和想象，这无疑也创造出社区的地方动员所需的集体意义。

此外，在社区建设方面，桃米社区在行政院农业委员会的补助，生物研究保育中心的专业指导下，已创设、改善或设置解说设施之人工湿地有中路坑湿地、组合屋生态池、茅埔坑湿地公园及草湳湿地等，不仅引入生态工法之观念，也提供了更多适合生态旅游及观察学习的湿地景观。“9·21”地震后，桃米社区在各界资源的投入及辅导下，逐渐从传统农村，转型成为结合生态保育、休闲农业和民宿体验的“生态旅游、教育”。因此，衍生了多样性发展，如民宿及餐饮等，使桃米社区深切与环境结合，重新出发建立生态理念规划。因此，现在社区规划中，“社会”逐步取代“空间”，重新回归生产的目标核心：构建多元主体共建、共治、共享的行动模式，以空间为主要生产手段，营造有主体意识和发展能力的社区共同体。[20]

6 从桃米社区的经验中反思北京大栅栏社司的社区媒介发展

北京的大栅栏有着其十分悠久的历史文化，它曾经是最古老最繁华的商业娱乐中心之一，过去人们常以“京师之精华尽在于此，热闹繁华，亦莫过于此”来称赞大栅栏。作为一个城市地理概念，传统的大栅栏主要是指前门大街及两侧街巷所构成的名店老字号云集的古老商业街区。可是，在面对中国社会进入的快速转型时期，其所繁衍的社会冲突亦不断加剧。当中，大栅栏地区成为高密度、老龄化、低收入、弱势群体集聚的城市底层的蜗居之所。显然，社会如果要维持一个基本整合的状态以使自身能够持续发展下去，就不仅仅要致力于对“断裂”状态下社会成员经济和政治地位差异的弥合，还要致力于对社会意识和文化认同的疏导和管理，通过信息沟通机制的完善为不同的社会利益表达和文化认同维系提供畅通的渠道，从而在信息和文化层面上为社会主体利益的公平博弈提供可能性。[21]

在桃米社区的发展过程中，媒体起了极为重要的作用。其媒体报道最初切入的角度不是经济视角，而是以“台湾本地生态生命力”的角色出发，以教育、引路的方式来报道。这些对树立桃米人的形象，开拓人们的视野有很大的帮助。[18]大栅栏自 2010 年开始以历史保护的角度，以渐进式的方法进行更新并同时注重社区营造来关注社会层面。同时，大栅栏更新计划于 2011 年启动，其主要是在地区政府的支持下，由北京大栅栏投资有限责任公司作为区域保护与复兴的实施主体进行微循环改造的旧城城市有机更新计划。[22]伴随着的是北京国际设计周进入大栅栏社区，其尝试以各种新媒体作为社区媒介（表 2）来行销社区更是得到了社会大众的关注。利用各种新技术的数字影像和活动的呈现方式来与民众互动，重拾大栅栏历史街区的传统风貌来重塑大栅栏旧城形象。此外，亦成立了一个开放的公众平台——大栅栏跨界中心（Dashilar Platfrom），以多元参与主体的理念探索历史街区的更新。

表 2　　大栅栏的社区媒介类型

社会资本类型	社区媒介类型		营运主体	功能	范围
粘合型社会资本	社区报纸	《北京大栅栏》	中共北京市西城区委大栅栏街道工委、北京市西城区人民政府大栅栏街道办事处	小区居民认同、对外展示	小
	社区活动	朗诵队、前西助老服务队、合唱队活动、养犬俱乐部	大栅栏街道社区营造项目团队	社区居民认同、培训社区种子	小
桥梁型社会资本	小区导览	导览解说员：《听本地居民讲述大栅栏的历史》； 《老北京遛弯儿》； “胡同漫游——一场社区分享之旅”； “行走在胡同·追忆旧时光”	广安控股大栅栏跨界中心； 北京文化遗产保护中心； 大栅栏街道办事处； 大栅栏街道三井社区	社区居民认同、培训社区种子、文化传播	中
	社区生活节	大栅栏生活节：“胡同漫游——一场社区分享之旅”、胡同食趣漫游、动动俱乐部、大“拾”栏、胡同共生空间、杨梅竹社群YMZ CIRCLE、“四名”汇智计划……	大栅栏街道办事处	支持社区建设、培训社区种子、居民培力、宣传、文化传播	中
	社区生活月	杨梅竹生活月·大栅栏一夜	大栅栏当地政府、大栅栏本地商家、社区居民、各方长期合作者	对外展示、宣传	中
	社区市集	杨梅竹循环市集、大栅栏市集……	大栅栏街道办事处	社区居民认同、对外展示	中
	社区平台	大栅栏领航员计划	大栅栏跨界中心	支持小区建设、居民培力	中

续表

社会资本类型	社区媒介类型		营运主体	功能	范围
连结型社会资本	社区网站(政府主导)	大栅栏街道办事处	西城区人民政府	社区居民认同、政务发布、对外展示	大
	社区网站(商业主导)	大栅栏	广安控股大栅栏跨界中心	支持社区建设、文化传播	大
	社区即时通信工具-微信	大栅栏	广安控股大栅栏跨界中心	对外展示、宣传	大
	社区工作坊	大栅栏手工艺者之家	广安控股大栅栏跨界中心	居民培力、文化传承、对外展示	大
	社区游戏APP	探秘大栅栏——在游戏中发现文化的角落	领域 Domain	对外展示、宣传、文化传播	大
	社区杂志	《北京规划建设》大栅栏特辑； 《一点儿北京·大栅栏》； 《帝都绘》	同济大学出版社	对外展示、宣传、社区居民认同	大
	社区影像	《大栅栏》《媒市街》(记录片)； 《这里是北京》——大栅栏 你不是一条街(电视)； 《进观新罗天》(建筑投影秀)； 大栅栏互动卷轴"胡同茶馆 2.0"	德国联邦文化基金会与歌德学院北京分院； 中央电视台； 北京国际设计周； archifiction inc.	对外展示、宣传、文化传播	大
	社区展览(国际、国内)	第十四届威尼斯双人展——"穿越中国—从北京出发"； 鹿特丹国际建筑双年展——大栅栏更新计划； 北京国际设计周	意大利威尼斯市政府、北京市西城区人民政府、北京国际设计周； 鹿特丹国际建筑双年展、北京国际设计周； 北京国际设计周	支持社区建设、对外展示、宣传、文化传播	大

大栅栏亦实施了“人学习-人”生活化的传播模式。主要是大栅栏街道三井社区中的爱心畅行指南针便民服务岗的队员同时兼任了社区导览队员。进一步唤醒了居民对美好家园的热爱意识，从而实现社区居民民心聚集形成较深的社群意识和集体价值。除外，大栅栏在地居民的胡同舞台：延寿单弦队、大栅栏统战艺术团、前西养犬俱乐部的表演对于社区内部组织网络结构的丰富与互动，通过社交网络的频繁互动，可以促进社会资本的流动，从而使社会资本更具生长性[23]。

但根据大栅栏社区媒介的主体参与，大栅栏的成功是在于其长久的历史和商业文化与外部组织建立许多密切联系，使其得到更多外界甚至是国际的支持，令社区媒介传播范围更为扩大。其更丰富的社区媒介和参与主体为其建构连结型社会资本提供了良好的基础。但是，这些社区媒介更多的是增强了大栅栏经济上的联系而并不是社会上的联系，主要原因是形成的集体社会资本主要来源于商业企业和政府部门而并非主要来源于非政府非营利组织。其立足点更多是品牌形象的推广和服务，对居民的信息需求满足层次较浅，与社区生活的嵌入程度较浅。同时，这些活动形式的参与具有时限性，像是设计周撤出后，社区的丰富度和关注度便会明显下滑。

因此，这种传播模式容易使社区成员或当地组织有限地、被动地参与，所建立的粘合型社会资本将会十分之薄弱。此外，与桃米社区不同的是在社会资本的主体参与并非是非政府非营利组织，其居民的媒体近用功能却较弱。如大型投资公司在主导各类活动的时候与社区负责人和居民的交流会不到位，使居民公众参与的方式主要还是停留在被告知或者被动参与这种阶段，主动参与的机会不是很多。对于其社区内部进一步凝聚共同的价值观将会受到影响和约束。社区传统产业亦将会依赖企业和政府的带动，失去了激发社区居民作为主体自主参与的热情，变得较为被动。

4 结语

在中国，过往的社区媒介明显以政府、商业机构为主导。因此，社区媒介的主流新闻被官方媒体、商业媒体占据，从而失去了以居民自主参与的主体角色。其中，官方媒体所建立的社区媒体其主要功能为政府工作的一种延伸，主要是用于自上而下的政务宣传，同时也较为制度化地提供居民利益表达和问题协商的平台，减少了居民自发、自为状态。可是对增强居民的社区荣誉感、增进邻里互相了解亦有积极作用。而商业机构所建立的社区媒介，则用以推广和服务促销，与社区生活的嵌入程度较浅。现时中国社区正从单位制社区转型到新型社区，在新中国实行福利分房制度，兴建了大批单位制小区，地缘和工作相似增加了社区联系。可改革开放后式微，商品房增多，使居民联系减弱，打破了过往的社会基础，使人与人之间的交流变得松散。因此，面对中国社交网络日益深入和需求，现今中国的社区媒介亦是处于重大的转型时期。

因此，北京大栅栏的更新计划以文化的传播和传承作为感染体，为中国改变旧往“自上而下”的单一主体实施形成强烈的“触媒效应”。虽然其参与主体集中于企业和政府，但是对于本地居民建立自主和社会资源共同参与的主动参与空间提供了前景。同时，未来中国的社区媒介是要引导居民自主参与社区，以信息流动为手段来培植社区力量形成“社区粘合-连结”模式。从而通过信息流动培植社会资本和真正的社区。建立社群从自在(in itself)到自为（for itself）并形成能够自我主导生活方式的能力，包括社区参与意识和实际的参与行动[24]。

作者简介

程情仪，清华大学建筑学院城乡规划系硕士研究生。

刘佳燕，清华大学建筑学院城乡规划系副教授。

本文由清华大学（建筑学院）旭辉控股（集团）有限公司可持续住区联合研究中心课题"基于存量空间资源挖掘的社区营造研究"（20152001392）经费支持。

参考文献

[1] 帕特南. 独自打保龄：美国社区的衰落与复兴[M]. 北京大学出版社，2011.

[2] 施拉姆，等. 传播学概论[M]. 陈亮，译. 北京：新华出版社，1984：32.

[3] 陈统奎. 台湾桃米社区的重建启示[J]. 南风窗，2010(1)：57-60.

[4] HOWLEY K. Community Media：People，Places，and Communication Technologies[M]. Cambridge：Cambridge University Press，2005.

[5] 李艳红. 传媒产制的第三部门：北美和澳大利亚社区媒体的实践、制度及民主价值[J]. 开放时代，2009(8)：5-32

[6] LOURY G C. A Dynamic Theory of Racial Income Differences[J]. Discussion Papers，1976. WALLACE P A E，LAMOND A M E. Women，Minorities，and Employment Discrimination[J]. Industrial and Labor Relations Review，1977，23(23)：217.

[7] 布迪厄. 文化资本与社会炼金术[M]. 上海：上海人民出版社，1997.

[8] COLEMAN J S. Social Capital in the Creation of Human Capital. The American[J]. American Journal of Sociology，1988，(94)：95-120.

[9] XU J. Community Organizing：Building Social Capital as a Development Strategy[J]. Contemporary Sociology，2018，29(2)：352-354.

[10] GRANOVETTER M. The Strength of Weak Ties：A Network Theory Revisited[J]. Sociological Theory，1983，1(6)：201-233.

[11] 黄源协. 小区社会资本与小区发展关联性之研究[J]. 公共行政学报，2010(34)：29-75.

[12] WOOLCOCK M. Social Capital and Economic Development：Toward a Theoretical Synthesis and Policy Framework[J]. Theory and Society，1998，27(2)：151-208.

[13] GROOTAERT C，IBRD W，NARAYAN D，et al. Measuring Social Capital：an Integrated Questionnaire[J]. World Bank Publications，2013，49(2)：201-220.

[14] PUTNAM R D. Bowling alone：The Collapse and Revival of American Community[M]. New York：Simon and Schuster，2000.

[15] 陈炳森. 以文化角度看农村小区之灾后重生：以埔里桃米小区及古坑华山小区为例[J]. 农业推广文汇，2012：271-297.

[16] TUANY F. Community，Society，and the Individual[J]. The Geographical Review，2002，92(3)：307-318.

[17] ELIASOPH，NINA，LICHTERMAN，et al. Culture in Interaction[J]. American Journal of Sociology，2003，108(4)：735-794.

[18] 孙兆慧. 社会力量助推台湾桃米生态社区的建设和发展[J]. 海峡科技与产业，2013(8)：34-35.

[19] 佚名. 关于廖嘉展联合报[N/OL]. 联合报，1999-4-14 [2015-10-1]. http://www.docin.com/p-4617224.html.

[20] 刘佳燕，邓翔宇. 基于社会-空间生产的社区规划——新清河实验探索[J]. 城市规划，2016，40(11)：9-14.

[21] 黄典林. 媒体主流叙事的边缘解读及其社会逻辑——以北京大栅栏地区为例[C]. 2006 中国传播学论坛论文集(Ⅰ)，2006.

[22] Dashilar. Updated Plan [EB/OL]. [2017-10-7]. http://www.dashilar.org/#A.

[23] 张荣. 从社区社会资本的培育探究和谐社区的创建[J]. 济南大学学报，2006(2)：14-17.

[24] 张春炎. 地方文化传播与社区营造：苗栗湾宝社区动员之初探研究[J]. 新闻学研究，2013(116)：173-206.

资本、权力及人文博弈下的历史街区空间再生产研究

——以厦门沙坡尾为例

张若曦　林小琳　兰　菁

摘　要　从空间生产理论的视角来看，空间影响着人类的生存方式，同时又可转化为复杂的社会关系结构。空间生产的社会属性决定其生产过程充满了相关各方群体的诉求权衡及利益博弈。文章以厦门市典型历史街区沙坡尾为研究对象，梳理沙坡尾物质空间演变、海洋产业发展及社会空间变迁历程，分析沙坡尾空间再生产过程中空间建构者、生产关系、社会关系的改变。剖析嬗变背后的资本、权力及人文的作用及博弈关系，并基于空间正义，对历史街区的空间再生产提出建议。

关键词　空间生产；历史街区；博弈；沙坡尾；空间正义

Spatial Reproduction of Historical Districts under the Game of Capital, Power and Humanity

— Taking Shapowei in Xiamen as an Example

Zhang Ruoxi, *Lin Xiaolin*, *Lan Jing*

Abstract　From the perspective of the theory of the production of space, space affects human living in the real world, and can be transformed into a variety of complex structure of social relations, is the dialectical unity between production and production by. Taking Shapowei, a typical historical district in Xiamen, as the research object, this article combines the material spatial evolution and the process of social space background such as development of marine industries, and analyzes the changes of space construction, production relations, and social relations during the spatial reproduction of Shapowei, to show the game relationship of capital, power and humanity behind the evolution, and to put forward some suggestions on the spatial reproduction of historical districts based on spatial justice.

Keywords　spatial reproduction; historical districts; game; Shapowei; spatial justice

1　引言

伴随存量规划时代的推进，众多历史街区被设定为新的城市增长极，其作为居民一般生活场所的使用价值日渐式微，而其交换价值却日益彰显。屡见不鲜的是，资本群体愈发看重其商业意义，将谋求通过改造更新而实现空间重构，进而带来最大的投资回报[1]。在诉求权衡及利益博弈的时代背景下，历史街区更新都或多或少打上了资本积累与增值的烙印，历史

街区再开发模式已从单一政府控制转向多元主体参与及利益平衡，参与博弈的主体不断增加。厦门市沙坡尾片区是厦门的城市脉源，自沙坡尾片区更新改造以来，代表资本、权力及人文的不同主体先后参与其中，沙坡尾片区的改造更新逐渐成为多方共同影响下的产物。

2 概念解析

列斐伏尔(Lefebvre)提出，“空间是人类社会活动的产物，空间就是社会”[2]。空间的生产类似于商品的生产，不断引导、影响、限制着人类在现实世界中的生存方式；同时空间作为一种物质力量，其生产力自身的成长和认知在物质生产中不断介入，从而转化为多种复杂的社会关系结构，具有生产与被生产的辩证统一关系[3]。空间生产理论为城市社会科学研究开辟了一个新视角，已逐渐为各界所关注。

相关学者已从多方面对城市空间重构与再生产现象进行探讨[4-7]。关于城市中的空间再生产的实证研究已有一定数量。马学广以广州海珠区 20 个城中村为例，总结了城中村空间生产的经济基础、属性特征、类型、过程、模式和治理机制，认为城中村空间的生产是制度变迁和社会行动者互动博弈的产物[4]。张京祥等人以南京市城中村江东村为研究对象，对空间生产的历史性变迁、社会关系的再生产、制造的新空间三个方面进行分析，提出城中村改造为现代社区后，将建立起新的生产关系和社会结构，在此过程中生产和塑造的不仅仅是空间，更是社会的新界限[5]。胡志强等人从空间生产的视角出发，分析了楚河汉街空间生产的三大博弈主体(政府、开发商和公众)各自的利益诉求，提出空间群体博弈的结构性失衡是导致楚河汉街出现空间特色危机、空间正义危机和人性化危机的主要原因[6]。袁奇峰等人从汕头小公园历史街区改造困境出发，探讨权力与资本主导下的历史街区空间再生产，得出小公园街区的改造，已沦为权力和资本主导下以土地效益为目标的城市开发活动[1]。洪世键等人通过分析租差的形成，认为包括绅士化和再开发在内的城市空间再生产是资本和权力共同驱动的成果[7]。总体而言，从研究对象上，已有研究多聚焦于城中村与历史街区这两类具有特殊性的社会空间，对其更新改造中的空间再生产进行分析。从研究内容上，或集中于资本与权力的博弈，或侧重于政府、开发商和居民间的博弈，对空间再生产过程中原住民利益之外的人文因素涉及较少。基于此，本文从空间生产理论切入，以典型历史街区厦门市沙坡尾为例，对历史街区空间再生产前后的产业变迁、人群结构演变及社会生产关系等社会空间变化进行梳理。对沙坡尾历史街区空间再生产及背后的资本、权力与人文多方博弈进行探讨；并在此基础上提出引导策略，以期为历史街区再开发提供借鉴。

3 沙坡尾历史街区空间演进脉络

沙坡尾历史街区位于厦门岛西南端，西侧与鼓浪屿跨海相对，东侧毗邻厦门大学和南普陀寺，南面隔海与漳州龙海市相望，距今已有 600 多年历史，是厦门岛内现存的唯一避风渔港。本次研究范围约 44.7 公顷，其中重点研究范围约 6.9 公顷(图 1)。结合社会与物质空间的变迁情况，将沙坡尾发展历程划分为四个阶段：

图1　本文研究区域图

3.1　渔民迁入，开埠通商

自唐宋时期，丰富的海洋资源在闽南地区酝酿形成一个初具规模的渔港，即厦门港的雏形。沙坡尾原为海边沙滩，有天然沉积沙层，是“天然避风港”。明末清初时期，郑成功曾以厦门岛为据点，在厦港玉沙坡地区屯兵操练，期间还大力发展对外贸易，带动了厦门港海上航运、商贸的发展，因此九龙江流域地区的渔民及以造船为生的渔工逐渐向此地迁移聚集，玉沙坡沿岸港口开始形成，并成为对台贸易往来的重要渡口[8]。人群的迁入与对外贸易的兴盛使这一带沿海区域兼具渔港、商港、军港的属性，并盛极一时。

1843年厦门开埠通商后，原渔商混用的港口开始功能分化，玉沙坡一带成为大小渔船的集中停泊地，进入围绕渔业集捕捞生产、鱼行商贸、生活服务为一体的街市港区近百年的鼎盛时代。此时“渔行”成为沙坡尾的重要业态，其通常由富商独资或合资经营，并与地方势力结合，通过同时垄断渔业的生产及销售权，达到控制渔民的目的，既使渔民收入被剥削，也使渔业产生依附性，从而控制渔区经济的命脉。

3.2　生产起落，因战而衰

1930年初，厦门设市，码头、港口的改造成为市政建设的重要内容，渔港因沙坡头堤岸修筑，外移至沙坡尾新建避风坞，同时，为扩大城市用地面积，开山填海，奠定了沙坡尾避风坞的近现代雏形：以大学路、民族路为界，临水一侧主要为生产区，分布有船坞、船厂、商店和打铁铺等场所，当时的沙坡尾沙滩上（今避风坞南侧）分布大量的造船工场、修船厂和一些渔民栖身的船厝。靠山一侧则主要是鱼市场、商业街市和居民区（图3）[9]。据记载，1937年沙坡尾渔港登记有大小渔船597艘，渔业人口总计5189人，其中下海渔民2490人。当时该地区手工业包括造船、打绳、制钓、打铁、桨橹、船帆、染汁等30多个行业，形成一个为渔业生产

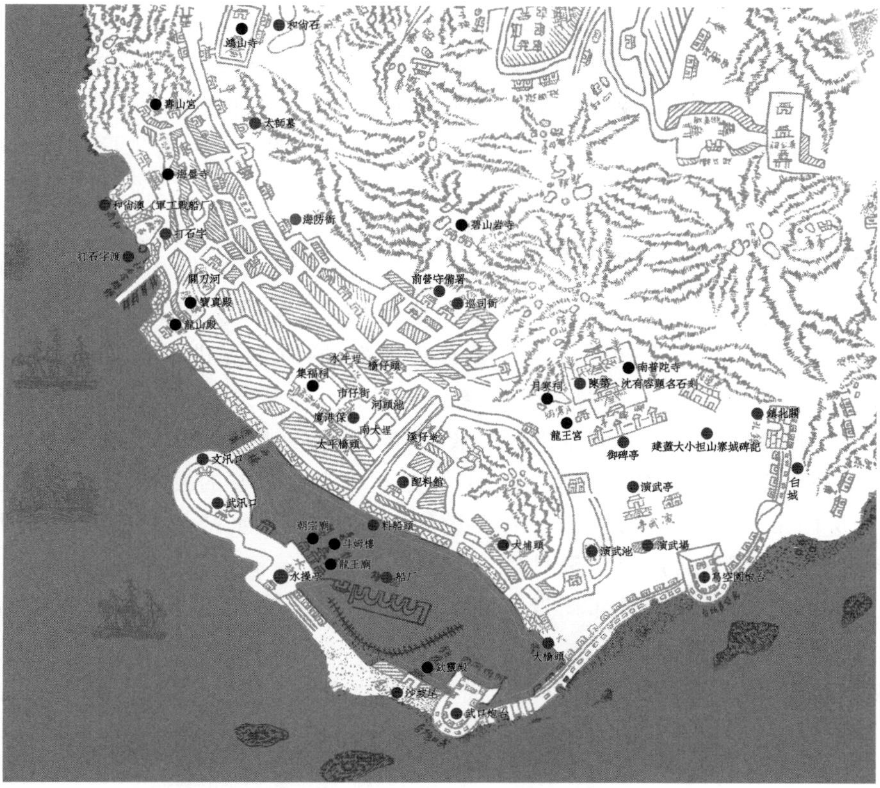

来源:作者根据清同治年间厦门旧城市图绘制

图 2　清同治年间的玉沙坡海港图

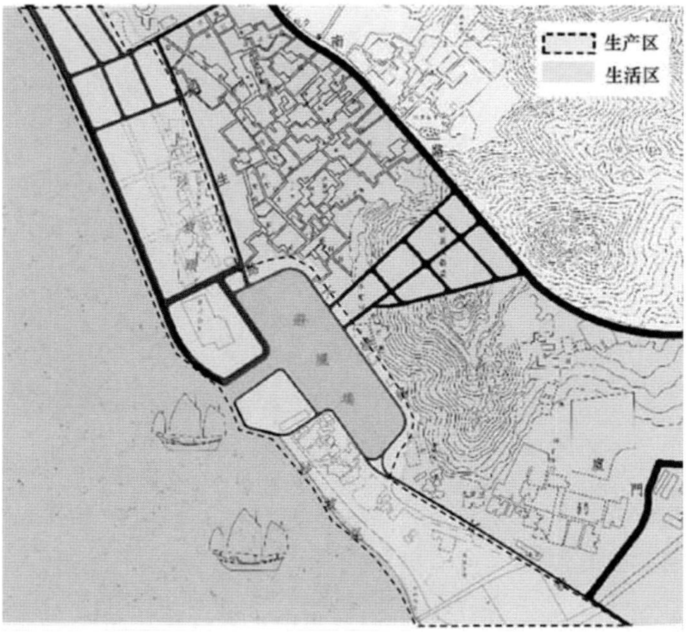

来源:作者根据 1938 年厦门全市图绘制

图 3　1930 年代厦门市沙坡尾片区功能分区

服务的供应网，一度成为整个厦门地区最繁盛之处。

1938年5月起，日军占领厦门长达7年。在此期间，港口被封锁，厦港船只、居民区被大量烧毁，渔业在武力统制及经济剥削下受到双重打击，广大渔民生计受到威胁[8]。据记载，至1941年渔民数量仅剩战前的一半。这一阶段，沙坡尾的海洋渔业生产经历了明显的起落变化。

3.3 渔业体制变革，渔港发展

1945年抗战胜利后，沙坡尾地区渔业百废待兴。自中华人民共和国成立初开始，多阶段的体制及技术改革，不仅使渔民摆脱了封建剥削，同时也促进了国营渔业机构的迅速扩展。从1953年起，政府先后通过清淤修缮、砌堤竖界、修建道路与灯塔等措施，改善避风坞的物质条件，沙坡尾的物质空间基本发展成型(图4)，这一时期，沙坡尾地区渔业年产量大幅攀升，也带动了以渔业为核心的制造、加工等工业化产业集群的发展，该片区也由传统渔村发展成为厦门市三大工业区之一，设有大量的机电造船厂、水产品加工厂、发电厂等。发展至20世纪七八十年代，冷冻厂、渔具厂、造船厂、造帆厂等渔业相关产业在沙坡尾地区随处可见。最辉煌时，沙坡尾渔港年产量达到3.5万吨，一个完整的产业链在避风坞周边展开。以沙坡尾为代表的厦港地区渔业人口一度占据80%，下海渔民达到5000人[8]。伴随渔业兴起，众多与航海、渔业有关的民间信仰宫庙也随之出现。

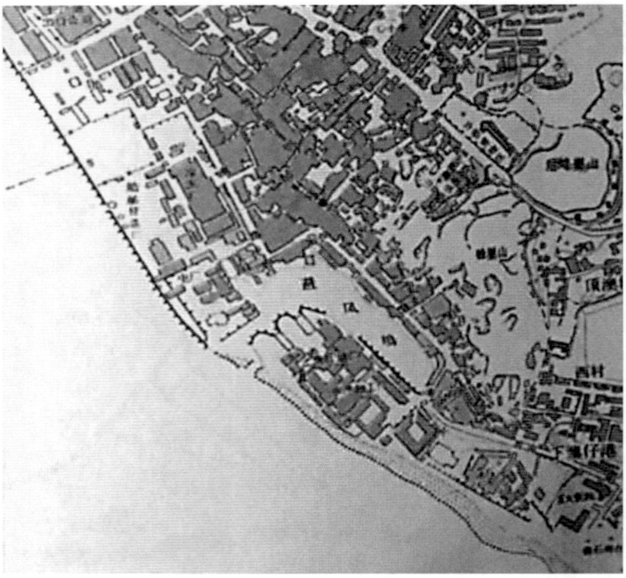

来源：《沙坡尾——一个厦门渔村的社会与文化》

图4 1967年厦门沙坡尾片区地图

3.4 渔业没落，渔民消退

20世纪90年代中期开始，厦门公共财政集中于新区开发，旧城改造资金相对短缺，物质结构呈现老化趋势。在生产方面，沙坡尾虽历经清淤整修，但渔业生产环境仍不佳；加之近海渔业资源的枯竭导致捕捞量急剧下降，渔业开始走向衰败；与之相关渔业工业开始出现外三现象，昔日繁盛的渔港走向没落。2003 年厦门市海湾型城市建设规划及环岛路的建设使厦港避风坞的功能进一步受限，渔民逐渐消退。面对物质空间环境品质日益下降的现状(图5)，局部的空间更新改造逐渐发生。

来源：http://travel.sina.com.cn/china/2015-03-12/0911301010_3.shtml.

图 5　沙坡尾避风坞老化的物质空间

3.5　渔港退渔，整体改造

2015 年思明区政府、厦门市海洋与渔业局发布了《关于厦港沙坡尾避风坞封闭管理》的公告，宣布沙坡尾片区将进行整体改造更新，通过给予本地渔船渔民适当补贴的方式，引导渔民退渔上岸转产。沙坡尾传统生产性渔港功能彻底消逝，其物质空间与生产关系发生重大转变，建立在业缘基础上的社会关系发生改变，新社会空间逐渐形成。

4　沙坡尾退渔后的空间再生产

4.1　空间建构者的置换

空间建构者是社会空间的重要组成部分，其变化能反映出社会的变化。据街道统计数据，2000 年沙坡尾 18%的居民为渔民，其他职业主要为造船工人、船工、商人。居民主要来源包括从古至今生活在此的原住民及渔民、周边地区汇入的渔民与船工、清代中叶汇入的商人。渔民区主要包括大埔头、小埔头、圆山宫、福海宫[8]。此后十年间，伴随物质空间老化，户籍人口与渔业工作者有所减少，但打鱼作业者仍是重要的空间使用主体。

2010 年以来大量外来人口涌入沙坡尾，沙坡尾人口呈现外来人口聚集，本地人口老化趋势。2011 年社区总户数 2070 户，常住人口 4998 人，流动人口 2150 人。其中在中山路附近上班的打工者是流动人口的重要组成部分。与此同时，距离此处不远的另一渔村曾厝垵由于受到众多文艺青年的追捧而迅速走红，许多原先在曾厝垵工作的文艺青年在房租推力下，迁往沙坡尾，加入沙坡尾的社会空间建构中。

伴随空间再生产的推进，近年来沙坡尾片区内的房租迅速上涨，拥有较高付租能力的外来人口逐渐取代原先租住在沙坡尾的打工者及部分文艺青年，在沙坡尾工作、学习的非原住民及游客渐渐成为空间主要建构者，空间构建者呈现“绅士化”发展趋势。

4.2 生产关系的变迁

对重点研究区域内业态情况进行统计分析(图 6)，可见，沙坡尾传统业态占据一定比例，片区仍具有一定生活气息。但渔业及相关业态已彻底消逝，能体现沙坡尾传统地方特色的商铺日益减少。2015 年退渔后，以小吃店为主的新业态取代渔业及便民类传统商铺的趋势日益明显，产业特征由传统型向现代型转变。代表外来文化和创意文化的咖啡厅、外国料理店、创意料理店、蛋糕甜品店快速兴起，并在餐饮行业内占据较大比例，成为沙坡尾片区生产关系的新标签。

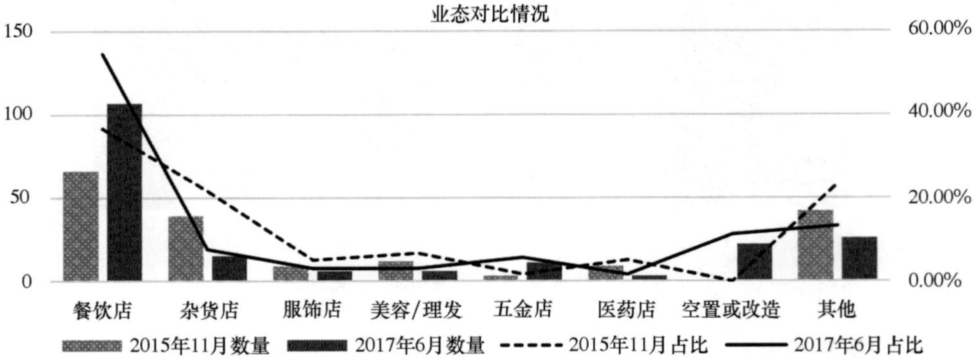

图 6　2015 年 11 月业态统计情况

4.3 社会关系的演变

沙坡尾由传统渔港向文化创意港转变的过程中，居民的社会空间关系也发生变化。当地居民的传统生产资料渔船不再出海作业，居民与原本的生产资料及生活方式相分离，改变了传统的渔业生产关系，渔民这一职业群体逐渐走向终结。伴随片区再开发的推进，同其他历史街区相似，住房在沙坡尾地区也成为新的生产资料，市场经济作用下居民纷纷将个人生产资料——住房投入空间创造价值的过程中，将住房外租用于商业使用，创造经济价值，原住民的身份转变为房东，以实现其利益的兑现。在这个转变的过程中，原先在沙坡尾片区内租住或工作的空间建构者也呈现核心—边缘结构。由于缺乏可成为新生产资料的住房，外来打工者、文化青年及疍民在空间再生产过程中处于不利地位，沦为空间再生产过程中的边缘人群。

4.4 新社会空间的诞生

历史街区的改造不简单是一个外在景观环境的重塑过程，本质上更是对历史街区的社会空间再生产过程，新物质空间的生成，也生产出新的生产关系与社会关系。从沙坡尾的案例可看到，新的空间的诞生不仅仅是文化创意港对渔港、外来人口对原住民的置换和取代过程，也包含了随之而来的日常生活空间的形成[10]。大型商业综合体世茂中心、聚集创意店铺的艺术西区，以及众多的咖啡、酒吧及甜品店等(图 7)，这些新社会场所的出现，预示着新的生产关系的建立，其生产和塑造的不仅仅是空间，更是一种社会结构与界限。旧的生产关系在新的空间中不复存在；依赖于地缘和本土历史网络所构成的传统空间界限也一同消失，在空间业态类型不同的表象背后实质上是主导资本、阶层和社会关系的不同[5]。在物质空间与社会关系的改造中，沙坡尾逐渐加入日常生活的再生产过程，与传统社会空间的逐渐分离。

来源：网络图片

图 7　沙坡尾的新兴店铺

5　影响因素分析

5.1　消费资本的驱动

资本的本性决定其空间生产过程始终以利润最大化作为其首要目标，获取剩余价值作为终极目标。资本顺应并利用了空间生产逻辑，实现了资本空间化向空间资本化转变，空间就像物质资料一样成为资本存在的具体形式，这就极易出现背离“以人为本”的空间生产终极价值的现象[6]。沙坡尾片区内私房较多，18%以上的住房具有两户以上的产权人，复杂的产权一定程度上使其免遭“大拆大建”式的商业地产开发。而消费文化为主导的私人资本，在市场驱动力的作用下，以“小规模渐进式”进入沙坡尾，使越来越多的居民逐渐放弃住房的居住使用价值，从而推动沙坡尾社会空间的重构。

当空间就像物质资料一样成为资本存在的具体形式，就极易出现利益驱动的空间生产现象[6]。近年来小吃餐饮类在沙坡尾的业态占比中迅速增加，一方面，餐饮类业态能在较短的时间内带来大量资金流，与资本利润实现最大化的目标相匹配，盈利空间较小的传统业态因此被迫逐渐退出片区；另一方面，以资本附加值为中心的生产方式使商铺租金日益高昂，又间接推高了商品的价格。从本质上看，这种以新型消费空间为主的社会空间只是满足了部分具有“文艺情怀”人群的需求，一定程度上忽视了原住民及渔民等边缘人群的诉求，是对“绅士化”的变相推进；而空间生产通过对特定消费群体的划分和吸引，也挤压了低收入市民对空间的部分享有权，代表空间公平与正义的天平开始倾斜。

5.2 政府干预的推进

在多数已有的历史街区改造中，政府在博弈中处于绝对的领导地位，有着城市管理者、利益参与者和仲裁者多重身份。政府通过行政权力管理城市的空间资源，加强了对空间生产的干预[11]。在城市历史街区的更新过程中，政府较重视历史街区的发展价值，将其打造为新的城市增长空间，而资本则看重其经济价值，两者的诉求在空间生产中存在一定程度的契合点，形成了权力与资本控制下的空间生产[1]。

通过规划与公告的颁布，厦门市政府确立了其在沙坡尾空间再生产过程中的主导者地位。2012年厦门市政府审批并通过《沙坡尾海洋文化创意港行动规划》，确定了沙坡尾文化创意休闲功能的功能定位。2015年思明区政府、厦门市海洋与渔业局发布了《关于厦港沙坡尾避风坞封闭管理》的公告，提出沙坡尾今后将不再作为渔船停泊点。通过规划与公告的颁布，政府的政策推动已确立了其在沙坡尾空间再生产过程中的引导者地位。沙坡尾片区的更新改造，未来不仅将提升厦门老城区的城市风貌，同时也将增加片区的旅游到访量与经济消费量，兼顾了空间治理与经济收益的诉求。同年年底，经过多轮群众意见征集、专家论证后，形成《厦港避风坞景观改造提升方案》。在沙坡尾的更新改造中，政府的角色一定程度上从“决策者”“主导者”转向“推动者”“参与者”，权力在沙坡尾更新运动中由最初“一家独大”转向为多方博弈协调。

5.3 人文情怀的反思

在国内历史街区的空间再生产中，人文要素是最容易被忽视的，恰恰与此相反，在沙坡尾的空间再生产过程中，包括了当地原住民诉求与泛化的城市精神等的人文情怀发挥了重要作用，这与厦门推动的“美丽厦门，共同缔造”参与式社区规划的政策背景，以及基于互联网的现代媒体的发展密不可分。

2015年的沙坡尾退渔激发起了社会各界的关注，沙坡尾的百度搜索指数及以此为题的新闻在此之后逐步攀升(图8，图9)。除了原住民表达“自下而上”建构社会空间要求之外，市民的文化认同也逐渐觉醒，促进了公众、政府等各界对沙坡尾改造的重新思索与讨论。在2016年组织的沙坡尾共同缔造工作坊中，以讨论“渔船该如何回归”及凝练沙坡尾未来发展愿景为目的的调研访谈、公众意见征集及制度设计逐步展开，为各方群体的发声提供了平台，促进其直接参与到片区的空间再生产中，以此表达诉求，进而谋取自身的空间权利。渔民、本地原住民、专家学者、热心人士及商家代表组成的社会各方群体，均在公众意见征询会上表达了观点和诉求，并混编分组针对大家共同关注的议题进行讨论(图10)，其中包括对沙坡尾片区未来的发展愿景，如何保护渔港文化及记忆，渔船以何种形式回归、如何进行社区营造等。可见，代表人文思考的社会群体对常见的以权力和资本主导的历史街区空间再生产进行了反思，自沙坡尾退渔以来，人文思考参与空间再生产博弈的特征更加明显。

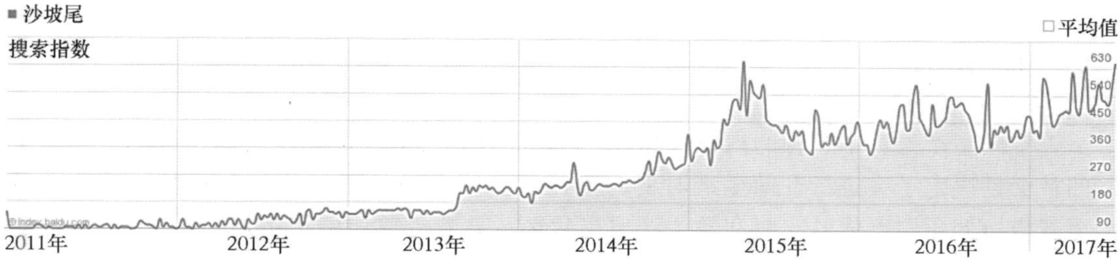

来源：http://index.baidu.com/? tpl=trend&word=%C9%B3%C6%C2%CE%B2.

图 8　沙坡尾百度指数变化情况

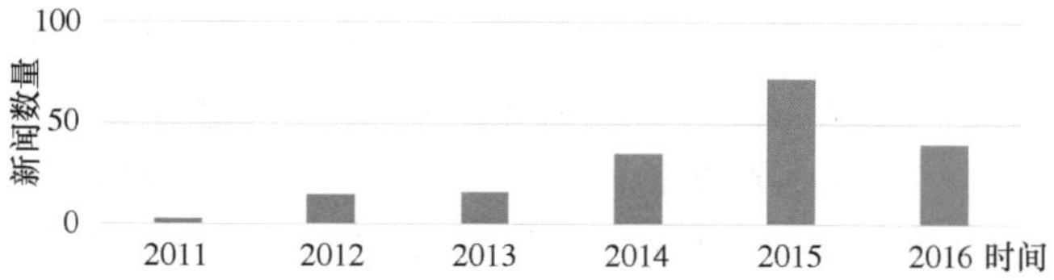

来源：http://news.baidu.com/ns? cl=2&rn=20&tn=news&word=%E6%B2%99%E5%9D%A1%E5%B0%BE.

图 9　新闻数量变化情况

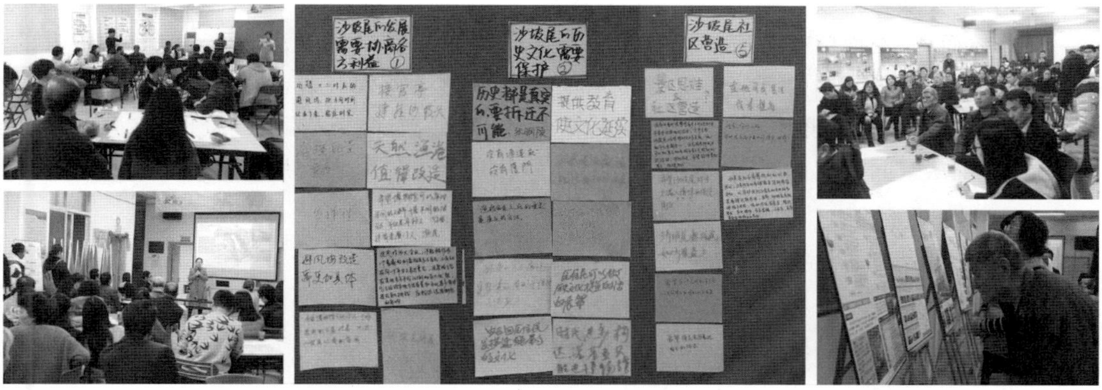

图 10　沙坡尾工作坊的公众意见征询会现场

5.4　三方博弈的契合

在列斐伏尔看来，城市空间是各种力量博弈的结果，不同权力、利益、集团在此相互竞技和争斗[6]，在自身空间利益的驱动下，不同的群体之间形成了合作或竞争的关系。在沙坡尾更新博弈机制中，分别代表资本、权力和人文的影响因素相互制约，由传统的权力或资本的“一家独大”转向进行多方融合及协调，进而逐渐走向平衡。沙坡尾片区的空间生产由资本主导下的空间使用者置换与生产关系转变，发展至政府干预下的新社会空间形成，人文因素在其中始终对空间再生产发挥着一定的修正作用。三种博弈主体在争取共同利益最大化的基础上、采取不同的形式在空间生产中互相博弈、达到均衡。

6 结语

空间生产是资本扩张的内在逻辑，资本扩张的必然结果是导致边缘化问题。然而空间的社会性决定了在进行空间生产时要时刻注意空间公平与正义[12]。"空间正义"要求城市更新应协调不同群体的空间利益。沙坡尾片区承载着老厦门的记忆，其蕴含的文化特色容易因空间再生产的资本逐利性而被忽视。要实现沙坡尾的可持续发展，应在空间再生产中考虑不同利益者的需求，具体来说包括以下几个方面：

首先，政府应积极发挥管理者的作用，针对不同空间主体实施差异化政策，为以渔民及文艺青年为代表的被边缘化群体提供相应策略，满足其空间权益，降低其被边缘化的压迫感。同时建议，通过增设片区内的共享公共空间等手段，加强居民交流，密切邻里关系，重建居民的社会网络。其次，对资本进行合理的控制及引导，通过设置同类业态的上限占比，对以消费主导的资本进行准入限制，防止同质资本对空间的霸占；结合税收减免等政策鼓励渔业等相关的传统业态回归，弱化资本的空间蔓延，保育片区文化。此外，深化公众参与机制，借助工作坊等形式创造良好氛围，形成对权力与资本的监督及有效制约，促进代表人文情怀的原住民及社会力量积极参与空间再生产过程，在城市更新的过程中体现公众的思想，形成一个权力、资本、人文力量共同作用的城市空间治理结构。在沙坡尾的空间再生产过程中，要达成合作共赢局面，各博弈主体间需构建起良性互动关系，各利益方应对空间再生产达成共识，方能实现可持续发展。

总体而言，在厦门市政府开放的管理环境、市场的积极响应以及市民意识日益提升的背景下，沙坡尾片区较国内其他历史街区，空间再生产社会条件较好，各方博弈力量较均衡，在未来应继续引导多方群体共同参与，同时需要政府部门着眼全局，协调资源，整合各种社会力量，实现从空间调配到时间调配的投入运筹，让更多主体分享到片区更新的红利。

作者简介

张若曦，博士，厦门大学建筑与土木工程学院城市规划系助理教授。

林小琳，厦门大学建筑与土木工程学院城市规划系硕士研究生。

兰菁，厦门大学建筑与土木工程学院城市规划系本科生。

参考文献

[1] 袁奇峰，蔡天抒. 基于空间生产视角的历史街区改造困境——以汕头小公园历史街区为例[J]. 现代城市研究，2016(7)：68-77.

[2] Lefebvre H. The Production of Space[M]. Oxford：Basil Blackwell，1991：112-120.

[3] 张京祥，邓化媛. 解读城市近现代风貌型消费空间的塑造——基于空间生产理论的分析视角[J]. 国际城市规划，2009，24(1)：43-47.

[4] 马学广. 城中村空间的社会生产与治理机制研究——以广州市海珠区为例[J]. 城市发展研究，2010，17(2)：126-133.

[5] 张京祥，胡毅，孙东琪. 空间生产视角下的城中村物质空间与社会变迁——南京市江东村的实证研究[J]. 人文地理，2014(2)：1-6.

[6] 胡志强，段德忠，曾菊新. 基于空间生产理论的商业文化街区建设研究——以武汉市楚河汉街为例[J]. 城市发展研究，2013，20(12)：116-121.
[7] 洪世键，张衔春. 租差、绅士化与再开发：资本与权利驱动下的城市空间再生产[J]. 城市发展研究，2016，23(3)：101-110.
[8] 张敏. 厦港沙坡尾船坞周遭海洋性聚落形态变迁[D]. 2013.
[9] 王楠. 沙坡尾——一个厦门渔村的社会与文化[D]. 2016.
[10] NEIL SMITH. The New Urban Frontier：Gentrification and the Revanchist City[M]. London：Routledge，1996：79.
[11] 何森. 城市更新中的空间生产：南京市南捕厅历史街区的社会空间变迁[D]. 南京大学，2012.
[12] 陆小成. 新型城镇化的空间生产与治理机制——基于空间正义的视角[J]. 城市发展研究，2016，23(9)：94-100.
[13] 沙坡尾共同缔造工作坊. 沙坡尾的第 101 种可能[R]. 中山大学，香港理工大学，华侨大学，厦门大学，2017.

城市历史文化遗产密集区发展困境与路径研究

——以上海虹口港地区为例

郭谌达

摘　要　本文将当代城市历史文化遗产保护理念不断演进的国际语境与我国拥有大量历史文化遗产的现实国情相结合，选取了历史文化遗产密集分布的城市区域作为研究对象，调查分析了研究对象在其发展历程中所遇到的困境和机遇，在此基础上借鉴历史性城镇景观(HUL)的保护方法和理念，将历史文化遗产作为一种城市发展的驱动力，探究了其在当下可持续与包容性发展的全球共识和"中国话语"中可以起到的重要驱动作用，从而提出了城市历史文化遗产密集区在保护和传承历史文化遗产前提下的可持续与包容性发展路径。

关键词　历史文化遗产密集区；历史性城镇景观；发展困境；发展路径

Study on the Development Dilemma and Path of Urban Area with Abundant Historical and Cultural Heritage

Guo Chenda

Abstract　Combined the international context of the evolution of the protection of urban historical and cultural heritage in contemporary with the reality that China has abundant historical and cultural heritage, this paper selects the urban area with rich historical and cultural heritage in its development area as the research object, then investigates its dilemma and opportunity in the development process. On this basis, drawing on the protection methods and concepts of Historic Urban Landscape (HUL) the paper takes the historical and cultural heritage as a driving force for urban development to explore what it can play in both worldwide consensus and Chinese discourse of current sustainable and inclusive development. At last, the paper puts forward the sustainable and inclusive development path of urban area with abundant historical and cultural heritage under the premise of protecting and inheriting historical and cultural heritage.

Keywords　area with abundant historical and cultural heritage; HUL; development dilemma; development path

1　引言

历史文化遗产一般指具有历史、文化价值的与人类生活相关的历史留存物，包括物质性和非物质性的。本文所指的是物质性历史文化遗产。城市历史文化遗产在本研究中特指位于城市规划范围内的历史留存物，可以理解为一种整体的历史文化环境[1]。这些环境中包含了一座城市产生发展演变过程中某一或某些阶段重要的历史文化信息,记载了一座城市的一段或几段集体记忆,对城市以及相当部分的原住民而言,具有不可替代亦不可复制的历史价值和文化价值,包括情感价值,是城市特色的重要构成部分。本文所指的城市历史文化遗产密集区是指城市规划范围内仍现存较大量历史文化遗产的城市建成区。不同于目前已挂牌的历史文化风貌保护区、历史文化风貌区、风貌保护街坊等,本研究所涉及的研究区域,除其中少量已挂牌单体历史保护建筑以外,尚无法定保护地位。

2005年世界遗产中心在“世界遗产与当代建筑——管理历史性城镇景观”国际研讨会上通过了一项致力于保护历史性城镇景观的新的备忘录,即《维也纳备忘录》,提出了“历史性城镇景观”(Historic Urban Landscape,简称“HUL”)的概念,以促进城市的保护及其与新城市的发展的结合。基于《维也纳备忘录》,2011年联合国教科文组织通过了《关于历史性城镇景观的建议》(*Recommendation on the Historic Urban Landscape*,简称《HUL建议》),为处于不断变化的环境中的城乡遗产在识别、评估、保护和管理方面提供一种在可持续发展框架内的综合的方法。2015年世界遗产委员会最终确定将“历史性城镇景观”(HUL)确定为一种文化遗产的保护方法(而非一类新的世界遗产类型)纳入《实施世界遗产公约操作指南》(2013版)[2]。

从这一过程可以看出,国际上HUL的产生语境是对于城市尺度而言的,着眼于新建区域与历史区域之间的关系,关注历史的层积性和延续性在空间的体现。历史的信息通过层积,共同构筑了城市遗产的价值[3]。这些时间累积下来的信息,通过空间上的延续,也带来了城市独特的魅力。本文借鉴这一理念,选择具有多个历史时期信息层积并与新城市区域有密切联系的虹口港地区作为研究对象。将关注点从整个城市的尺度聚焦在若干街区的尺度,试图用HUL的视角与方法来研究城市历史文化遗产密集区的保护和发展问题,探索其可能的发展路径。

2 研究范围及其发展历史

本研究所指的上海虹口港地区是指北至海伦路,南至黄浦江北岸,东至梧州路、西安路、旅顺路,西至四平路、吴淞路、峨眉路、武昌路的一片区域(图1)。

虹口港地区的发展可以按以下几个阶段进行划分(图2)[4]。

(1) 开埠前(1848年前)

1848年之前,虹口港地区由于毗邻河道,逐渐形成了一些小渔村。随着人口的不断积聚繁衍,集市开始出现,其中较为繁华的是一条“虹口老街”(今东汉阳路219弄)。目前该老街的肌理及老街两侧的部分历史建筑仍然存在,但老街自身的功能已由集市功能完全演变为居住功能(图3)。

(2) 美租界形成时期(1848—1863年)

1848年美国开始在虹口港地区划设租界。此后,虹口港地区规划修建了一系列城市道路(表1)。这一时期港口和航运业也开始了较快的发展。

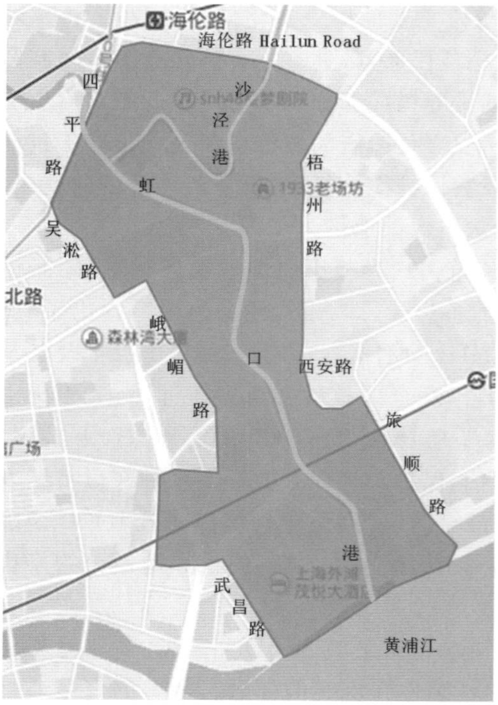

来源：作者根据百度地图自绘

图 1　虹口港地区研究范围示意图

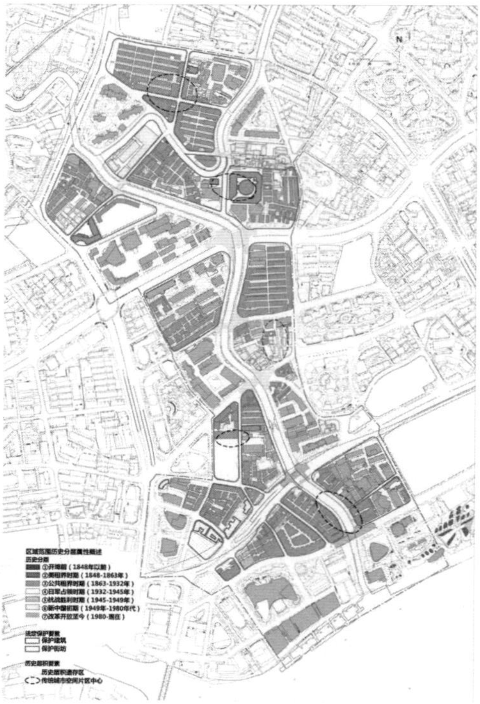

来源：作者与李燕宁博士共同完成

图 2　虹口港地区历史分层图示

图 3　现在的虹口老街

表 1　　虹口港地区道路历史信息列表

现路名	起讫	始建时间	曾用名
东大名路	惠民路—溧阳路	1864 年	百老汇路、东百老汇路
东长治路	海门路—溧阳路	1881 年	东熙华德路、熙华德路
东汉阳路	新建路—溧阳路	1892 年	汉璧礼路、东汉璧礼路
东余杭路	溧阳路—大连路	1912 年	东有恒路
东嘉兴路	辽宁路—溧阳路	1912 年	/
沙泾路	溧阳路—海伦路	1913 年	/
沙泾港路	海伦路—香烟桥路	1930 年代	/
吴淞路	北苏州路—虬江路	1864 年	/
余杭路	九龙路—吴淞路	1891 年	有恒路
武昌路	黄浦路—江西北路	1864 年	广东路、西武昌路、自来火街、东武昌路
周家嘴路	东长治路—大连路	1920 年代	东鸭绿路
南浔路	黄浦路—汉阳路	1883 年	/
沙泾路	溧阳路—海伦路	1913 年	/
沙泾港路	海伦路—香烟桥路	1930 年代	/
吴淞路	北苏州路—虬江路	1864 年	/
余杭路	九龙路—吴淞路	1891 年	有恒路
周家嘴路	东长治路—大连路	1920 年代	东鸭绿路
南浔路	黄浦路—汉阳路	1883 年	/
拓皋路	辽宁路—拓皋路桥		拓皋路
哈尔滨路	吴淞路—海伦路	1904 年	汤恩路
海宁路	九龙路—河南北路	1902 年	东段:鸭绿路
海伦路	周家嘴路—邢家桥北路	1908 年	东洋街、欧嘉路、库伦路
海伦西路	邢家桥北路—秦关路	1913 年	士庆路
海拉尔路	梧州路—高阳路	1913 年	海勒路
鸭绿江路	周家嘴路—溧阳路	1908 年	东鸭绿路
峨嵋路	天潼路—海宁路	1875 年	密勒路
梧州路	东汉阳路—沙泾路	1904 年	/
溧阳路	黄浦江—四川北路	1889 年	狄思威路
新嘉路	东嘉兴路—溧阳路	1930 年代	/
塘沽路	大名路—河南北路	1850 年代	文监师路、蓬路
嘉兴路	吴淞路—九龙路	1904 年	/
汉阳路	汉阳路桥—塘沽路	1864 年	汉璧礼路
辽宁路	溧阳路—海伦路	1907 年	奉天路、墨克登路
五台路	辽宁路—东嘉兴路	1912 年	东新嘉路、东五台路
九龙路	扬子江路—虬江路	1877 年	斐伦路
长治路	大名路—九龙路	1864 年	熙华德路
黄浦路	青浦路—大名路	19 世纪中叶	/
闵行路	黄浦路—吴淞路	1864 年前	/

(3) 公共租界时期(1863—1932 年)

这一时期从 19 世纪中叶到 20 世纪上半叶持续了将近七十年,也是国际上政治经济等格局风云多变的一个时期。虹口港地区在社会、经济、市政建设等各方面也都呈现出较明显的发展,比较突出的有商业、工业的繁荣和文化产业的兴起。这体现在城市面貌上,主要是码头、仓库业等与航运业相关的城市功能和行业兴盛起来,这也进一步刺激了道路、建筑等城市建设活动(如表 1 所示),逐渐形成了目前基本尚存的城市肌理。同时这也带来新的城市移民,因此社会公共活动开始丰富,戏院、电影院出现,电影制片业也随之产生。

(4) 日本军事占领时期(1932—1945 年)

这一阶段虹口港地区的发展遭受重创,商业、工业、文化业均陷入低迷,社会萧条,多片街区包括里弄住宅遭日军炸毁。现存被炸痕迹最为明显的是百福里,原百福里中部完全被炸毁,现仅存原西端(今东大名路 353 号,如图 4 所示)和东端(今旅顺路 15 弄 9 号,如图 5 所示)各几户人家。

图 4　百福里西端(东大名路 353 号)

图 5　百福里东端(旅顺路 15 弄 9 号)

(5) 抗战胜利后(1945—1949 年)

这一阶段时间较短,大量的逃难的居民涌入这一区域生活,城市建设和部分中小型工商业开始恢复。城市空间的变化不大。

(6) 1949 年后(1949—1990 年)

这一时期,大部分里弄街区和公共建筑基本被保留下来,其中多数仍基本按原功能被继续使用。

(7) 20 世纪 90 年代后(1990 年至今)

由于虹口港的区位及上海城市产业转型的需要,该地区的大部分工厂停产,截至目前传统的航运功能也完全停止。同时,在若干轮城市更新中,部分棚户区、里弄街区和建筑被拆除,取而代之的是现代住宅区或办公楼;部分里弄街区和工业建筑被改造成新的业态和空间;还有一部分里弄街区如瑞康里、常乐里、春阳里、百福里等(图 6),以及部分历史建筑如宰牲厂、和记洋行、虹口救火会、嘉兴路巡捕房等仍然存在(图 7)。同时,由于虹口港河道的存在,该地区的水陆关系仍得以保存。

图 6　春阳里

图 7　虹口救火会(今虹口消防支队消防中队)

目前虹口港地区的功能主要有四类,包括居住、公共服务、创意产业和新航运业。居住主要里弄街区(图 8)和现代多层高层住宅小区,公共服务主要有医院、国家电网、消防站、学校等,这两类功能目前所在的位置,在历史上也基本上是类似的功能。现代住宅小区大多建于 20 世纪末至 21 世纪初,少数是近年所建,整体都具有较完备的生活设施和较适宜的居住环境。里弄建筑具有很高的历史文化价值,记载了不同时期的里弄住宅特征(图 9),但里弄街区的居住状况和环境状况则差强人意。公共服务设施除虹口消防中队、北虹中学等沿用了历史建筑外,其他多以新建为主。创意产业主要分布在北部哈尔滨路附近里弄街区周边,也大都是较早出现的,如有 1933 老场坊、1913 老洋行、上海音乐谷等,稍晚成形的有北部三角地艺术园(嘉兴路 260 号)、毗邻老洋行的半岛湾(溧阳路 735 号,如图 10 所示)和南部的北外滩 111 艺术园区(溧阳路 111 号)。这些与历史上的功能发生了很大变化。新航运业(为区别于历史上虹口港地区的航运业,本文称之为“新航运业”)

图 8　里弄住宅街区

图 9　不同时期的里弄住宅的特征举例

即南部沿黄浦江一线的国际航运中心。

经过对研究区的时空梳理，可以发现这一区域保留了从出现至今各历史时期的部分留存物，包括路网格局、部分建筑群和建筑单体，见证了上海城市从最初发展到辉煌及至今日的各个过程，浓缩式地彼此集中地体现了历史信息的层积性，并在相当程度上保留着在空间上的延续性，从而形成了城市独特的历史文化内涵。因此，这一区域适宜从HUL的视角进行分析和研究。

图10　半岛湾

3　发展困境

虹口港地区的发展困境主要表现为城市活力衰落，有待复兴，更深层的原因是尚未能很好地适应当下经济和社会结构的变化。就研究对象本身而言，目前面临着许多问题，主要可以归纳为保护和传承的问题、复兴和发展的问题。保护和传承方面，首要的冲击来自外界环境的变化。整个城市的现代化进程给本区域带来了不可避免的影响，特别是扩路、拆迁等现实情况给该区域由密集的城市历史文化遗产所营造出的城市空间氛围、城市特色、社区结构等都带来不可逆的损毁[3]。同时，部分历史上的工业厂房被转化为创意文化产业的空间，吸引了相应的从业群体和新的社会关注，这需要该区域能更好地适应这些新变化。其次，这一区域仍然保留着多处里弄街区、历史建筑和城市空间。这些建筑物随着使用年限的增长，如果缺乏保养，会不可避免地出现衰败的迹象，目前已有不少建筑出现这类情况。再次，人文氛围方面，虹口港地区历史上曾繁荣一时的文化气象已相对较弱，社会文化生活也相对贫乏。该区域的物质环境和社会文化环境都在发生着明显的变化，给保护历史肌理、传承城市文脉都带来巨大的挑战。

复兴和发展方面，历史文化遗产为虹口港地区带来崭新的发展机遇。2006年，1933老场坊创意产业集聚区正式启动建设，历史上的工部局宰牲厂被改造为创意文化产业的聚集地，吸引了一批时尚创意从业人员入驻。在随后的十年间，1933老场坊成为虹口港地区的新名片，带给整个地区新的活力，一大批文化创意产业集聚地出现，如人力车夫互助会旧址所在的三角地被发展成为三角地艺术园，1913年成立的“和记洋行上海分行”被改造成1913老洋行创意文化园区，始建于1929年的哈尔滨大楼现成为半岛湾文化创意产业园，均有多家文化、艺术、设计类公司和工作室入驻。以国家音乐产业基地为核心的上海音乐谷，则是全国首个正式获批的国家级音乐产业集聚区，集合了音乐制作、音像制品集散、艺术培训和音乐产权交易。见证了20世纪前半叶上海电影院发展黄金时期的嘉兴大剧院，现名为SNH48星梦剧院，仍是一处门庭若市的剧院。但不容忽视的是，经过十余年的发展，这些在当时属于十分新兴的创意文化产业，也面临着其他区域产业均质的威胁，运营情况和商业活力已不如创建之初。近年来，全市以及全国文化创意产业都风起云涌，造成市场的生存缝隙较之以往变得更小，市场对产业发展模式的要求变得更高。肯定不能哪里都是田子坊、哪里都是新天地，也肯定不会哪里都是1933老场坊。此外，虹口港地区在空间上的一大特征是滨水，但目前该区域内滨水空间的活力很弱，有些沿河步道形同虚设，有些防洪墙阻断了人与水的亲近，也破坏了景观视线。

同时，本区域还面临着民生发展的困境。一是里弄住宅环境不尽如人意，建筑内部表现为人均住房面积十分狭小，搭建改造严重，一个门牌号可以住三四家人甚至更多，如图11所示，一个电表、一个水表对应一户人家，里弄超负荷地承载了大量的居民。由于空间紧缺，在建筑内部加建隔层成为普遍现象，也造成很多无窗房间的存在，带来通风不畅、自然采光受限、消防隐患等弊端，室内居住环境较差（如图12左图、中图所示）；在建筑外部，里弄街区内的公共空间也显得十分拥挤，洗菜洗衣甚至洗澡都可能是在弄堂里完成的，也普遍存放着较多杂物，缺少必要的公共活动空间（如图12右图所示）。近年来在里弄内增加公共卫生间、垃圾站点、健身设施等措施起到一定的改善效果，但空间紧张仍然是难以回避的问题。里弄之外，紧邻街区的河道水系也尚未对居民的生活环境起到明显的积极作用，滨水空间几乎没有居民活动的身影。同时，复杂的产权关系也使居民很难自发修缮维护居住环境，加上居民也普遍缺乏用于这些项目支出的资金，居住状况堪忧。另一个表现是本区域内常住居民的经济活动能力衰退。随着社会经济发展和转型，目前这些街区以中低收入居民为主，一部分是已在此生活十几二十几年甚至更长的本地居民，主要为老年人，其中多为单位退休职工；一部分是以青壮年外来务工人员为主的租客，其中相当一部分在附近从事日常性服务业。社区老龄化和外来较低收入人群聚集也给民生带来很大的压力。

图11　里弄超负荷地承载了大量的居民

图 12 里弄较差的居住环境

4 发展路径

面对当下可持续发展、包容性发展的全球共识，城市历史文化遗产密集区如何发展需在此框架下进行。我国提出“城市修补”，明确指出要“发掘和保护城市历史文化和社会网络”。基于这样的全球共识和中国语境，本研究借鉴 HUL 的理念，将历史文化遗产作为城市发展的一种驱动力，从新建区域与历史区域之间关系的角度，强调历史的层积性和延续性在空间上的体现，应对处于不断变化的环境中的虹口港地区的发展困境，实现该地区的可持续发展、包容性发展。

(1) 尊重和传承历史层积性——将历史文化遗产作为活力激发点，驱动城市活力再生点的形成

对于目前尚存的各历史时期的建筑单体、建筑群、里弄街区肌理予以保护，既不能任其自然消亡，也不能随意使其突变再生。这是虹口港地区的吸引力所在，是未来该区域活力的激发点。首先要对历史建筑、建筑群及里弄的建筑结构进行普查和结构修缮强化，确保建筑质量安全。其次，针对不同的功能选择不同的复兴措施。里弄建筑、救火会和北虹中学教学楼，以及一部分仍在使用中的工业建筑，可以沿用原有的功能；另一部分已经停产的工业建筑，可以根据自身空间特点和区位市场的需求，转为其他功能。新建建筑群也是对当下的见证，站在历史的角度来看，也将是走向未来的历史。已新建落成的建筑不需要全盘推倒重来，筹备新建的建筑无须仿古，新老建筑毗邻而立，可以作为虹口港地区的历史文化遗产的特色(图 13)，将可以进一步增强历史文化遗产的吸引力、扩大城市活力的范围。

(2) 修补和营造空间的延续性——使区域特色更加突出，驱动城市活力的可持续性复兴

近年来国家提出“城市双修”，城市修补成为一个热门话题。本文认为修补不是复古重建，而是要注重在即将规划的空间中挖掘历史的元素，注重守护和修补其在空间上的延续性。具体到研究区域内，主要体现在河流水系、街道、里弄街区方面。这是本区域有别于其他区域的重要特质，也是本区域可以促进活力复兴的一种不可再生的稀缺资源。历史上，河

图 13　从长治路向南看平安里和东方明珠等

河水运的交通系统为上海城市初期的发展带来了巨大的动力，虹口港也经历过这一辉煌时期。水系带动经济发展的同时，也带来居民的聚集，进而带动周边日常生活和社会文化的繁荣，表现在空间上就是水系和居民居住建筑、消费娱乐设施等的密切关联。因此，如何恢复滨水空间的生活活力、消费娱乐活力是虹口港地区的一大重任。虹口港地区目前的水系位置与历史上几乎没有变化，这也为该区域延续历史空间提供了有利的条件。街道对城市肌理的延续起着至关重要的作用。由于街道不像河道那么难以被人为变换，因此对于街道肌理的保护更要重视。目前大名路、长治路已被较大尺度地拓宽，但沿河及里弄街区之间的小路，仍保留着历史地图上的基本面貌，更应尽力保留。里弄街区也是虹口港地区的重要历史元素之一，它们经历了上海 20 世纪初繁荣发展的时代历程，也记录了当时人们应对人口激增的一种具有上海特色的居住策略，并承载了由此产生形成的社会文化。保护里弄住宅即是在保护城市发展的一段历史。从最近一次的全市里弄街区普查工作中得知，里弄建筑存量已十分有限，随着它的逐渐稀缺，更应该全力保护。里弄住宅与新建住宅共同构筑了城市住宅形式跨越时间的多元性留存，对于保护城市发展脉络具有十分重要的意义。

(3) 关切社会结构的持续性——驱动包容性发展

人是社会的主体，历史文化遗产的价值离不开历史上各阶段的人的参与。因此，在区域发展过程中，应关注存在于该区域中的人。大拆大建带来的不仅是区域内空间的断裂，也带来了人的割裂式大换血，这对于延续空间和文化都是极为不利的。因此，在制定政策时，应充分考虑区域内各类居住者、工作者的生活模式、能力和需求，有意识地保持它们在该区域内一定程度上的多样性。而多样性是城市活力的重要驱动力之一。正如田子坊，由于旅游消费型商业和日常式居住的混合形态，使外来游客置身其中时，可以既保留自身的消费娱乐习惯，又可以参观甚至体验到老上海居民里弄生活的特色；同样，居民也可以在一定程度上保留自己的生活习惯，又可以观察外来游客的、新兴的生活消费方式，对他们的生活发展也是一种开拓。既尊重历史的形式和内涵，也尊重时代带来的新变化，并给予各类生活者一定的自我完善的机会，这也是包容性发展的题中之意。

前两者可以通过地方规定的确立和相应的城市设计手段来逐步落地，第三方面则更有赖于相关政策的大力扶助，在需要时可启动社区规划师进行辅助。基于这些原则和认识，凝聚社会、市场、居民、规划技术的综合力量，参言参事复兴地区综合活力。

5 结语

适应当下可持续和包容性发展的全球共识和我国“城市修补”的语境，本文从研究区域的历史演变和现状出发，梳理分析了城市历史文化遗产密集区所面临的历史文化遗产保护和城市区域发展的困境，并从其在发展演进中新旧关系的角度讨论了其发展路径。主张在城市发展进程中，尊重和传承城市空间的历史层积性、修补和营造现代与历史空间的延续性、关注社会结构的包容性发展，结合政策制定、规划技术支撑等手段来共同实现研究区域活力的复兴和发展。

作者简介

郭谌达，同济大学建筑与城市规划学院博士研究生。

参考文献

[1] 周俭. 城市遗产及其保护体系研究——关于上海历史文化名城保护规划若干问题的思辨[J]. 上海城市规划，2016(03)：73-80.

[2] 邵甬，朱丽娜. 历史性城镇景观方法纳入操作指南的过程和意义[J]. 世界遗产，2015(09)：58-59.

[3] 顾玄渊. 历史层积研究对城市空间特色塑造的意义——基于历史性城镇景观(HUL)概念及方法的思考[J]. 城市建筑，2016(16)：41-44.

[4] 上海市虹口区志编纂委员会. 虹口区志[M]. 上海：上海社会科学院出版社，1999.